Scholarship for Sustaining Service-Learning and Civic Engagement

a volume in
Advances in Service-Learning Research

Series Editor:
Shelley H. Billig
RMC Research Corporation, Denver

Advances in Service-Learning Research

Shelley H. Billig, Series Editor

From Passion to Objectivity (2007)
edited by Sherril B. Gelmon and Shelley H. Billig

Advancing Knowledge in Service-Learning:
Research to Transform the Field (2006)
edited by Karen McKnight Casey, Georgia Davidson,
Shelley H. Billig, and Nicole C. Springer

Improving Service-Learning Practice:
Research on Models to Enhance Impacts (2005)
edited by Susan Root, Jane Callahan, and Shelley H. Billig

New Perspectives in Service Learning:
Research to Advance the Field (2004)
edited by Andrew Furco and Shelley H. Billig

Deconstructing Service-Learning:
Research Exploring Context, Participation, and Impacts (2003)
edited by Janet Eyler and Shelley H. Billig

Service Learning Through a Multidisciplinary Lens (2002)
edited by Shelley H. Billig and Andrew Furco

Service Learning: The Essence of the Pedagogy (2002)
edited by Andrew Furco and Shelley H. Billig

Scholarship for Sustaining Service-Learning and Civic Engagement

edited by

Melody A. Bowdon
University of Central Florida, Orlando

Shelley H. Billig
RMC Research Corporation, Denver

Barbara A. Holland
Service-Learning Clearing House

Information Age Publishing, Inc.
Charlotte, North Carolina • www.infoagepub.com

Library of Congress Cataloging-in-Publication Data

Scholarship for sustaining service-learning and civic engagement / edited by
Melody A. Bowdon, Shelley H. Billig, Barbara A. Holland.
    p. cm. — (Advances in service-learning research)
  "In October of 2007 ... in Tampa, Florida, for the 7th International Research
Conference on Service-Learning and Community Engagement"—ECIP data view.
  Includes bibliographical references.
  ISBN 978-1-60752-002-3 (pbk.) — ISBN 978-1-60752-003-0 (hardcover)
1. Service learning—Congresses. 2. Service learning—Research—Congresses.
I. Bowdon, Melody, 1967- II. Holland, Barbara A., 1950- III. Billig, Shelley.
IV. International Research Conference on Service-Learning and Community
Engagement (7: 2007: Tampa, Florida)

  LC220.5.S36 2008
  378.1'03—dc22

                                             2008039023

Printed in the United States of America

CONTENTS

PART III:
SUSTAINING FACULTY ENGAGEMENT IN
SERVICE-LEARNING AND COMMUNITY ENGAGEMENT

PART IV:
SERVICE-LEARNING AND ETHICS EDUCATION

ACKNOWLEDGMENTS

We wish to acknowledge the following for their support and assistance with this project:

Jeffrey Anderson
Christine Batson
Margaret Boreman
Min Cho
Deborah Collins
David Deggs
Florida Campus Compact
Leena Furtado
Sherril Gelmon
Aileen Hale
Linda Hargreaves
Gary Homana
George Johnson
Christopher Koliba
Lynn McBrien
Barbara Moely
Eileen Quinn-Knight
Dee Dee Rasmussen
Luciano Ramos
J. Blake Scott
Robert Shumer
Shawna Smith
University of Central Florida
Steve Willis
Adrian Wurr
Amy Zeh
All of our authors and others who
submitted manuscripts for consideration

FOREWORD

Shelley H. Billig
Series Editor

Service-learning research has come a long way both in terms of the rigor of the studies and their more widespread dissemination. The strategic planning that occurred at the turn of the decade was in part responsible: the plan included deliberate attempts to provide incentives to the field to develop a network with robust, highly credible venues for deliberative dialogues, presentations, and publications.

As part of this strategic plan, the *Advances in Service-Learning Research* series was created in 2001. At the time, there were few outlets dedicated to the advancement of service-learning research through rigorous peer-reviewed publications. Along with the International Service-Learning Research Conference, this series was meant to provide a place for the presentation of new research, the discussion of promising theoretical orientations and methodologies to guide the research agenda for the field, and the generation of ideas that could be replicated or extended to advance the practice of service-learning.

Over the past eight volumes, there have been an impressive array of chapters discussing important issues such as field-building and institutionalization at both the higher education and K-12 levels; theory generation and testing to better understand how service-learning leads to social-

Scholarship for Sustaining Service-Learning and Civic Engagement
pp. ix–xii
Copyright © 2008 by Information Age Publishing

emotional and ethical development, civic engagement and development, academic engagement and development, and career exploration; and methodological discussions to show how to increase the quality and quantity of high level research with implications for improvement of practice. Studies have also begun to examine the variables associated with implementation that serve as mediators or moderators of outcomes, and many of the studies presented within this series served as part of the research base used to develop the new K-12 standards and indicators of high quality practice (Billig & Weah, 2008). The power of this type of research should not be underestimated: if disseminated appropriately, these standards will transform practice.

The series has also been among the first to provide a vehicle for dissemination of international research on service-learning and community engagement. Over the years, chapters have reflected research conducted not only in the United States, but also in Australia, South Africa, Ireland, Great Britain, and Canada. These chapters allow the reader to discern how service-learning has evolved throughout the world, and they provide informed analyses for nations to learn from each other.

The wisdom of creating a professional association for service-learning researchers was first argued in this series, and the association came to fruition in 2006. The International Association for Research in Service-Learning and Community Engagement was created as a membership organization to serve active researchers in the field in every nation. The Founding Board developed an infrastructure, became chartered, and is growing continuously, with active committees and structures that increase the probability that the conference and the book series will endure over time. Scholarships for emerging researchers, prizes to recognize quality, and differentiated sessions to help professionals advance their thinking have all been added over the years. Receiving books from this series is also one of the benefits of the organization.

Yet while both the research and the practice of service-learning and community engagement are growing, there is still a long way to go. After all these years, there still is not conceptual clarity in the field such that service-learning and community engagement have a clear and distinct identity well known and articulated by those conducting the research or implementing the practice. The standards and indicators in the K-12 field are driving some change in this area, since they are being embraced by practitioners as a way to maximize impact. However, there is no parallel attempt yet in higher education. On the other hand, in higher education, studies that appeared here and elsewhere have been used to build models of institutionalization that have been widely shared and implemented. However, this type of dissemination has not yet prompted similar action in K-12 education.

Overall, there are too few studies of service-learning that have been replicated, so it is not clear whether the findings hold under different conditions and with different populations. There is too little study of important topics such as diversity, community impacts, academic impacts at the higher education level, teacher impacts at the K-12 levels, and the association between service-learning and later dispositions or utilization of skills as determined in longitudinal studies. There is too little theory testing to know which theories actually ground the practice and explain why service-learning works.

In addition, many of the submissions for peer review for this series still lack the methodological and theoretical rigor needed to be considered valid and reliable and necessary for advancing the field. There are still too few experimental or quasi-experimental study or even studies employing mixed methods. Too many of the studies remain primarily descriptive in nature.

The last common research agendas for the field were published in 2001 and there has been little analysis of what actually has been done as a result of the agendas that were published. While summaries of impacts exist, they are not yet found in series of these types and there have been few, if any, meta-analyses.

Thus while there is great cause for reflection and celebration, there is more work to do. To have a thriving and robust research community, more people need to be involved in the research network. More mentoring needs to occur, more coherence needs to be brought to the field, and deeper, more complex studies need to be conducted. When promising or even negative results occur, they need to be written up in a way that links them better with a theoretical foundation so the field can better understand when and why service-learning works. Publications need to be more self-critical and more thoughtful about how results can be interpreted and understood. More effort needs to be placed on disseminating research that can be used for improving practice. More time needs to be devoted to learning from each others' nations and how the philosophical, political, social, religious, and other cultural aspects of societies influence motivation, implementation, and results. More funding needs to be generated. More effort needs to be placed in advocacy so that the field recognizes the ways in which the research serves as a critical catalyst for high-quality practice. Finally, researchers need to find ways to help inform national, regional, and local policy.

It can be argued that research is currently in its hey day, with more attention being paid to the "evidence base" than ever before. It is time to create common agendas and build the type of research base that will help the field grow and prosper. This book series has been one of many factors instrumental in growth and we invite all of you readers to join in promoting "more and better" research.

REFERENCE

Billig, S. H., & Weah, W. (2008). K–12 service-learning standards for quality practice. In J. C. Kielsmeier, M. Neal, N. Schultz, & T. J. Leeper (Eds.), *Growing to greatness 2008: The state of service-learning project* (pp. 8–15). St. Paul, MN: National Youth Leadership Council.

INTRODUCTION

Scholarship for Sustaining Service-Learning and Community Engagement

Melody A. Bowdon

In October of 2007, more than 400 participants assembled in Tampa, Florida, for the 7th International Research Conference on Service-Learning and Community Engagement. Two hundred fifty presenters from across the United States and around the world shared their research in 65 sessions, addressing topics ranging from international service-learning models to youth mentoring to community impacts of research and learning outcomes for students from K-12 through graduate education. The conference theme was Sustainability and Scholarship: Research and the K-20 Continuum and indeed the event itself—sponsored by Florida Campus Compact and a consortium of member campuses including the University of South Florida, Florida State University, University of Central Florida, Miami Dade College, and the University of Miami—offered an intriguing model for sustaining research on service-learning and community engagement through its cross-institutional and interdisciplinary collaboration that incorporated new and diverse voices in the planning of the conference with guidance from International Association for Research

Scholarship for Sustaining Service-Learning and Civic Engagement
pp. xiii–xix
Copyright © 2008 by Information Age Publishing
All rights of reproduction in any form reserved.

in Service-Learning and Community Engagement (IARSLCE) leaders. The richness of the program demonstrates the vibrancy of our organization's diverse constituency and the followings essay from an expanding range of disciplines represent examples of the exciting scholarship shared during that gathering. These essays, which underwent a rigorous peer review process, approach questions from multiple perspectives, but considered together they underscore the importance of continued meaningful research into student learning outcomes, community impacts, institutional and disciplinary effects, and best practices of service-learning and community engagement. Each emphasizes the importance of reliable and valid assessment for the sustainability of service-learning and community engagement on classroom, program, institution, discipline, and field levels.

In chapter 1, Jessica Katz-Jameson, Patti H. Clayton, and Robert G. Bringle take up a challenge offered by several scholars and suggested by their own previous work to formally study the outcomes of a structured system for reflection among students in a growing interdisciplinary academic minor in nonprofit studies at North Carolina State University. The authors build on existing research on learning outcomes of service-learning in individual courses and on models for service-learning reflection to assess the value of a scaffolded curriculum that relies on articulated learning throughout a sequence of related courses. This piece underscores the importance of assessment to the process of developing and sustaining interdisciplinary programs, and it offers a useful example of a multiyear study approach.

Chapter 2 offers results of a programmatic evaluation of a different nature. Trae Stewart applies Chickering's seven-point model of undergraduate student psychosocial development to assess the effects of a semester-long service-learning experience for 119 honors students at the University of Central Florida. The chapter presents research related to first-year experiences and honors curricula and describes the program's partnership with a local Junior Achievement chapter. The study examines the effects on students' sense of self-efficacy and argues that this type of experience can help students to recognize their ability to contribute to their communities.

Shelley Billig, Dan Jesse, Marc Broderson, and Michelle Grimley offer a rich discussion of service-learning and sustainability in K-12 environments in chapter 3. This chapter features case studies of Philadelphia middle and high schools where service-learning was found to be associated with gains in civic engagement and citizenship, prosocial attitudes and behaviors, and resilience and academic efficacy. This chapter combines comments from K-12 educators and administrators with results from surveys and objective measures of students' academic performance and school behavior to make a compelling argument for the value of character education in secondary education, and it suggests strategies for making such programs effective and sustainable.

In chapter 4, Marjori Maddox Krebs extends research conducted by Billig (2001) to offer the perspective of K-12 teachers on service-learning sustainability. With this previous research in mind, Krebs interviewed six central and northwest Ohio teachers about their experiences implementing and sustaining service-learning projects. Analyzing the results using a phenomenological approach, she confirms and extends the findings of the previous study through the powerful voices of her faculty participants. This work documents the significance of faculty attitudes in program sustainability.

Chapter 5 also focuses on connections between research with faculty and program sustainability. Shelley Henderson, Megan Fair, Paul Sather, and Barbara Dewey argue that pedagogical outcomes and community impacts are improved when faculty members at the University of Nebraska Omaha receive meaningful and institutionally validated feedback on student and community perceptions of their service-learning work. These authors contribute to ongoing conversations about faculty development by using results from focus groups of students, community partners and faculty to shape their study. Through multiple relevant instruments, they secured feedback that challenged faculty to improve their courses. Reviewing study results with community partners and peers particularly helped faculty to make clearer connections between their community-based activities and course objectives. Results of this work will shape a statewide P-16 initiative.

Sally Blomstrom and Hak Tam consider service-learning assessment from a discipline-based perspective in chapter 6 by applying an assessment framework inspired by the 2006 Report of the Commission on Public Relations Education in a student study. They surveyed public relations students at Chadron State University to determine the extent to which the students perceived improvements in targeted personal and intellectual skills after participating in service-learning. They compared outcomes of these majors with a group of students from other majors taking similar courses as well. The results offer some interesting insights into discipline-based assessment and its importance for field-level service-learning sustainability.

In chapter 7, Susan Waters and Elizabeth Carmichael Burton present a study of student moral development associated with service-learning. They compare results from an ethics survey of students at who took a service-learning course with those from comparable students in a course that did not include service-learning. Further, they compare these student results with those of professionals in both the business and nonprofit sectors to suggest that civic engagement can help students to develop ethical reasoning skills.

In chapter 8, Brian Hoyt presents data from a research study involving over 800 students engaged in service-learning experiences at 21 universities to consider impacts of this pedagogy on ethical decision making. Applying a number of experiential education theories, Hoyt concludes that service-learning experiences positively shape students' moral development measurably only when they are particularly intense, and he articulates some criteria for intensity that will be valuable to other researchers and practitioners. This study is an example of a multi-institutional large-scale approach, which can be valuable for sustainability of service-learning and community engagement research throughout a discipline.

MOVING FORWARD: SUSTAINABILITY AND CIVIC ENGAGEMENT

In 2002, the United Nations Educational, Scientific, and Cultural Organization (UNESCO) declared 2005-2014 the Decade of Education for Sustainable Development (DESD). The essential thrust of education for sustainability development from UNESCO's perspective is to prepare "people of all walks of life to plan for, cope with, and find solutions for issues that threaten the sustainability of our planet" (United Nations Educational, Scientific, and Cultural Organization [UNESCO], 2005, p. 7). The broad focus is on finding ways to preserve and maintain the Earth's integrity and ability to continue to support life, but UNESCO and affiliated organizations recognize that this objective involves far more than overtly environmental issues. It encompasses social and economic considerations as well, including gender equity, human rights, poverty reduction, and corporate responsibility and accountability. Clearly much of the work that we do in service-learning and community engagement research is relevant to this agenda. The leaders of UNESCO and affiliated organizations determined long ago, when they began referring to the concept of sustainable development in the early 1990s, that education was a crucial aspect of this movement and that without broad support and participation from our planet's inhabitants, no program for sustainability would succeed and, further, that education was the key to such participation. Whether we share the explicit values of these member organizations or agree entirely with any one particular assessment of planetary conditions and prognoses, we can agree that education for civic engagement is crucial for the future of our planet. And as we move forward in our efforts to research and assess outcomes of our service-learning and community engagement, I hope we'll be mindful of this model of action that emphasizes "improving access to quality basic education, reorienting existing education programmes, developing public understanding and analysis, (and) providing training" (UNESCO, 2005, p. 6).

For some time our efforts as a professional community have been focused on demonstrating learning outcomes for students, benefits for institutions, and, increasingly, impacts on our communities. As service-learning becomes ever-more institutionalized and valued on our campuses, even in the midst of budget crises, we must certainly maintain and indeed strengthen our efforts in all of these areas. According to the Web site (http://www.researchslce.org/Files/aboutus.html), the mission of our organization is "To promote the development and dissemination of research on service-learning and community engagement internationally and across all levels of the education system" (IARSLCE) and I believe that there is room within this vision for joining forces to consider the global concerns that unite our international constituency in urgent ways as we move forward. Sustainability of service-learning and campus-based civic engagement demands research that demonstrates the impacts of our work with students and our partnerships with organizations, but to participate meaningfully in global sustainability efforts we will need to raise questions about the ways in which what we do shapes our communities socially, economically, and environmentally. What impact does service-learning and community engagement have on local and global economies and ecosystems? How does our work fit into a broader context?

Nadinne Cruz and Dwight Giles (2000) called on service-learning and community engagement scholars to conduct more research with community partners in "Where's the Community in Service-Learning Research?" in a special issue of the *Michigan Journal of Community Service Learning* called "From Yesterday to Tomorrow: Strategic Directions for Service-Learning Research." Their article advocates collaborative research between partners and scholars and offers a model of inquiry based on participatory action. In subsequent years studies have been published in that journal and others on relationships between university representatives and partners and on attitudes of partners toward their work with service-learners (e.g., Basinger & Bartholomew, 2006; Dorado & Giles, 2004; Kecskes, 2006; Miron & Moely, 2006; Sandy & Holland, 2006; Worrall, 2007). These, in addition to many other studies on community-based research, are critical for our work, but moving forward it will be valuable to invite into our conversations even more of the people served by these partnerships. We need studies that move beyond the pedagogy and partnership aspects of service-learning to assess community impacts on a campus and program level. Certainly in my own field of composition studies, for example, researchers are looking at ways in which community collaborations impact people served by our partners as we assess clients' reception of and uses for the documents we create through these campus-community collaborations. As we move toward a more interdisciplinary attitude toward research, it will be crucial to study ways in which, for example, universities with large-scale multidimensional service-learning and community engagement programs are affecting local communities, not only in terms of attitudes toward the institution but also in terms of humanistic impact and community sustainability.

According to the highlights of Campus Compact's 2007 report, "Nearly one-third of students on member campuses participated in campus-organized service and service-learning projects during the 2006–2007 academic year, contributing $7 billion in services to their communities" (p. 2). The report shows significant participation by community partners in course-related activities, including visits to classes and feedback to shape programs and courses, but the need continues to integrate partners and the clients they serve more fully into our programs, activities, and research. Data from such work could be used to sustain our programs in times of budget uncertainty by helping researchers and educators to secure funding for our work, but it could also be used formatively, to help us design courses and programs that will better address human needs on a global scale. My coeditors and I hope that you will find the following essays informative and inspiring and we look forward to the 2008 conference with its theme, "The Scholarship of Engagement: Dimensions of Reciprocal Partnerships."

REFERENCES

Basinger, N., & Bartholomew, K. (2006, Spring). Service-learning in nonprofit organizations: Motivations, expectations, and outcomes. *Michigan Journal of Community Service Learning, 12*(2), 15-26.

Cone, D., & Payne, P. (2002). When campus and community collide: Campus community partnerships from a community perspective. *The Journal of Public Affairs, 6*, 203-218.

Cruz, N., & Giles, D. E. (2000). Where's the community in service-learning research? [Special Issue]. *Michigan Journal of Community Service Learning, 7*(2), 28-34.

Dorado, S. and Giles, D.E. (2004, Fall). Service-learning partnerships: Paths of engagement. *Michigan Journal of Community Service Learning, 11*(1), 25-37.

Campus Compact. (2007). *2007 annual survey statistics highlights.* Retrieved August 1, 2008 from http://www.compact.org/about/statistics/

International Association of Research in Service-Learning and Community Engagement. (n.d.). *IARSLCE: About Us.* Retrieved August 28, 2008, from http://www.researchslce.org/Files/aboutus.html

Kecskes, K. (2006, Spring). Behind the rhetoric: Applying a cultural theory lens to community-campus partnership development. *Michigan Journal of Community Service Learning, 12*(2), 5-14.

Miron, D., & Moely, B. (2006, Spring). Community agency voice and benefit in service-learning. *Michigan Journal of Community Service Learning, 12*(2), 27-37.

Sandy, M., & Holland, B. A. (2006, Fall). Different worlds and common ground: Community partner perspectives on campus-community partnerships. *Michigan Journal of Community Service Learning, 13*(1), 30-43.

United Nations Educational, Scientific, and Cultural Organization. (2005). *International implementation scheme.* Retrieved August 28, 2008 from http:// 209.85.165.104/search?q=cache:mmG2--3MMggJ:unesdoc.unesco.org/ images/0014/001486/148654e.pdf+unesco+international+ implementation+scheme&hl=en&ct=clnk&cd=3&gl=us

Worrall, L. (2007, Fall). Asking the community: A case study of community partner perspectives. *Michigan Journal of Community Service Learning, 14*(1), 5-17.

PART I

SUSTAINING INTERDISCIPLINARY PROGRAMS IN HIGHER EDUCATION

CHAPTER 1

INVESTIGATING STUDENT LEARNING WITHIN AND ACROSS LINKED SERVICE-LEARNING COURSES

Jessica Katz Jameson, Patti H. Clayton, and Robert G. Bringle

This chapter summarizes the design, preliminary results, and primary challenges of a multiyear investigation of student learning within and across a sequence of service-learning enhanced courses. The investigators are assessing written student reflection products that are guided by specific prompts designed to facilitate higher order reasoning in the context of specific learning objectives, which are shared by multiple courses in a nonprofit studies minor. The results of the research, based on independent assessment of student products and in line with the intent of the minor's developmental design, demonstrate that student learning in later courses is more advanced in terms of Bloom's Taxonomy than student learning in earlier courses. Although limited in scope, this study represents the first evidence we are aware of in the research literature demonstrating that instructional methods intentionally designed to build on earlier service-learning enhanced courses do lead to higher order thinking and progressively more sophisticated understanding of course material. This ongoing research project demonstrates an intentional, analytical process of curriculum design and evaluation

Scholarship for Sustaining Service-Learning and Civic Engagement
pp. 3–27

that should lead to the sustainability of the minor. The chapter examines the challenges that underlie the limitations of the study and suggests practical implications for continued scholarship of teaching and learnings work and for the institutionalization of other interdisciplinary programs.

EDITORS' NOTE: The poster presentation associated with this article was recognized for Outstanding Achievement in Research at the International Research Conference on Service-Learning and Community Engagement.

Although service-learning courses include a variety of components that can be implemented in different ways, there is widespread agreement that reflection is central to the learning process (Bringle & Hatcher, 1999; Conrad & Hedin, 1990; Eyler & Giles, 1999; Eyler, Giles, & Schmiede, 1996; Hatcher & Bringle, 1997; Stanton, 1990). As many authors have noted, however, more research is needed to document how and under what conditions reflection helps students achieve course objectives and other desired learning outcomes (Hatcher & Bringle, 1997; Maki, 2004; Strouse, 2003). This discussion reports the third phase of a multiyear scholarship of teaching and learning (SoTL) project that examines the use of critical reflection to generate, deepen, and document student learning.

This SoTL project responds to challenges of service-learning research noted by Eyler (2002) and by Bringle (2003), who have suggested that the field needs more rigorous research designs, more specificity in the identification of independent variables, more precise definition and measurement of outcomes, and more explicit theoretical grounding. It also directly responds to Eyler's concern that "there are few researchers who have developed a sustained research plan with multiple studies building on previous work" (p. 5). The article includes a brief overview of previous assessments in addition to a rich description of the research project.

The most persuasive evidence of service-learning's contributions to academic outcomes comes from studies that include an independent assessment of learning (versus self-reports of perceived learning by students). Markus, Howard, and King (1993) incorporated service-learning into half of the sections of a large political science course. All sections took a common final examination to assess mastery of course content. The students in the service-learning sections demonstrated significantly better learning than students in the other sections. Osborne, Hammerich, and Hensley (1998) assessed learning using independent raters' evaluation of student products written during and at the end of the course for the degree to which they met four course objectives centered on communication issues: (a) complexity of communication, (b) integration of practical examples into communications, (c) sensitivity of communication, and (d) awareness of diversity. Students in the sections that included a community service component produced higher quality written products on all but complexity of communication, compared to students in the traditional sections. Kendrick (1996) found that student performance in sections including service-learning was better on essay examinations, but not multiple-choice examinations, when compared to students in previous semesters of the course that did not include service-learning. Kendrick suggests this pattern indicates that "service-learning promotes quality of thought, even though it may not improve knowledge content" (p. 79).

The work of Vogelgesang and Astin (2000) is one of the few longitudinal studies that have assessed the effects of service across courses. However, they relied on self-report measures of academic outcomes (grade point average, growth in writing skills, critical thinking skills) to compare students who had service-learning course experiences to students who had participated in other forms of service, after controlling for characteristics of students when entering college and for college size and type. The results indicate that both cocurricular community service and service-learning were associated with higher academic outcomes, but service-learning had a larger degree of association and was independent of participation in co-curricular community service. The excessive use of self-report measures of outcomes has been questioned (Steinke & Buresh, 2002). Although they can provide useful information for some research questions, such data do not provide convincing evidence for one of the most important, fundamental questions about service-learning: what is the learning that results from service-learning? The current study attempts to examine this question by applying the process of independent assessment of student learning to a multicourse setting.

This chapter summarizes the design, preliminary results, and primary challenges of a multiyear investigation of student learning that does not rely on student surveys or anecdotal data but rather assesses written student reflection products that are guided by specific prompts designed to facilitate higher order reasoning in the context of specific learning objectives. Using reflection as a service-learning assessment strategy has been promoted by Strouse (2003), who suggests: "Deliberately conceptualizing and utilizing student reflection as an authentic assessment strategy can concurrently stimulate student learning and provide teachers with guidance to improve subsequent instruction" (p. 75).

Extending the earlier phases of this SoTL project (see Ash, Clayton, & Atkinson, 2005), this research is grounded in the theoretical framework provided by Bloom's Taxonomy, which is used to develop hierarchically expressed learning objectives and associated reflection prompts. In the earlier work, Ash et al. applied two rubrics to student reflection products from two unrelated courses in an investigation of changes in student learning over time within the semester. This chapter builds on that work by documenting learning through reflection on experience as students progress through the multiple courses composing a minor enhanced with threaded (or cumulative) service-learning. The development of an interdisciplinary minor in nonprofit studies provided a valuable opportunity to start a dialogue among program faculty (those faculty developing the minor and teaching related courses) regarding learning outcomes, teaching philosophies, and the design of service-learning experiences. As Maki (2004) suggests, the next logical step in the development of the minor is to assess to what extent students are achieving the desired learning outcomes and then to use this data for program evaluation purposes, leading to ongoing refinement of the individual courses and of the course sequence as a whole.

This investigation has several goals. First and foremost, the ongoing assessment of student products allows us to refine our reflection prompts and guides course and program design, implementation, and development. This course development has in fact been ongoing since the inception of the project, with reflection prompts and rubrics refined each semester. Continuous examination of reflection products as students move through the program allows the research team to be intentional in both course and curricular revision and supports efforts to sustain both the interdisciplinary and linked service-learning roots of the minor. A second goal is to test Ash et al.'s (2005) use of Bloom's Taxonomy to develop hierarchically expressed learning objectives and associated reflection prompts and rubrics not only within but also across courses. A third goal is to explore the relationship between learning outcomes in various linked courses, which may encourage additional faculty to adopt the threaded service-learning model (Berle, 2006). An important outcome of our examination of the difficulties encountered in obtaining a complete data set is the identification of several challenges that may be common in this type of scholarship and, more generally, in implementing a curriculum with linked service-learning. Some of these challenges are associated with the service-learning process per se, some are "people" problems, and some emerge from institutional contexts. Naming these challenges better positions practitioner-scholars and their institutions to address and overcome them and thereby to facilitate institutionalization of engaged teaching and scholarship.

BACKGROUND ON THIS SOTL PROJECT: INVESTIGATING THE DEAL MODEL FOR INTEGRATING CRITICAL REFLECTION AND ASSESSMENT

Ash et al. (2005) presented the results of the first phase of the SoTL project that laid the groundwork for the present study. The critical reflection and assessment model developed by Ash and Clayton and their faculty and student colleagues at North Carolina State University (NC State) is grounded in the conviction that reflection is the component of the service-learning process that maximizes the quality of both learning and service and, therefore, that effective reflection requires intentional design driven by the desired outcomes (Ash & Clayton, 2004; Ash et al., 2005; Clayton et al., 2005). The DEAL model is an adaptable, three-step structure for guiding reflection, which is integrated with a critical thinking rubric (grounded in the work of Paul & Elder, 2002) and a set of learning objective-based rubrics grounded in Bloom's Taxonomy (1956). The model moves students from *Description* of their service-learning experiences through *Examination* of those experiences in accordance with specific learning objectives (generally, in the case of service-learning, in the categories of academic enhancement, civic engagement, and personal growth) to *Articulation* of *Learning* outcomes. The final written product of the DEAL model, called an Articulated Learning (AL), is structured to answer the questions "What did I learn," "How did I learn it," "Why does it matter," and "What will I do in light of it." The Examine step of this model is structured in terms of hierarchically expressed (per Bloom) learning objectives, customized for each learning goal, to move student reasoning from lower to higher levels, with the highest level desired being determined by each instructor for each course. The two rubrics (i.e., one based on Bloom for learning objectives; one based on Paul and Elder for critical thinking) are used to provide students with feedback, to build their capacity to examine and enhance the quality of their own thinking, and, as desired by the instructor, to provide a summative assessment. They also provide a basis for collecting evidence about student learning that can be used in the scholarship of teaching and learning and in program evaluation.

Ash et al. (2005) described a study design in which students reflected using the DEAL model on several occasions throughout the semester; students submitted draft ALs after each of four reflection sessions for two rounds of feedback, and the first and final drafts of each were collaboratively scored (blind to student author, draft, and date submitted) by a faculty-student team using the two rubrics. The following three research questions guided the study: (1) Do the assessment tools improve the ALs across drafts within a reflection session, from first to final version? (2) Do the assessment tools improve the first drafts of the ALs over the course of the semester, from early to later reflection sessions? and (3) Are there differences in the degree to which students achieve mastery among the three categories of learning goals (academic enhancement, civic engagement, and personal growth)?

The researchers found that although scores on written products for both the learning objective and critical thinking rubrics did improve across drafts and over the course of the semester, students showed greater improvement in critical thinking. For the three categories of learning, students had the most difficult time with the academic objectives, which more than the other two required students to critique course material and theory. The authors posited that service-learning is a "counter-normative" approach to learning (Clayton & Ash, 2004; Howard, 1998) that poses significant learning challenges to students, who are used to listening to and absorbing lecture material rather than being expected to analyze and evaluate it. Therefore, both instructors and students may need additional support to help them make the "shifts in perspective and practice" required for and fostered by service-learning, particularly with respect to the role of writing as a learning process, not simply a learning product (Clayton & Ash, 2004). This study resulted in the development of new instructional tools, (e.g., a tutorial on critical reflection in service-learning), revised reflection prompts, and enhanced faculty development (including for faculty in the nonprofit studies minor). It was built on in an interinstitutional Phase II, which is an ongoing process of adaptation, implementation, and investigation conducted by practitioner-scholars on partner campuses under the guidance of Clayton (Clayton et al., 2006; Clayton & McGuire, 2007; Henry & Clayton, 2007; McGuire et al., 2007). This initial work was also critical to the development of new service-learning based curricula, such as the minor in nonprofit studies that extends this study by serving as the context for Phase III.

BACKGROUND ON PHASE III: ASSESSING LEARNING THROUGH CRITICAL REFLECTION IN LINKED COURSES

With initial funding provided by the Kellogg Foundation and with support from the university's Institute for Nonprofits and Service-Learning Program (now the Center for Excellence in Curricular Engagement), faculty and students at NC State collaborated during 2003-05 to develop an interdisciplinary minor in nonprofit studies. Housed in the College of Humanities and Social Sciences, the minor is open to undergraduates in any discipline and is designed around what we call "threaded service-learning." Threaded service-learning is the intentional use of service-learning as a vehicle to connect the teaching and learning processes across one or more courses or other experiences in a developmentally-sequenced and progressive fashion, which is designed to increase student learning and critical thinking. It is a process of learning through reflection on multiple experiences that build cumulatively over time (Clayton, Jameson, Metelsky, & Summers, 2007). In the case of the NC State non-profit studies minor, the threaded service-learning component is hierar-chically structured using Bloom's Taxonomy to articulate common, cross-course learning objectives within five themes, which were identified by the collaborating faculty as the primary challenges facing leaders (broadly defined) in the nonprofit sector:

1. Aligning mission, methods, and resources;
2. Balancing individual interests and the common good;
3. Earning and maintaining the public trust;
4. Capitalizing on opportunities associated with diversity; and
5. Moving beyond charity toward systemic change.

Each "leadership challenge" is expressed in terms of six levels of Bloom-based learning objectives, and the courses cumulatively challenge and support the students to ever-higher levels of reasoning within each. The introduction to nonprofits course targets levels 1–3 (knowledge, com-prehension, and application) across the five leadership challenges, setting the stage for students to progress up to levels 4, 5, and 6 (analysis, synthe-sis, and evaluation) in the intermediate courses; in the capstone course student reflection is structured to support their thinking at the level of evaluation across all five leadership challenges and in the context of inte-grating the multiple service-learning experiences they have had in previ-ous courses. The DEAL model for integrating critical reflection and assessment is used across the course sequence, with the Examine step structured to facilitate meaning making up to the target level of learning objectives in each leadership challenge. The six-level learning objective rubrics are available for student and faculty use both formatively (giving feedback) and summatively (assigning final grades). The core conviction underlying this approach to the design of the minor is that iteratively and cumulatively examining actual experiences through guided reflection that continually pushes their thinking to deeper and more complex levels will help students internalize and therefore be able to act on a truly sophisti-cated understanding of the leadership challenges.

Instructors of the courses in the nonprofit minor worked with the uni-versity's service-learning professional staff and followed the Phase I and Phase II SoTL process of scoring student products (ALs) and revising reflection prompts and rubrics, including, over time, producing reflection assignments specifically customized to each course level (introductory, intermediate, capstone) in the minor (see Appendix). Specific research questions guiding Phase III include (1) Do the reflection and assessment tools facilitate student learning to the level of reasoning desired within each course? (2) Do the reflection and assessment tools facilitate student learning to the level of reasoning desired across the courses in the minor? and (3) Is there greater evidence of higher level reasoning in some leadership challenges than in others?

METHOD

The data for this study came from students in three core courses in the minor: Introduction to Nonprofits, Nonprofit Leadership and Development (a required intermediate course), and the Capstone course. Faculty assigned reflection activities using reflection prompts developed in accordance with the targeted level of reasoning within each leadership challenge; students in each course wrote one articulated learning (AL) for each leadership challenge, using the prompts associated with the relevant learning objectives rubric to guide their thinking, and ALs were submitted to instructors for assessment as a course assignment. AL assignments were collected and scored by a faculty-student team, blind to author (note that, unlike in Phase I, the products were not blind as to date produced, due to the progression across leadership challenges as the semester unfolded).

A team of three raters scored the ALs against the learning objectives rubrics, noting which level each AL demonstrated (see Appendix). For example, for leadership challenge one, "Aligning Mission, Methods, and Resources," the following four items provide evidence that students have achieved level five, "synthesize": (a) provides a new idea for better aligning mission, methods, and resources; (b) explains why new idea might lead to improved alignment, in light of evaluative criteria; (c) discusses changes that need to occur for the new idea to be implemented; (d) discusses likelihood of new idea being carried out. Each AL was given a score of 1 (identify) to 6 (evaluate), reflecting the highest level at which the student demonstrated at least some thinking. In order to distinguish between partial and complete achievement of a given level, scorers gave a "+" or a "−" in addition to the number of each score (e.g., a product that only included responses to "a" and "b" at level 5, would be scored as a "5−"). Raters discussed scores and reached consensus on most ALs.

Examples of student writing at different levels demonstrate the learning outcomes achieved. For example, the rubric for the level 3 learning objective within the leadership challenge of "Aligning Mission, Methods, and Resources" asks students to "provide an example from your partner organization that illustrates the relationship among mission, methods, and resources." A student in the intro course demonstrates achievement of level 3, application, when s/he writes:

> The community kitchen has utilized its resources such as donations from the community around it [sic], to aid in providing real meals with fresh ingredients, allowing those in need of the program's assistance to keep hope and not feel like they should give up trying to climb back into the world of stability.

An example of student writing from the leadership course achieves level 6 (evaluation) by identifying challenges a leader may face when implementing a recommendation for improving staff communication:

> In the short-term ... I believe the staff should work on internal relations. By eliminating personnel-related distractions, they would be better able to focus on ensuring they are working towards optimal alignment. However, I understand it is difficult for an individual to openly acknowledge "issues" that he or she might have with others in the office, thus slowing down any progress that might be made on fixing the problems and creating an environment where people talk about problems "behind each others' backs."

RESULTS

Due to differences in teaching styles and in implementation of reflection assignments, the investigators did not collect the intended complete sets of comparable products from each of the three classes (see Exhibit 1.1). While this limits our ability to answer the original research questions comprehensively, the results led to the identification of several obstacles related to assessment, linking learning outcomes across a curriculum, and institutionalization of interdisciplinary programs, to be discussed below.

The first research question is whether the reflection and assessment tools facilitate student learning to the intended level of reasoning. Exhibit 1 demonstrates that 29 of 34 (85%) students in the Introduction to Nonprofits course demonstrated learning at the highest level expected, level 3. To break this down further, six of these 29 students received a "3–" (they only addressed one of the two subitems), five students achieved a "3" (they partially addressed both subitems) and nine students achieved a "3+" (they completely addressed both subitems). In the nonprofit leadership course, in which the desired level of learning is level 6, 89% of students reached level 3, and not surprisingly the numbers decrease at levels 4, 5, and 6. Nonetheless, with 21% of students achieving level 6, there is

Exhibit 1.1.   Summary of Student ALs Included in Dataset per Course

	Introduction to Nonprofits (n = 34)	Nonprofit Leadership & Development (n = 38)	Capstone (n=1)
None	2 (6%)	4 (10%)	
Level 1: Identify	32 (94%)	34 (89%)	1 (100%)
Level 2: Describe	32 (94%)	34 (89%)	1 (100%)
Level 3: Apply	29 (85%)	34 (89%)	1 (100%)
Level 4: Analyze	NA	33 (86%)	1 (100%)
Level 5: Synthesize	NA	23 (60%)	1 (100%)
Level 6: Evaluate	NA	8 (21%)	1 (100%)

some evidence that the reflection tools facilitate student learning to the desired level of reasoning.

The second research question is whether the tools facilitate student learning across courses. The limitations of the student products collected make it difficult to answer this question at this preliminary stage. While some of the students in the nonprofit leadership course had taken the introductory course previously, they did not complete the AL assignment as we expected, so we could not compare their written products across the two courses. One interesting finding is that two of the nine students who achieved the highest level of learning in the Introduction to Nonprofits course had taken the nonprofit leadership course previously. The AL written by the student in the Capstone course was compared to earlier writing from a previous course taken by the same student. The capstone AL demonstrated higher levels of reasoning than the AL written on the same leadership challenge when the student was in the leadership and development course. The current data is therefore promising, but it will be necessary to collect and score more student products in order to make strong claims about the ability of the reflection tools to facilitate learning across courses. The team will work with faculty during future semesters to achieve better consistency in reflection assignments and thereby increase the size of the sample of student products.

The third research question is more specifically related to the curriculum and involves whether there is evidence of higher level reasoning for some leadership challenges than others. Students in the nonprofit leadership course wrote ALs for all five challenges. Only those ALs that followed the correct format and that were revised following instructor feedback were scored, accounting for differences in the number of products for each leadership challenge. Exhibit 1.2 illustrates the levels of learning objectives achieved for each set of leadership challenges.

Exhibit 1.2.   Learning Objectives Achieved Across Leadership Challenges: Nonprofit Leadership and Development (Intermediate Course)

	LC 1 (n = 9)	LC 2 (n = 6)	LC 3 (n = 3)	LC 4 (n = 11)	LC 5 (n = 9)
Level 1: Identify	8 (89%)	0	1 (33%)	7 (63%)	4 (44%)
Level 2: Describe	5 (55%)	4 (66%)	2 (66%)	10 (91%)	7 (78%)
Level 3: Apply	9 (100%)	6 (100%)	3 (100%)	11 (100%)	9 (100%)
Level 4: Analyze	8 (89%)	6 (100%)	3 (100%)	9 (82%)	7 (78%)
Level 5: Synthesize	6 (66%)	4 (66%)	1 (33%)	6 (54%)	5 (55%)
Level 6: Evaluate	2 (22%)	1 (16%)	1 (33%)	2 (18%)	2 (22%)

The results in Exhibit 1.2 are inconclusive but illustrate some interesting patterns. Students attain learning objective levels 3 and 4, apply and analyze, most consistently across all five leadership challenges. This may indicate that the prompts at these levels were the most helpful in facilitating student reasoning. It may also be the case that students have more experience applying course concepts to experiences and analyzing alternative approaches than they do generating recommendations and evaluating the challenges associated with implementing them, and therefore these learning objectives are more easily achieved than others. It is also notable that very few students achieved levels 5 and 6 across the leadership challenges, suggesting that we need to help students reach these higher levels of reasoning regardless of the specific content.

The low numbers of ALs that demonstrated reasoning at level 1 and level 2 may be surprising, since students should not achieve level 3 or higher without demonstrating the ability to identify and describe the phenomenon of interest. This is an artifact of the rubrics and a result of lack of consistency in the actual implementation of the AL assignment, however. For example, to demonstrate level 1, "identify," students were asked to use course readings to define the key concept(s) within the given leadership challenge. In some cases relevant readings were not provided, and therefore students were unable to meet the requirements of the rubric. Nonetheless, many of these same students were able to achieve level 3 and higher objectives, which demonstrates that they understand the concepts and are often able to discuss them at more sophisticated levels of reasoning.

DISCUSSION

This research offers preliminary results of assessing student learning outcomes across sequentially ordered courses using quantitative scoring of student products. This approach is unique in that most assessments of student learning are based on self-reports in a single course at the end of the semester.

From a curricular perspective, the approach to developing the minor in nonprofit studies demonstrates the importance of specifying learning objectives and specific aspirations for those objectives in hierarchically ordered courses. This approach is different than focusing only on one course and demonstrates how civically engaged work can benefit from different units of analysis (e.g., department, major, degree; see Kecskes, 2006). It is also different than the work reported in Berle (2006), which describes the progressive integration of service and service-learning across a course sequence but does not investigate associated learning outcomes. Berle does point to the value of the sequential design that underlies his own courses and the structure of our minor, suggesting that "a sequence of service-learning courses might maximize the potential civic and academic outcomes of service-learning" (p. 43). Furthermore, in the nonprofit studies curriculum, the level of mastery that is expected of students is shared with them as an integral part of both instruction and assessment of student performance. These are all strengths of curriculum development that Marsh (2007) views as being central to good SoTL:

> One of the reasons learning outcomes are taking "center stage" is because research on this topic asserts that learning is enhanced when students are made aware of the mastery expectations for their courses and degree programs (Appleby, 2003; Chappuis & Stiggins, 2002; Halonen, Appleby, Brewer, Buskist, Gillem, Halpern, Lloyd, Rudmann, & Whitlow, 2002; McKenney, 2003).

Although these data are based on relatively small samples at this point in the development of the minor, they suggest several important lessons. First, an examination of a multi-course, interdisciplinary curriculum in terms of common learning objectives provides a basis for curricular development, faculty development, and design and evaluation for program sustainability. Second, theories of learning (e.g., Bloom; Paul & Elder) can provide a basis for informing the development of learning objectives and the assessment of outcomes (see Hutchings, 2007). Third, all three phases of this SoTL project illustrate how cross-sectional and longitudinal designs can be used to track student learning across time within a course (Ash et al., 2005) and across courses (current research). Fourth, as suggested by Steinke and Fitch (2003), assessment procedures can be developed for both content specific learning objectives (e.g., Leadership Challenges) and general reasoning (critical thinking), as demonstrated in written student work.

The results of the research, based on independent assessment of students' written products and in line with the intent of the minor's developmental design, demonstrate that student learning in later courses is more advanced in terms of Bloom's Taxonomy than student learning in earlier courses. This may be particularly significant as the academy continues a trend toward increasing interdisciplinary and cross-disciplinary curricula, which require students to make conceptual and analytical links within and across courses. Although limited in scope, this study represents the first evidence that we are aware of in the research literature demonstrating that instructional methods intentionally designed to build upon earlier service-learning enhanced courses do lead to higher order thinking and more sophisticated understanding of course material.

LIMITATIONS, CHALLENGES, AND FUTURE DIRECTIONS

This study illustrates the utility of SoTL projects in the continuous improvement of courses and curriculum, although we note several limitations. The nature of the data collection to date makes it difficult to make strong claims regarding our research questions at this point. With respect to the first research question, whether the reflection and assessment tools help students achieve desired levels of reasoning within courses, there is some evidence to suggest that the tools help, but confounding factors include the instructors' willingness and capacity to use the tools, the type and duration of service-learning activity, and differences in individual student ability coming into the course. A significant difference across courses is instructors' use of feedback to facilitate student learning: due to time constraints, no feedback-revision process was used for the ALs in the introductory or Capstone courses, while there was a feedback-revision process in the leadership course.

The second research question is whether the reflection and assessment tools help students achieve desired levels of reasoning across the courses in the minor. Again, there is limited evidence suggesting that the students who achieved the highest levels of reasoning were those who had taken more than one course in the minor, but there were not enough of those cases to make a strong claim to that effect. Another difficulty of cross-course assessment is that students do not always take the courses in the intended sequence of Introduction to Nonprofits, Nonprofit Leadership and Development, other intermediate courses, internship, and Capstone. When students take courses out of sequence it is difficult to examine systematically the relationship between learning in one course and learning in another.

Since only the students in the Nonprofit Leadership and Development course wrote ALs within all five leadership challenges, we also need more data to answer the third research question: whether there is greater evidence of higher level reasoning in some leadership challenges than others. In this case it is also important to note that a confounding factor is the point in the semester at which a student writes a given AL: as found in the first phase of this research (Ash et al., 2005), we would expect ALs written later in the semester to demonstrate higher levels of reasoning than those written at the beginning of the semester, as students develop their reasoning abilities and their capacity to gauge and improve the quality of their own thinking. The team will need to find a way to overcome this potential confounder in order to accurately investigate the third research question in the future.

The difficulties encountered in this study heightened the research team's awareness of three types of obstacles to consider in future SoTL research and curriculum development: those related to process, to people, and to context. Greater attention in all three areas is needed to facilitate effective faculty adoption of critical reflection and overall sustainability of an interdisciplinary minor, not to mention in order to improve the quality and value of assessment activities such as the current project. At the process level is the nature of service-learning itself and, within that, the nature of critical reflection, and, within that, the nature of the particular model for critical reflection under investigation. A significant commitment of time is needed to build instructors' capacity to integrate service-learning with course content and to facilitate meaningful learning through critical reflection on experience. As indicated above, the pedagogy is counternormative and does not easily lend itself to widespread adoption by faculty who do not or cannot choose to devote time to their own and their students' capacity building. One of the main objections we have heard is that time in class must be devoted to content, and instructors do not have time to have students review tutorials or other tools that would help them learn how to learn this way. Given the topic area of our minor (nonprofit studies), instructors see the value of having students spend time working with a nonprofit in an existing course, but they sometimes resist the notion that their pedagogy must change as well.

Related to the challenge of process are issues associated with people. Both individually and collectively, instructors need to be motivated to adopt service-learning and to devote significant time and effort to doing it well. Berle (2006) also discusses this challenge in his efforts to integrate service-learning into a horticulture curriculum. He notes that time, inadequate understanding of the benefits, and lack of knowledge about how to use service-learning are all barriers. While he had some success introducing a series of three linked service-learning courses to students, he commented that he taught all three courses, making it easier than coordinating among multiple professors. As the team has learned through this project, faculty also need to have a collaborative approach to course and curriculum development, which may also run counter to typical academic values of independence and academic freedom. One question this project has raised is how such programs can motivate additional faculty to participate in both the teaching and the research project. The program's current emphasis on promoting engaged scholarship provides one example of how it might be possible to encourage faculty to integrate their teaching and service into their research such that all three aspects of their work are enhanced and lead to scholarly publication.

Institutional norms and values comprise challenges of institutional context. University norms do not currently support a requirement for students in the minor to take the courses in sequence. This is due to a typical disciplinary minor structure that allows students to declare a minor after they have taken the required number of courses. The nonprofit minor is itself structurally counternormative, in that we want students to declare it in advance and take courses in the intended sequence. A second contextual challenge relates to priorities and reward structures that privilege research over teaching and likewise value scientific (or social scientific) scholarship over the scholarship of teaching and learning (typical in research-extensive universities). This makes it difficult for faculty to justify devoting significant time to building capacity for service-learning or SoTL work. Finally, while it has recently become popular to promote interdisciplinary work, historical academic structures that create "turf wars" and competition for scarce resources have built walls around departments and disciplines that make it difficult to engage in collaboration. As we have found, even when a small group of faculty are willing to collaborate and embrace service-learning in principle, all of the preceding challenges impede progress.

Despite the challenges and limitations, preliminary results indicate that future research is warranted and beneficial. We hope and intend that our continued research and promulgation of the results will provide persuasive evidence for the value of the threaded service-learning approach, leading to increased faculty adoption of service-learning and to the sustainability of the minor within our institution as well as to the use of this model for integrated curricular development at NC State and beyond. To that end we will continue to collect and score student products, until we have a more complete data set for curricular-level assessment. Based on the limitations of relying solely on the learning objectives rubrics in formative assessment and in research, we will integrate the critical thinking standards into future research design, as suggested and modeled by Ash et al. (2005). In order to ensure that the rubrics are not limiting our understanding of student learning, we also plan to supplement this approach with a qualitative method of narrative analysis. Using the critical thinking standards and a more qualitative reading of the ALs will allow us to more readily document and analyze reasoning that is not captured by our existing learning objectives rubrics. We also want to document student learning in the other categories of learning at stake in service-learning, such as civic engagement and personal growth (Ash & Clayton, 2004; Strouse, 2003). A related project involves broadening the emphasis on investigating student learning in the minor to encompass faculty learning as well. A pilot inter-institutional project investigating student learning, faculty learning, and the relationship between them is underway as part of Phase II of this DEAL-based SoTL project (McGuire et al., 2007), and the current study will be expanded similarly to include faculty teaching in the minor in the coming semesters. We believe that as faculty become more conscious of the ways in which they learn the service-learning pedagogy through professional development and through their own reflective practice, they also become more aware of the challenges associated with such learning (i.e., of a new pedagogy), with the result that they are more effective teaching with this counter-normative pedagogy. And it may be the case that this broader investigation will help with recruitment of additional faculty into the teaching and research project, as the scholarship and enhanced practice that should result from it may be strong motivators for participation. A final goal is to leverage our experience with this SoTL project and our institution's current interest in engaged scholarship to enhance the perceived legitimacy of service-learning, the scholarship of teaching and learning, and interdisciplinary collaboration.

APPENDIX: SAMPLE REFLECTION PROMPTS
AND RUBRIC FOR LEADERSHIP CHALLENGE 1:
ALIGNING MISSION, METHODS, AND RESOURCES

DEAL Nonprofit Minor Reflection Framework
Leadership Challenge 1
Aligning Mission, Methods, and Resources
Introduction to Nonprofits Course

DESCRIBE

A.   Objectively describe what you have done and observed in interactions with your community partner *(Who did it in involve? Who was not there? What occurred? What did you do? What did others do? When did it happen? Where did it take place? Why did it occur this way?)*

B.   Use the course readings to define *mission, methods,* and *resources.*

C.   Based on A and B above discuss your organization's missions, methods and resources: Complete Steps 1 and 2 for Diagram A.

- What is your organizations' *mission?* Explain it in your own words.

- What are the *methods* used in pursuit of this mission (e.g., services provided, educational programming, etc.)? What do the methods accomplish and how do they accomplish it?

- What are the *resources* needed to implement these methods (e.g., money, volunteers, facilities, staff, time)? What are the current resources used by your organization and how does the organization attain them?

EXAMINE

A.   Complete Steps 3 and 4 for Diagram A.

B.   What are the relationships between mission, methods, and resources in your organization?

- What internal and external factors help to explain the selection of this mission, these methods, and these resources?

- Does any one of these three drive the others?

- Which would you say is the most influential in shaping the others?

- Why is it this way?

ARTICULATED LEARNING

What did you learn?

How did you learn it?

Why does it matter?

What will you do in light of it?

DEAL Nonprofit Minor Reflection Framework
Leadership Challenge 1
Aligning Mission, Methods, and Resources
Nonprofit Leadership and Development Course

Step 1: DESCRIBE

A.   Objectively describe what you have done and observed in interactions with your community partner since the last reflection session. *(Who did it in involve? Who was not there? What occurred? What did you do? What did others do? When did it happen? Where did it take place? Why did it occur this way?)*
B.   Use the course readings to define *mission, methods,* and *resources.*
C.   Based on A and B above discuss your organization's missions, methods and resources: Complete Steps 1 and 2 from Diagram A

- What is your organization's *mission?* Explain it in your own words.
- What are the *methods* used in pursuit of this mission (e.g., services provided, educational programming, etc.)? What do the methods accomplish and how do they accomplish it?
- What are the *resources* needed to implement these methods (e.g., money, volunteers, facilities, staff, time)? What are the current resources used by the NPO and how does the NPO attain them?

Step 2: EXAMINE the Ideas from Step 1

A. Complete Steps 3 and 4 from Diagram A
B. What are the relationships between mission, methods, and resources in your organization?

   • What internal and external factors help to explain the selection of this mission, these methods, and these resources?
   • Does any one of these three drive the others?
   • Which would you say is the most influential in shaping the others?
   • Why?

C. Consider Diagram B: Chart the organization using the evaluative criteria and add other criteria you believe are central to your community partner as necessary: [Note: Diagram B not included in Appendix]

   • For each, on a scale of 1–10 [1 = *not at all*, 10 = *extremely*] to what extent does your experience with the organization suggest that, in its mission, it

      (a) Says it prioritizes the criterion in question?
      (b) Actually embodies the criterion in question?
           If there are differences between (a) and (b), what do you believe explains them?

   • For each, on a scale of 1–10 [1 = *not at all*, 10 = *extremely*] to what extent does your experience with the organization suggest that, in its methods, it

      (a) Says it prioritizes the criterion in question?
      (b) Actually embodies the criterion in question?

           If there are differences between (a) and (b), what do you believe explains them?

   • For each, on a scale of 1 – 10 [1 = *not at all*, 10 = *extremely*] to what extent does your experience with the organization suggest that, in its resource acquisition and allocation, it

      (a) Says it prioritizes the criterion in question?

      (b)   Actually embodies the criterion in question?

           If there are differences between (a) and (b), what do you believe explains them?

D.   Consider A and B above to analyze your organization's alignment. By "alignment" we refer to the extent to which methods and resources advance the mission in accordance with the evaluative criteria.

- Where are they aligned?
- Where aren't they aligned?
- What influences (both internal and external) have driven their decisions?
- What helps them become aligned?
- What stands in the way of alignment?

E.   Consider Alternatives

- Brainstorm alternative missions, methods, and or resources; and or possible relational shifts that could help the organization increase alignment. Use Diagrams A and B to facilitate discussion of how alternatives might reflect movement on the continua toward greater alignment with evaluative criteria.
- What are the benefits of implementing these alternatives?
- What are the costs of implementing these alternatives?

F.   Propose a New Idea

- Based on your understanding of the current situation and alternatives, propose an idea for improving the alignment of mission, methods and resources for this organization.
- Use Diagrams A and B to explain why your idea would improve the current situation.
- How likely is it that your idea could be carried out under the current conditions?
- What would need to change in order to make it happen? What are the costs of implementing this change?

G.   Recommendations for Implementation

- What do you recommend that the organization do in the short term to move towards optimal alignment?
- What do you recommend the organization do for the long term to move towards optimal alignment?
- What challenges might you face as a nonprofit leader when attempting to follow through with these recommendations?
- How would you deal with these challenges?

Step 3: ARTICULATE LEARNING

What did you learn?

How did you learn it?

Why does it matter?

What will you do in light of it? (Set specific, measurable, realistic goals)

Leadership Challenge 1: Aligning Missions Methods and Resources [July 2007]

Students should be able to articulate their understanding of the relationship between nonprofit organizations' missions, methods, and resources in a way that reflects the implications of choices that nonprofit leaders make regarding missions, methods, and resources. Students should generate recommendations for improved alignment of missions, methods, and resources in terms of the evaluative criteria (effectiveness, efficiency, integrity, sustainability) and in light of the challenges nonprofit leaders face.

LO1: Identify: Use course readings to define the concepts of mission, methods, and resources	__ Identifies definitions of mission according to readings. __ Identifies definitions of methods according to readings used in pursuit of this mission. __ Identifies definitions of resources according to readings needed to implement these methods.
LO2: Describe: Explain the concepts of mission, methods, and resources in your own words	__ Explains mission in own words. __ Explains methods in own words. __ Explains resources in own words.

LO3: Apply:
Provide examples from your partner organization that illustrates the relationship between mission, methods, and resources

__ Identifies the mission of the organization, the methods used in pursuit of it, and the resources needed and resources used to implement those methods.
__ Uses a specific example to illustrate relationship between mission, methods, and resources at the organization.

LO4: Analyze:
Analyze the alignment in the current relationship between mission, methods, and resources in terms of the evaluative criteria.

Compare/contrast with possible alternatives for increased alignment in accordance with evaluative criteria.

__ Discusses current organizational choices that impact alignment of mission, methods, and resources, in terms of their strengths and their limitations (in light of the evaluative criteria).
__ Discusses internal and external factors that influence alignment.
__ Considers alternative choices that would alter alignment.
__ Compares current alignment with that potentially produced through alternative choices, in light of evaluative criteria.
__ Contrasts current alignment with that potentially produced through alternative choices, in light of evaluative criteria.

LO5: Synthesize:
Propose an idea for improved alignment in light of the evaluative criteria.

__ Provides a new idea for better aligning mission, methods, and resources.
__ Explains why new idea might lead to improved alignment, in light of evaluative criteria.
__ Discusses changes that need to occur for the new idea to be implemented.
__ Discusses likelihood of new idea being carried out.

LO6: Evaluate:
Provide *BOTH* short-term and long-term recommendations for improved alignment while addressing associated challenges.

__ Provides short-term recommendations for moving toward optimal alignment.
__ Provides long-term recommendations for moving toward optimal alignment.
__ Discusses challenges faced when implementing these recommendations.
__ Provides ways to deal with challenges of implementing recommendations.

REFERENCES

Appleby, D. C. (2003). *The first step in student-centered assessment: Helping student understand our curriculum goals.* Retrieved April 24, 2003, from http://www.apa.org/ed/helping_students.html

Ash, S. L., & Clayton, P. H. (2004). The articulated learning: An approach to reflection and assessment. *Innovative Higher Education, 29,* 137-154.

Ash, S. L., Clayton, P. H., & Atkinson, M. P. (2005). Integrating reflection and assessment to improve and capture student learning. *Michigan Journal of Community Service-Learning, 11*(2), 49-59.

Berle, D. (2006). Incremental integration: A successful service-learning strategy. *International Journal of Teaching and Learning in Higher Education, 18*(1), 43-48.

Bloom, B. S. (1956). *Taxonomy of educational objectives, Handbook I: Cognitive domain.* New York: David McKay.

Bringle, R. G. (2003). Enhancing theory-based research on service-learning. In S. H. Billig & J. Eyler (Eds.), *Deconstructing service-learning: Research exploring context, participation, and impacts* (pp. 3-21). Greenwich, CT: Information Age.

Bringle, R. G., & Hatcher, J. A. (1999). Reflection in service learning: Making meaning of experience. *Educational Horizons, 77*(4), 179-185.

Chappuis, S., & Stiggins, R. J. (2002). Classroom assessment for learning. *Educational Leadership, 60*, 40-43.

Clayton, P. H., & Ash, S. L. (2004). Shifts in perspective: Capitalizing on the counter-normative nature of service-learning. *Michigan Journal of Community Service Learning, 11*, 59-70.

Clayton, P. H., & McGuire, L. (2007, May). *Structured critical reflection: A strategy for implementing a new paradigm for teaching and learning.* Presentation at International Service-Learning and Civic Engagement Symposium, University of Indianapolis, IN.

Clayton, P. H., Ash, S. L., Bullard, L. G., Bullock, B. P., Moses, M. G., Moore, et al. (2005). Adapting a core service-learning model for wide-ranging implementation: An institutional case study. *Creative College Teaching, 2*, 10-26.

Clayton, P. H., Jameson, J. K., Molee, L. M., & McGuire, L. (2006, October). *Inter-institutional research on integrating reflection and assessment to generate, deepen, and document student learning.* Presentation at 6th Annual K-H Service-Learning International Research Conference, Portland, OR.

Clayton, P. H., Jameson, J. K., Metelsky, B., & Summers, B. (2007, February). *Design and assessment of threaded service-learning in a nonprofit studies curriculum.* Presentation at NC Campus Compact 9th Annual Service-Learning Conference, Elon University, Elon, NC.

Conrad, D., & Hedin, D. (1990). Learning from service: Experience is the best teacher—Or is it? In J. Kendall & Associates (Eds.), *Combining service and learning, 1* (pp. 87-98). Raleigh, NC: National Society for Internships and Experiential Education.

Eyler, J. (2002). Stretching to meet the challenge: Improving the quality of research to improve the quality of service-learning. In S. H. Billig & A. Furco (Eds.), *Service-Learning through a multidisciplinary lens* (pp. 3-13). Greenwich, CT: Information Age.

Eyler, J., & Giles, D. E. (1999). *Where's the learning in service-learning?* San Francisco: Jossey-Bass.

Eyler, J., Giles, D. E., & Schmiede, A. (1996). *A practitioner's guide to reflection in service-learning.* Nashville, TN: Vanderbilt University.

Hatcher, J. A., & Bringle, R. G. (1997). Reflection: Bridging the gap between service and learning. *College Teaching, 45*(4), 153-158.

Henry, M. B. & Clayton, P. H. (2007, October). *Assessing student learning through structured, critical reflection assignments.* Presentation at 7th Annual International Association of Research on Service-Learning and Civic Engagement Conference, Tampa, FL.

Howard, J. (1998). Academic service learning: A counter normative pedagogy. *New Directions in Teaching and Learning, 73,* 21-29.

Hutchings, P. (2007). Theory: The elephant in the scholarship of teaching and learning room. *International Journal for the Scholarship of Teaching and Learning, 1*(1), 1-4.

Kecskes, K. (2006). *Engaging departments: Moving faculty culture from private to public, individual to collective focus for the common good.* Bolton: Anker.

Kendrick, J. R. (1996). Outcomes of service-learning in an introduction to sociology course. *Michigan Journal of Community Service Learning, 3*(3), 72-81.

Maki, P. L. (2004). *Assessing for learning: Building a sustainable commitment across the institution.* Sterling, VA: Stylus.

Markus, G. B., Howard, J. P., & King, D. C. (1993). Integrating community service and classroom instruction enhances learning: Results from an experiment. *Educational Evaluation and Policy Analysis, 15,* 410-419.

Marsh, P. A. (2007). What is known about student learning outcomes and how does it relate to the scholarship of teaching and learning? *International Journal for the Scholarship of Teaching and Learning, 1*(2). Retrieved March 15, 2008 from http://academics.georgiasouthern.edu/ijsotl/v1n2/essays/march/index.htm

McGuire, L., Ardemagni, E., Wittberg, P., Strong, D., Lay, K., & Clayton, P. H. (2007). *Faculty learning, student learning, and the relationship between them: A collaborative scholarship of teaching and learning project.* Indianapolis, IN: Assessment Institute, IUPUI.

McKenney, K. (2003). The learning-centered institution: Key characteristics. *Inquiry & Action, 1,* 5-6.

Osborne, R. E., Hammerich, S., & Hensley, C. (1998). Student effects of service-learning: Tracking across the semester. *Michigan Journal of Community Service Learning, 5*(1), 5-13.

Paul, W. L., & Elder, L. (2002). *Critical thinking: Tools for taking charge of your professional and personal Life.* Upper Saddle River, NJ: Pearson Education.

Stanton, T. K. (1990). Liberal arts, experiential learning and public service: Necessary ingredients for socially responsible undergraduate education. In J. Kendall & Associates (Eds.), *Combining service and learning, 1* (pp. 175-189). Raleigh, NC: National Society for Internships and Experiential Education.

Steinke, P., & Buresh, S. (2002). Cognitive outcomes of service-learning: Reviewing the past and glimpsing the future. *Michigan Journal of Community Service-Learning, 8*(2), 63-71.

Steinke, P., & Fitch, P. (2003). Using writing protocols to measure service-learning outcomes. In S. H. Billig & J. Eyler (Eds.), *Deconstructing service-learning: Research exploring context, participation, and impacts* (pp. 171-194). Greenwich, CT: Information Age.

Strouse, J. H. (2003). Reflection as a service-learning assessment strategy. *Journal of Higher Education Outreach and Engagement, 8*(2), 75-88.

Vogelgesang, L. J., & Astin, A. W. (2000). Comparing the effects of community service and service-learning. *Michigan Journal of Community Service Learning, 7,* 25-34.

CHAPTER 2

COMMUNITY SERVICE SELF-EFFICACY AND FIRST-YEAR UNDERGRADUATE HONORS SERVICE-LEARNING

Trae Stewart

This chapter uses psychosocial student development theory to frame first-year undergraduate honors students' completion of service-learning hours in underserved elementary schools. Information on the use of service-learning in the first-year experience is offered. Analyses of pre-/postre-sponses administered to 119 participating honors undergraduates showed that student community service self-efficacy was significantly increased. Gender, number of previously completed nonrequired service hours, and religious activity were significantly correlated to the measures. A discussion on the major findings in relation to previous research and their implications is provided. Limitations and opportunities for further research conclude the chapter.

EDITORS' NOTE: The poster presentation associated with this article was recog-nized for Outstanding Achievement in Research at the International Research Conference on Service-Learning and Community Engagement.

Scholarship for Sustaining Service-Learning and Civic Engagement
pp. 29–53

In 2005, the *Journal of the National Collegiate Honors Council* (JNCHC) published a forum on "What is Honors?" evidencing a need for those working with undergraduate honors students to reflect on the past, present, and future approaches of the field. In this forum, Mullins (2005) argued that although "honors" is difficult to define, due to its identity relative to the population it serves, honors programs appear to be "cut from the same cloth" (p. 19). In his review of honors program Web sites, he found a repeating set of adjectives (e.g., "challenging," "innovative," "intellectually rigorous," "enriching," "enhanced") used to describe the programs. He concluded that regardless of these myriad descriptors, honors overall seems to be a "system that exposes students of exceptional ability or promise to an equally exceptional educational experience" (pp. 19-20), a definition left purposefully broad in order to allow each program to structure itself according to its particular mission, students, faculty, and community.

Similarly, commentary on honors teaching has focused on the need for instructors to be pedagogically flexible and experimental, recognizing that honors students do not have one particular learning preference and that various pedagogies can play different roles depending on the objective or question at hand. Schuman (2005) has argued, in fact, that "great teaching can happen in virtually any pedagogical venue, and when it does, it can be great honors teaching" (p. 31).

This chapter uses psychosocial student development theory to understand the outcomes from first-year honors students' completion of service-learning hours in underserved elementary schools. Information on the use of service-learning in the first-year experience will be offered. Findings from a pre-/poststudy administered to 119 participating honors undergraduates will be presented, including data on their community service self-efficacy. Correlations between outcomes and students' previous engagement in volunteer activities and select demographic variables will be highlighted. A discussion on the major findings in relation to previous research and their implications will elucidate the findings. Limitations and opportunities for further research will conclude the chapter.

STUDENT DEVELOPMENT IN HIGHER EDUCATION

Student development theories examine how post-secondary learners develop cognitively and psychosocially in educational settings. Contemporary student development theories evolved from seventeenth century European universities' practice of in loco parentis. Because the average age of students at the time was 14, schools accepted the role of a student's parent while s/he was in residence (Dwyer, 1989). In this regard, student development was focused on instilling traditional values, often through the enforcement of strict social norms via disciplinary actions. Character development outweighed intellectual development under this model until the late nineteenth century when a new paradigm of student development was influenced by psychology, namely psychoanalysis and behaviorism. This "student service" approach argued that while character development is important, attention should be placed on providing students with the services that they require in order to develop cognitively (Creamer, 1980). These changes in student affairs paralleled the rapid growth and depersonalization of higher education at the time (Upcraft & Moore, 1990).

In the 1950s, there was increasing acceptance that student learning is influenced by milieus that extend beyond the walls of the classroom (e.g., residence life, extracurricular activities). Educational institutions should ensure, therefore, that every aspect of a student's life was attended to and that the educational environment, and the resources available therein, served not only to support students to meet challenges intentional to the learning and development process. Under this student development paradigm, each student is unique and has different educational and developmental needs. Another change was that the primary responsibility for a student's personal and social development shifted from the institution to the student (Rodgers, 1989).

Because student development theory is founded in part on the individual characteristics, personalities, learning styles, and needs of students, there is no grand narrative that explains this paradigm. However, the theories that address the cognitive and psychosocial development of students are the most well-known and applied (Miller & Winston, 1991). In this study, academic and cognitive outcomes from students' participation in the service-learning course were not related to the primary research questions. For this reason, Chickering's (1969) theory of undergraduate student psychosocial development theoretically framed the study.

CHICKERING'S THEORY OF STUDENT PSYCHOSOCIAL DEVELOPMENT

Arguably the most known and applied theory of undergraduate student psychosocial development, Chickering's (1969) seven-point model extends Erikson's (1968) *identity versus identity confusion* stage, which includes the traditional 17-18-year-old first-year undergraduate students in this study. Chickering developed vectors along which traditional-aged college students develop: (1) developing competence, (2) managing emotions, (3) developing autonomy, (4) establishing identity, (5) freeing inter-

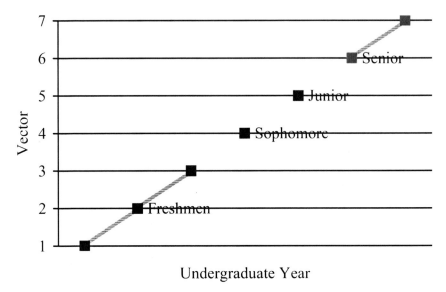

Exhibit 2.1.   Chickering's expected vector of psychosocial development by undergraduate year.

personal relationships, (6) developing purpose, and (7) developing integrity.

Like Erikson, Chickering's theory assumes that identity development is an evolutionary process. Individuals continually rework themselves and their relationships with others. Challenges, or "crises" as termed by Erikson (1968), that we encounter force us to question our conceptualizations of phenomena. Although there is a presumed progressive linearity to the vectors, students may progress at different rates and may even recycle through some vectors. These vectors and the expected progression that traditional-aged undergraduates should make by year of enrollment are illustrated in Exhibit 2.1.

Chickering argues that students' experiences are not sufficient for them to mature through the developmental vectors if they are not accompanied by external support systems. This realization is not surprising, given that students at this developmental stage still have egocentric tendencies and therefore look for acceptance/approval by those important to them. Undergraduates' persistence and ultimate success, in part, relies on their feelings about whether they *matter*/are appreciated or whether they occupy a more *marginal* position in which they feel ignored or unaccepted. Tinto (1993) echoes the mattering versus marginality theory, arguing that students are more likely to persist, and ultimately succeed, in college when they are academically and socially integrated. Academic integration manifests via interaction with faculty, staff, and fellow students. Social integration occurs inside and outside of the classroom, where the primary emphasis of the interaction is not focused on academics.

SERVICE-LEARNING IN THE FIRST-YEAR/FRESHMAN YEAR EXPERIENCE (FYE)

Although approaches to FYE are abundant and purposefully flexible in order to allow an institution to meet the needs of its specific student population, some colleges and universities have infused service-learning into first-year seminars or introductory courses populated primarily by freshmen. Part of the appeal of service-learning is that regardless of published "best practices" for the implementation and use of service-learning, its very foundation of addressing unique needs within a particular community, matching intimately to academic courses, and fitting with the teaching methods of the faculty, allows for immense flexibility. Service-learning's organic underpinnings parallel those of FYE programs. In addition, the teacher-student collaborative effort in FYE is also central to the philosophy behind and effective practice of service-learning (Zlotkowski, 2004). Mysteriously, however, first-year experience and service-learning programs have developed in relative isolation from one another, and connections between the two have been slow to develop (Zlotkowski, 2004).

With regard to the issues addressed by first-year programs, service-learning has been touted as a pedagogical approach to ease the transition from high school to college (Furco, 2002) because it provides a familiar cultural element to which students can automatically connect. This outcome has greater potential when we consider that since the early 1990s, service-learning's infusion in high schools has grown from barely 10% to over 50% (Duckenfield, 2002). Students are coming to college with backgrounds in volunteerism and are already acculturated to new pedagogies of engagement (Colby, Ehrlich, Beaumont, & Stephens, 2003; Gardner, 2002). Furthermore, the inclusion of service-learning and other experiential methods in FYE came from the realization that as students, especially nontraditional students, enter college with more and more life experiences, it will be become impossible to maintain the "campus" as the only significant milieu for learning.

Service-learning has also been found to increase retention and interpersonal engagement (Gallini & Moely, 2003). Through service-learning, like other cocurricular activities, students share "common" experiences and thereby feel connected and feel that they matter to other students and their instructors (Gardner, 2002). These connections also help to increase student interest and combat boredom. First-year students enrolled in required general education courses often experience boredom (Zlotkowski, 2002) because there is a lack of integration between their academic studies and social lives. Academic integration is proportionately related to the physical and psychological energy that a student devotes to an academic experience (Billson & Terry, 1986). Service-learning requires additional energy and could be an approach that institutions can embrace to increase student success and to confront the problems associated with retention (Aldridge & Delucia, 1989).

Service-learning in FYE courses addresses concerns beyond retention. In the past decade, institutions of higher education have been urged to return to the public foundations of their work (Harkavy, 2006). They have been asked to prepare their graduates not only for successful professional lives, but also for fulfilling and productive lives as moral citizens (Colby et al., 2003). Unfortunately, the first year of college is a time when students most often turn away from service (Vogelgesang, Ikeda, Gilmartin, & Keup, 2002). Colleges and universities must continue to promote the values of citizenship, democracy, and civic engagement (Battistoni, 2002), and FYE courses have been identified as excellent venues through which to initiate such value learning, character development, and civic involvement (Colby et al., 2003; Whiteley, 1989). Some concerns have been voiced that by infusing a civic-oriented service-learning component, the curriculum and goals of a FYE course will be watered down. These claims are unfounded, however. Bonstead-Bruns (2007) has concluded that integrating service-learning into a disciplinary FYE course can be useful both in meeting some FYE goals and in teaching disciplinary concepts.

FIRST-YEAR HONORS STUDENTS

First-year college honors students differ from their nonhonors peers and thus warrant distinct attention. Honors students are academically talented learners who have been accepted into the honors program of a postsecondary institution. Although requirements for admittance into an honors program differ by institution, invitations are generally sent to students who performed well in their high school classes, ranked in the top 10% of their graduating class, and earned top percentile scores on college admissions exams (e.g., SAT, ACT). Once in college, honors students tend to continue to exhibit a greater inclination toward academics. Their academic success has been attributed to good study habits, efficiency and promptness, and high levels of motivation that they developed early in their academic careers (Day, 1989; Mathiasen, 1985). Because of their motivation as their peers, honors students are often not as reliant on faculty for information. They are active, creative, and inferential learners (Palmer & Wohl, 1972). They play with ideas, think abstractly, problem solve easily, and make connections between seemingly disparate concepts.

Comfort with abstraction is evidenced in honors students' nonacademic interests as well. Academically talented students overwhelmingly value diversity (Mullins, 2005). Honors students do not simply interact with "others," but also consistently consider the realities of these individuals beyond the time and space of their interactions. Such altruism is extended by their willingness to delay or even resign their own needs and wants for those of another. Overall, honors students are "enthusiastic, determined, industrious, self-directed, goal-oriented, and actively involved freshmen" (Day, 1989, p. 353).

In spite of these strengths, like their younger gifted counterparts, college honors freshmen are not without their struggles. Retention among honors students, especially women, remains a challenge for many universities. Honors students accustomed to acknowledgements and rewards in high school find their accomplishments lost or scantly referenced in university honors programs where their peers arrive with equally impressive backgrounds. To compensate, some students hyperfocus on academics, risking psychological and social isolation which affects the building of a strong peer support group, a necessary factor in successful first-year experiences and subsequent success. In contrast to withdrawal tendencies, some honors students can also become too involved when they find a plethora of scholarly and social activities in college. Suffering from perfectionist tendencies, these naturally curious learners dangerously assume that they can continue the same level of involvement as they did in high school while maintaining a respectable grade point average. Like most first-year students, honors students are unprepared to deal with the anxiety, stress, overwork, and underconfidence that can result when all goals are not achieved (Day, 1989).

Service-Learning in Undergraduate Honors Education

Empirical studies on service-learning in undergraduate honors education are scarce. One reason for this deficiency is the relative absence of service-learning in college honors education. In its 2003 Annual Service Statistics publication, Campus Compact reported that only 19% of its responding member institutions had service-learning as part of their honors programs, which had only increased by 1% from the previous year's survey. No data on service-learning in honors courses have been reported from such surveys since.

A search for service-learning in honors programs in the *Journal of the National Collegiate Honors Council*, the primary academic journal focused on honors education at the tertiary level, yielded no results. Similar inquiries through the National Service-Learning Clearinghouse, university academic database search engines, and even Google Scholar resulted in numerous publications linking service-learning to honors education. However, these articles were anecdotal, highlighting specific honors program descriptions and syllabi. In one evidentiary article, for example, Jenkins (1991) chronicled the collaboration between student affairs and academic affairs in the establishment of a service-learning course requirement for an honors leadership program at one institution.

The few research articles that included honors students in service-learning did not purposefully explain why honors students were chosen for the study and did not explicitly connect literature reviews or conclusions to the development needs of honors students. Undergraduate honors students seem to have been solely a population of convenience in the service-learning literature. For example, Vozzola and Long (2007) examine whether participation in political campaigns constitutes service. Only six female undergraduate honors students enrolled in a service-learning course composed the study's population, but no rationale was provided for this choice. Discussions were not linked back to the honors group. Both authors were faculty associated with the honors program at the institution where the study was conducted.

In contrast to the literature on postsecondary honors education, numerous endorsements of service opportunities for academically talented middle and high schoolers have been offered (Bernal, 2003; Higgins & Boone, 2003; Johnson, 2001; Karnes & Riley, 1996; Lewis, 1996). These commentaries highlight that if gifted students' potential to contribute is to develop fully, they need to practice their talents in real-world contexts. Empirical studies on this topic (e.g., Keen & Howard, 2002; Matthews & Menna, 2003; Terry, 2000, 2003), however, are limited, poorly designed (Webster & Worrell, 2008), and are not generalizable to older college-level honors populations. With this in mind, and given the unique backgrounds and developmental needs of undergraduate honors students, research on the use of service-learning in first-year honors education is warranted.

THE CURRENT STUDY

The previous literature on student development, first-year experience, and service-learning suggests that in their first years of college, students should be developing a stronger sense of identity, autonomy, and competence, as facilitated by social interactions with diverse others and engagement in dynamic academic learning processes through which they can see that they play an important role in a larger community. Framed by these assumptions, the current study aimed to determine if after participating in a 15-hour required service-learning program, first-year undergraduate honors students would be more inclined toward making change through community service. Findings were further analyzed to determine which demographic variables were significantly correlated to each pre-/postmeasure.

Context

The Burnett Honors College:
History an Student Demographics

Established as a program in 1980, and accorded college status in 2002, The Burnett Honors College (TBHC) at the University of Central Florida combines the intimacy of a small liberal arts college with the benefits of a large, metropolitan research university. TBHC strives to create a diverse learning community that fosters the pursuit of excellence, a sense of social and civic responsibility, and a passion for life-long learning. Students are asked to participate in the learning experience instead of merely observing it, thereby developing their intellects in a way that will enhance them as thoughtful, productive, and creative individuals. These aims are succinctly stated in the college's goals:

- achieve national prominence in honors education;
- foster academic excellence, personal growth, and civic responsibility in our students;
- be UCF's premier program to foster intellectual curiosity, creativity, and undergraduate research; and,
- become more inclusive and diverse.

In affiliation with the National Collegiate Honors Council, TBHC is designed to attract and challenge students who have demonstrated an ability to achieve academic excellence. Honors students receive an education that prepares them to enter the best graduate and professional schools, as well as obtain distinguished careers in business and public service. The Burnett Honors College offers two distinct programs of study: University Honors and Honors in the Major.

University Honors provides a special course of study to the most promising undergraduate students at the university. This program is geared toward incoming freshmen or students transferring from a community college with an honors associate's degree. Primarily, the focus of Honors is to combine smaller classes with greater expectations for a student's performance. The University Honors Program is a 4-year course of studies that requires a minimum of 21 hours of honors courses. These courses include honors sections of UCF's General Education Program, upper-level honors courses, and interdisciplinary seminars. Students are also required to attend honors freshmen symposium in the semester in which they are admitted. Students who successfully complete the program with at least a 3.2 GPA (overall) and 3.0 GPA (honors) graduate with university honors distinction on their diplomas and transcripts.

Honors in the Major is a 2-year program designed to encourage the best junior and senior students to undertake original and independent research in their major field under the supervision of a faculty committee. This research culminates in a thesis or creative project. Because of the diversity of student interests, academic departments regulate Honors in the Major course work.

In fall 2006, TBHC enrolled more than 1,600 students. Honors freshmen are admitted in the fall semester of each year and 485 honors students were admitted in fall 2006. The mean total SAT score for this incoming class was 1354 and the mean high-school grade point average was 4.03 (unweighted). Students of all majors are accepted into TBHC. Overall, the largest concentration of majors is in the College of Arts and Sciences (32%) and the College of Engineering and Computer Science (27%).

Atrophy of Social Studies in Florida's Underserved Schools

Service-learners like those in this study and volunteers in K-12 classrooms can address numerous deficiencies. However, the needs in some classrooms are exacerbated by unique factors. In Florida's schools, for example, the need for assistance has increased in recent years due to the competing forces of legislation that limits class sizes to 20 students and Florida's growing population. Although this legislation makes sense pedagogically, Florida faces a deficit in qualified teachers. For the 2006-07 school year alone, state educational officials needed to recruit more than 30,000 teachers (Winchester, 2005), even if all already employed teachers returned for another academic year.

In addition, Florida is suffering from budget constraints that have led to significant reductions in budgetary appropriations to educational institutions. While county school officials have considerable flexibility in how they address these reductions, some have chosen to lay off paraprofessionals and teaching assistants, except when legally obligated (e.g., classrooms with high numbers of students with documented disabilities). Fewer students in classes does not mean that teachers no longer need extra assistance, however. Although Florida's K-12 educators are teaching in less-populated classrooms, their student populations have also changed. Florida's classrooms follow the inclusion model and have significant numbers of English language learners. An examination of county Web sites around the state reveals requests for adult volunteers to work one-on-one with students who are at risk or need additional help, as well as be an extra set of eyes, ears, and hands for everyday class activities/lessons. Although Florida needs more teachers, there are fewer funds with which to train and hire them. Therefore, the need is not being met. When asked by TBHC what needs they had that could be addressed by undergraduate honors volunteers, elementary teachers expressed the need for assistance in meeting state social studies benchmarks. Florida's Comprehensive Assessment Test (FCAT) assesses K-12 students' knowledge of reading/language arts, science, and math. Content areas not tested receive less teacher emphasis, instructional time, and student effort. Recent legislative mandates requiring elementary schools to offer 150 hours of physical activity each week have further reduced instructional time for non-FCAT subjects. Such reductions additionally impact schools that were identified as struggling, as determined by previous years' FCAT scores. These schools feel added pressure to increase their standardized test scores or risk state-levied penalties, including reduction in operating budget, terminations, or even closure. These schools are typically comprised of majority at-risk or minority student populations.

Coggins (2007) surveyed 1,766 elementary school teachers (K-5) to determine the extent to which there has been a substantial reduction of instructional time in social studies in Florida. Sixty-seven percent of respondents reported that they devoted no more than 2 hours a week to social studies while 21% spent 3 hours, and 11% spent 4 to 6 hours a week. In contrast, instruction in reading averages 8 hours, math 5 hours, and science 4 hours a week. Since science was added to the Florida's Comprehensive Assessment Test, 72% of teachers felt that 1-4 hours of instructional time per week that had been previously devoted to social studies instructions is now used for science lessons. When teachers were asked whether they thought that the reduction in instruction on Social Studies was connected to the introduction of the FCAT, 61% agreed or strongly agreed.

The implications from Coggins's study are more troubling than teachers emphasizing content areas that are tested on the FCAT while de-emphasizing time and effort on nontested subjects. By de-emphasizing social studies, we risk the atrophy, or even worse, the absence, of a civic understanding and associated behaviors, including civic participation.

Junior Achievement Service-Learning Program and Honors Freshman Symposium

To address the aforementioned needs in elementary schools and to prepare its graduates as socially responsible young women and men who fully understand the importance of being civically engaged, TBHC part-nered with Junior Achievement of Central Florida which provides struc-tured, standards-aligned lesson plans on the roles individuals, consumers, and workers play in an expanding cultural environment that extends from the self and family to global relations. It is implicit in these lessons that every student has the potential to succeed in life, regardless of his or her background or economic status.

To prepare honors students for their service activities, representatives from Junior Achievement provided an orientation to the organization and a training workshop on the curricula during the third week of classes. At that time, honors students were walked through each of the five lessons in their curricular packets, so that any misunderstandings could be addressed at that time.

For their service-learning, TBHC students served in one classroom in an underserved school where they taught five themed lessons. Themes by grade level include: Ourselves (K), Our Families (1st), Our Community (2nd), Our City (3rd), Our Region (4th), and Our Nation (5th). Honors students made six visits. The first visit was to orient the students to the school and hosts, and the K-12 students to their service providers. The remaining five visits were to teach each of the Junior Achievement les-sons. Total service time was 15 hours and included the teaching of the les-sons, visits to the schools, and preparation. Only about 5 hours were devoted explicitly to direct service-learning activities (i.e., teaching les-sons, helping in class).

Service experiences are linked to "The Evolution of a Community" Hon-ors Freshman Symposium. This course, required of all freshmen honors stu-dents, examines the historical, cultural, and psychosocial development of "community" with a particular emphasis on how traditional notions of com-munity have been defined and redefined in the context of American history. Another focus of the course is on the responsibility of the individual citizen in a democratic society and how the proper exercise of that responsibility is important both for those who contribute to and those who receive the benefits of community service. All students met once per week in a lecture class for two hours with the course instructor and team leaders. The role of group leaders was to help incoming students adjust to campus and college life, facilitate postlecture discussions and encourage student involvement, and to lead meaningful reflective activities about service experiences. For the first hour, all students met for a lecture by a guest faculty member. Stu-dents then met with small groups led by an upper-class honors team leader. Thirty minutes of the small group meetings were used to discuss the pre-ceding lecture and connect it to service-learning experiences and course readings. The remaining time was then devoted to first-year orientation topics (e.g., services on campus, wellness issues, study habits). Group leaders presented topics as well as answered questions from students. To facilitate the socialization process at the beginning of the semester, each group went on a field trip unrelated to course content.

Several assignments were related to service-learning activities. Throughout the semester, students had to complete service-learning reaction reports. Each report stemmed from a different prompt that required students to reflect critically on their experiential activities vis-à-vis course readings. At the end of the semester, students were to complete a summative reflection paper that synthesized their experiences, reactions, and readings across the entire semester and tie these conclusions to civic engagement and school reform. To ensure students' understanding of class readings, weekly online reaction postings to selected readings were required. These reactions were to enable students to move to a more critical discussion of their service-learning experiences in the reaction reports. Three texts were selected to address each of the main course themes. First, *Nickel and Dimed: On (Not) Getting by in America* by Barbara Ehrenreich (2004) was selected as a foundation on poverty, class, and the working poor. The need for school reform in low-income schools was covered by Jonathan Kozol's (2006) *The Shame of a Nation: The Restoration of Apartheid Schooling in America*. Lastly, the importance and impact of civic engagement was framed around selections from *The Impossible Will Take a Little While* by Paul Loeb (2004).

Method

Participants

This study's population was composed of 58 males (49%) and 61 females (51%). Seventy-eight percent of the student participants were Caucasian, 1% African-American, 3% Asian-American, and 12% Latino. Six percent of students represented other ethnic groups, including but not limited to Native American, Sub-Continent Indian, and Biracial. In terms of religious faith, 72% identified as Christian, 3% Jewish, and 6% other (e.g., Hindu, Wicken/Pagan, Buddhist). Nineteen percent replied that they did not follow a religious faith.

Students were also asked about their service experience in the previous 12 months. Students estimated how many required and nonrequired service hours they completed. Thirty-five percent of students had completed up to 10 hours of service, 16% had completed 11-30 hours, 13% had completed 31-50 hours, 6% had completed 51-70, 16% had done 71-99 hours, and 14% of students completed over 100 hours of service. These percentages do not mutually exclude the required and the nonrequired service hours. These data are elaborated in Exhibit 2.2.

Measure

The Community Service Self-Efficacy Scale (Reeb, Katsuyama, Sammon, & Yoder, 1998) consists of 10 items that assess student confidence in making significant contribution to community through service. The Com-

Exhibit 2.2.   Participant Demographics (*n* = 119)

Variable	n	%
Gender		
Male	58	48.7
Female	61	51.3
Race/Ethnicity		
Black/African American	1	0.8
Latino/Hispanic/Chicano	14	11.8
Native American/American Indian	1	0.8
Caucasian/White (not Hispanic)	93	78.2
Asian	3	2.5
Sub-Continent Indian	1	0.8
Biracial/Multiracial	4	3.4
Other	2	1.7
Required Service Hours		
0-10 hours	47	39.5
11-30 hours	17	14.3
31-50 hours	15	12.6
51-70 hours	7	5.9
71-99 hours	16	13.4
100+ hours	17	14.3
Nonrequired Service Hours		
0-10 hours	37	31.1
11-30 hours	22	18.5
31-50 hours	15	12.6
51-70 hours	7	5.9
71-99 hours	21	17.6
100+ hours	17	14.3
Religious Background		
Christian/Catholic	86	72.3
Jewish	4	3.4
Atheist	15	12.6
Agnostic	8	6.7
Hindu	1	0.8
Wicken/Pagan	1	0.8
Other	4	3.4
Religious Activity		
Extremely Active	21	17.6
Moderately Active	41	34.5
Hardly Active	32	26.9
Not Active at All	25	21.0

munity Service Self-Efficacy Scale's questions are rated on a 10-point range (1 = *quite uncertain,* 10 = *quite certain*). High scores show high community service self-efficacy. Exploratory and confirmatory factor analytic procedures reveal one-factor solution, consistent with unidimensionality, and coefficient alphas above .90 (Reeb et al., 1998). Reliability analyses for the current study echoed previous findings.

Procedure

A one-group, pre-/posttest research design was conducted with 119 undergraduate students enrolled in the fall 2006 "Honors Freshman Symposium" at the University of Central Florida to determine the impact of their participation in the mandatory 15-hour service-learning project on their inclinations toward making change through community service, feelings of self-efficacy, and an us-them mentality.

During the second class meeting, students over the age of 18 years were asked to complete an informed consent form that had been approved by the university's institutional review board in order to participate in the study. Students were not required to participate, and their results were not connected to the instructor evaluations of students or student evaluations of instructional teams.

Participating students completed the same surveys during the penultimate class meeting. Pre- and postresponses on surveys were then matched by the last four digits of a student personal identification number (i.e., not social security number). Incomplete surveys and surveys without a pre- or postmatch were deleted, leaving a final population of 119. Responses were then coded following the coding instructions of each measure, including filler items, reverse coding, and summed aggregate or clustered item totals.

Analyses were computed using the Statistical Program for Social Sciences (SPSS). Descriptive nonparametric statistics were used to describe the demographic data. Paired-samples t tests were calculated to determine significance in pre- and post-survey aggregate means on each instrument. An independent samples t test, ANOVA, and multivariate tests for repeated measures were calculated to determine relationships between survey scores and demographic variables.

Results

A paired-samples t-test analysis indicates that for the 119 subjects, the mean score on the postsurvey ($M = 78.75$) was significantly greater at the $p < .001$ level (note: $p = .001$) than the mean score on the presurvey ($M = 71.97$). These results indicate that a significant correlation exists between these two variables ($r = .578, p < .001$). Cronbach alphas for pre-

Exhibit 2.3.   Paired Samples Means and Significances

	Presurvey		Postsurvey		Paired Differences			
Scale	Mean	SD	Mean	SD	Mean	SD	t	Sig.
Community Service Self-Efficacy	71.97	16.61	78.75	15.07	6.77	14.61	−5.06	.001*

Note: *$p < .001$.

and postsurveys were .93 and .94, respectively, showing very high internal consistency.

An independent-samples t-test analysis indicates that the 61 females had means of 73.75 and 81.90 on the pre- and postsurveys respectively; the 59 males had means of 70.10 and 75.43. The presurvey means did not differ significantly ($p = .232$) between the gender groups. However, the post-survey means differ significantly at the $p < .05$ level (note: $p = .019$). Levene's test for equality of variances indicates variances for males and females on the postsurvey do not differ significantly from each other (note: $p = .841$).

A one-way analysis of variance (ANOVA) was conducted to determine if the means of the corresponding population distributions differ in comparison to pre-/postsurvey means. Two significant relationships were found. Based on a $p = .003$, extremely significant differences exist within comparisons of presurvey means among the number of nonrequired service hours students had completed in the previous year. Bonferroni post hoc test results indicate three pair of groups whose means differ significantly ($p < .05$ level) from each other. According to the data, students who had completed 11-30 hours ($M = 76.77$), 31-50 hours ($M = 79.07$), and over 100 ($M = 78.82$) nonrequired service hours in the past year all scored significantly higher on the community service self-efficacy presurvey than did students who had completed 0-10 hours ($M = 64.03$).

Another ANOVA procedure also showed a strongly significant difference between postsurvey means and students' level of religious activity ($p = .016$). Bonferroni post hoc test results indicate that students who reported that they were "hardly active" in their religion ($M = 83.06$) scored significantly higher ($p = .012$) on the post-survey than those that were not active at all ($M = 70.50$).

Discussion

By participating in mandatory service-learning, first-year undergraduate honors students gained significantly in their confidence to make significant contributions to community through service. Three demographic variables were found to have significant relationships to the community service self-efficacy findings: gender, previously completed nonrequired service hours, and religious activity.

Gender

The first variable found to correlate was gender. Both genders reported significant changes between their pre-/postcommunity service self-efficacy scores. However, female students not only began their service-learning activities with a higher level of community service self-efficacy, but also scored higher on posttests. Their pre-/postdifferences were also more statistically significant than male students.

Findings support previous research on gender and participation in community service activities. Female college and university students have been found to report more substantial involvement in community service than their male counterparts (Serow, 1990; Serow & Dreyden, 1999) and generally score higher on community service measures (Shiarella, McCarthy, & Tucker, 2000). Similar findings have been reported on K-12 student service-learners. Females have been found to volunteer beyond the required service hour minimum, engage in larger numbers, have more positive attitudes about mandatory community service programs, and are more likely to report intentions to engage civically via volunteerism in the future (Chapin, 1998; Miller, 1994; Stukas, Switzer, Dew, Goycoolea, & Simmons, 1999).

Service programs should be careful, however, not to equate community service with caregiver tendencies. This distinction will be particularly important for service-learning programs that ask students to complete stereotypical, socialized feminine/masculine tasks. For example, and pertinent to this study, women still make up an overwhelming majority of elementary school teachers and continue to be pushed into more humanistic, nurturing lines of work. This possibility has been highlighted by Chesler and Vasques Scalera (2000): "Female affinity for service work and preparation for service-oriented careers" (p. 20). In contrast, these findings also suggest that continued focus on male involvement in service activities is warranted. Most importantly, the data show that whenever one is introduced to service activities, regardless of gender, significant growth in community service self-efficacy can still occur in college.

Previously Completed Nonrequired Service Hours

The second variable to correlate was the number of nonrequired service hours completed in the year prior to entering college. Students who had completed 11-30, 31-50, or 100+ nonrequired service hours in their senior year of high school scored significantly higher on the community service self-efficacy presurvey than students who had completed 0-10 hours. This finding makes sense intuitively in that students who had completed more service hours voluntarily would report that they can make change through similar activities. If a student had completed just a few or no voluntary community service hours, s/he would not be expected to have such a realization.

What is most important to note, however, is that no significant differences were found between non-required service hour groups in the postmeasure. Coupled with an overall significant increase in honors students' community service self-efficacy, these findings indicate that previous service hours might not be as important in the development of students' confidence in making significant contributions to community through service and thus a likelihood to engage civically in the future. Exposure to community service via service-learning at even the postsecondary level of education might compensate for missed opportunities at the K-12 level.

Religious Activity

The last variable to correlate significantly to students' community service self-efficacy scores was religious activity. The connection between religion/spirituality and secular community engagement has been well documented. Even in the 1800s, Tocqueville (1835/1969) commented that religion should be considered America's first political institution. Although he did not use the terminology at the time, Tocqueville referenced the power of religious associations and structures to generate social capital (Coleman, 1988; Putnam, 1993), which has since been linked to civic health. Religion affects associational life by shaping how congregants view and relate to the world and each other.

Out of these religious associations and activities, church attendance has the strongest impact on civic involvement, even exceeding education (Smidt, 1999; Verba, Schlozman, & Bardy, 1996; Lopez, Pratap, & Conner, 2007). Given that participation in religious associations can provide "the social contacts and organizational skills necessary to understand political action and to exert effective influence" (Houghland & Christenson, 1983, p. 406), it is unsurprising that religious social capital supports both religious and secular volunteering (Greeley, 1997; Wuthnow, 1991).

In this study, honors students who reported that they were "hardly active" in their religion scored highest on the postsurvey, and significantly higher than those that were not active at all. These findings do not support previous research that documents a positive correlation between community service intentions and levels of religious involvement. However, Lopez et al. (2007) report that how often a young person attends religious services positively correlates with how often they had volunteered in the previous year and how likely they were to be regular volunteers. For example, 40% of regular attendees of religious service had volunteered in the past 12 months versus 37% of infrequent attendees and 29% who had not attended. Twenty-five percent of regular attendees were likely to volunteer regularly, while 17% of infrequent attendees and 11% of young people who did not attend religious services would volunteer on a regular basis. These data support earlier research on the analyses of students' participation in community service. Serow (1990) found that volunteers' community service involvement related positively and significantly to their spirituality. In a study surveying 1,960 students from eleven institutions in a southeastern state, Serow and Dreyden (1999) found again that spiritual/religious values were positively associated with community service.

From these findings, students who were "extremely involved" in their religions would be expected to score the highest, while those who were less involved would score lower with each reduced level of involvement. In this study, however, students who were "hardly active" outscored the two higher levels of religious activity. For more critical thinking honors students, religion might not play such a significant role in their decisions to be civically engaged as their peers, although the significant difference between the "hardly involved" and the "not involved at all" groups still indicate that religion does play some role and continues to deserve attention.

It should be noted, however, that these findings do differ somewhat from what previous research has found, partially because the focus of the research has been different. In this study, students' religious activity correlated to their feelings of making change through community service in the future, while other research has focused on the intersection between religious activity and civic engagement and volunteerism, in particular. Although not mutually exclusive, these differences are important to note as the former measures self-efficacy and change-oriented intentions; the latter measures simple engagement.

In addition, this study did not examine the meaning that students ascribed to their service activities (e.g., charity versus social justice). These inquiries are particularly important for studies that examine service-learning approaches that actively seek to conscientize students to social inequalities. Ross and Boyle (2007) studied the challenges that first-year undergraduates had when transitioning from high school service to college service-learning. They suggest that with the increasing number of high schools requiring service hours for graduation, college service-learning courses, especially those enrolling first-year undergraduates, should be reconceptualized to help students move from a charity to a more social action orientation. Given the relationship between civic engagement and religious activity found in this study and the published literature, and previous writings on the tensions between charity and social justice paradigms of service vis-à-vis religious identity (Marullo &

Edwards, 2000; Stewart, 2002, 2003; Youniss & Yates, 1997), research intersecting all of these variables is needed.

Future research should again ask students about their religious involvement at the postphase of data collection. College offers opportunities for students to interact with diverse individuals, sets of ideals, and practices, thereby challenging them to constantly self-reflect. In addition, some students away at college decrease religious activity because they consider their religious connection to be their parish, church, temple, or synagogue at home and do not want to connect intimately with another. Students might choose to engage in secular social or academic events instead of religious ones. Three to four months at college could therefore significantly influence the role that religious activity might play. One means by which to address this limitation might be to include an additional survey that measures religiosity (e.g., Multidimensional Measure of Religion/Spirituality [Fetzer Institute, 1999]), although distinctions can be made between the concept of religiosity and religious activity as a possible determinant of civic engagement.

LIMITATIONS TO THE STUDY AND OPPORTUNITIES FOR FUTURE RESEARCH

This study had several limitations and weaknesses. First, non-Hispanic White students were overrepresented. This skew is not typical of gifted and talented populations, which in general report large numbers of Asians as well. The generalizability across more diverse populations and other non-White honors subgroups are limited for this reason.

Second, this study has not included the impact of honors students' service-learning participation on community partners. Although this weakness is not a limitation in terms of study design and meaning of reported findings, the inclusion of community member perspectives and service activity impacts is inadequate and ironic given the reflexivity inherent in service-learning. To contextualize this request, future studies on service-learning in K-12 schools might consider how K-12 students benefit from the interaction with undergraduate honors students, especially with regard to mentorship/modeling, and how these outcomes correlated to the demographic differences between them and the service providers. Similarly, how the host teacher benefited and whether the initial need of addressing the social studies benchmarks was met are both essential considerations that exceed the purview of this study.

Lastly, this study inferred its findings from statistical data. Because of the psychosocial theory framing this study, no attention was applied to the academic subject-matter learning or cognitive development of participating students. In addition, and a general critique of quantitative studies, outcomes from students' participation are limited to the measures selected and analyses completed. Qualitative data may help to address these and other aforementioned limitations. In particular, given the importance of extracurricular experiences to student development, data collection of out-of-class or less-structured class activities should be attempted (e.g., bus rides to service sites, residence halls, small group meetings with team leaders).

CONCLUSION

This study aimed to determine if first-year undergraduate honors students would be more inclined toward making change through community service after participating in a 15-hour required service-learning program. Results suggest that service-learning during the first-year of college, as is configured in the study's honors program, can help to provide honors students with meaningful opportunities to develop confidence that they can make change in communities by engaging civically. To extend this finding to apply to student psychosocial development, honors service-learners realize that they have a role to play and thus matter. This realization evidences students' developmentally-appropriate progression toward Chickering's fourth vector, which is about establishing identity and is placed at the sophomore year.

To capitalize on service-learning possibilities as framed by student psychosocial development, however, service-learning program directors and faculty must acknowledge that although the freshman year is students' first year at college, they do not live in a vacuum prior to their matriculation. They arrive with myriad experiences, expectations, sets of knowledge, appreciations of diversity, and levels of confidence. In this study, students' gender, previously completed nonrequired community service hours, and levels of religious activity were found to correlate significantly and evidence that development is certainly a progressive process.

Regardless, first-year honors students engaged in service-learning are actively and collaboratively participating in academic, social, and community settings, thereby theoretically supporting smooth transitioning into the first year of college and future success.

REFERENCES

Aldridge, M., & Delucia, R. C. (1989). Boredom: The academic plague of first-year students. *Journal of the First-Year Experience & Students in Transition, 1*(2), 43-56.

Battistoni, R. M. (2002). *Civic engagement across the curriculum: a resource book for service-learning faculty in all disciplines*. Providence, RI: Campus Compact.

Bernal, E. M. (2003). To no longer educate the gifted: Programming for gifted students beyond the era of inclusionism. *Gifted Child Quarterly, 47*, 183-191.

Billson, J. M., & Terry, M. B. (1986). A student retention model for higher education. *College and University, 62*, 290-305.

Bonstead-Bruns, M. (2007). Assessing the use of service-learning for meeting the goals of the first-year experience course. *Teaching Forum*. Retrieved August 25, 2008, from http://www.uwosh.edu/programs/teachingforum/public_html

Chapin, J. R. (1998). Is service learning a good idea? Data from the National Longitudinal Study of 1988. *Social Studies, 89*, 205-211.

Chesler, M., & Vasques Scalera, C. (2000). Race and gender issues related to service-learning research. *Michigan Journal of Community Service Learning, 7*, 18-27.

Chickering, A. W. (1969). *Education and identity*. San Francisco: Jossey-Bass.

Coggins, P. C. (2007). *Evaluating the impact of FCAT upon civic and historical understanding in Florida: An analysis of the extent to which elementary teachers have reduced the amount of time devoted to social studies instruction*. Deland, FL: Stetson University, Florida Association of Social Studies Supervisors.

Colby, A., Ehrlich, T., Beaumont, E., & Stephens, J. (2003). *Educating citizens: Preparing America's undergraduates for lives of moral and civic responsibility*. San Francisco: Jossey-Bass.

Coleman, J. S. (1988). Social capital in the creation of human capital. *American Journal of Sociology, 94*(Supplement), s95-s120.

Creamer, D. G. (Ed.). (1980). *Student development in higher education: Theories, practices and future directions*. Cincinnati, OH: ACPA.

Day, A. L. (1989). Honors students. In M. L. Upcraft & J. N. Gardner (Eds.), *The freshman year experience: Helping students survive and succeed in college* (pp. 352-363). San Francisco: Jossey-Bass.

Duckenfield, M. (2002). Look who's coming to college: The impact of high school service-learning on new college students. In E. Zlotkowski (Ed.), *Service-learning and the first-year experience: Preparing students for personal success and civic responsibility* (Monograph No. 34) (pp. 39-50). Columbia, SC: University of South Carolina, National Resource Center for The First-Year Experience and Students in Transition.

Dwyer, J. O. (1989). A historical look at the freshman year experience. In M. L. Upcraft & J. N. Gardner (Eds.), *The freshman year experience: Helping students survive and succeed in college* (pp. 25-39). San Francisco: Jossey-Bass.

Ehrenreich, B. (2004). *Nickel and dimed: On(not) getting by in America*. New York: Holt.

Erikson, E. H. (1968). *Identity: Youth and crisis*. New York: W. W. Norton.

Fetzer Institute. (1999). *Multidimensional measurement of religiousness/spirituality for use in health research*. Kalamazoo, MI: Fetzer Institute.

Furco, A. (2002). High school service-learning and the preparation of students for college: An overview of research. In E. Zlotkowski (Ed.), *Service-learning and the first-year experience: Preparing students for personal success and civic responsibility* (Monograph No. 34) (pp. 3-14). Columbia, SC: University of South Carolina, National Resource Center for The First-Year Experience and Students in Transition.

Gallini, S. M. & Moely, B. E. (2003). Service-learning and engagement, academic challenge and retention. *Michigan Journal of Community Service Learning, 10*(1), 5-14.

Gardner, J. N. (2002). What, so what, now what: Reflections, findings, conclusions, and recommendations on service-learning and the first-year experience. In E. Zlotkowski (Ed.), *Service-learning and the first-year experience: Preparing students for personal success and civic responsibility* (Monograph No. 34) (pp. 141-150). Columbia, SC: University of South Carolina, National Resource Center for The First-Year Experience and Students in Transition.

Greeley, A. (1997). Coleman revisited: Religious structures as sources of social capital. *American Behavioral Scientist, 40*(5), 487-94.

Harkavy, I. (2006). The role of universities in advancing citizenship and social justice in the 21st century. *Education, Citizenship and Social Justice, 1*(1), 5-37.

Higgins, K., & Boone, R. (2003). Beyond the boundaries of school: Transition consideration in gifted education. *Intervention in School and Clinic, 38,* 138-144.

Houghland, J. G., & Christensen, J. A. (1983). Religion and politics: The relationship of religious participation to political efficacy and involvement. *Sociology and Social Research, 67,* 405-420.

Jenkins, T. S. (1991). Student affairs and academic affairs collaborate through a service-learning course requirement. *Journal of College Student Development, 32,* 79-80.

Johnson, K. (2001, Fall). Integrating an affective component in the curriculum for gifted and talented students. *Gifted Child Today Magazine, 24*(4), 14-18.

Karnes, F. A., & Riley, T. L. (1996, March-April). Competitions: Developing and nurturing talents. *Gifted Child Today Magazine, 19*(2), 14-15.

Keen, C., & Howard, A. (2002). Experiential learning in Antioch College's work-based learning program as a vehicle for the social and emotional development for gifted college students. *Journal of Secondary Gifted Education, 13*(2), 130-140.

Kozol, J. (2006). *The shame of a nation: The restoration of apartheid schooling in America.* New York: Three Rivers Press.

Lewis, B. A. (1996). Serving others hooks gifted students on learning. *Educational Leadership, 53,* 70-74.

Loeb, P. (2004). *The impossible will take a little while.* New York: Basic Books.

Lopez, M. H., Pratap, K. V., & Conner, S. L. (2007). *Religious service attendance and civic engagement among 15-25 year olds.* College Park, MD: University of Maryland, The Center for Information & Research on Civic Learning & Engagement (CIRCLE).

Marullo, S., & Edwards, B. (2000). From charity to justice. *American Behavioral Scientist, 43*(5), 895-911.

Mathiasen, R. E. (1985). Characteristics of college honors students. *Journal of College Student Personnel, 26,* 171-173.

Matthews, D., & Menna, R. (2003). Solving problems together: Parent/school/community collaboration at a time of educational and social change. *Education Canada, 43*(1), 20-23.

Miller, J. (1994). Linking traditional and service-learning courses: Outcome evaluations utilizing two pedagogically distinct models. *Michigan Journal of Community Service Learning, 1,* 29-36.

Miller, T. K., & Winston, Jr., R. B. (Eds.). (1991). Human development and higher education. In *Administration and leadership in student affairs: Actualizing student development in higher education.* Muncie, IN: Accelerated Development.

Mullins, D. W., Jr. (2005). What is honors? *Journal of the National Collegiate Honors Council, 6*(2), 19-22.

Palmer, A. B., & Wohl, J. (1972). Some personality characteristics of honors students. *College Student Journal, 6,* 106-111.

Putnam, R. (1993). The prosperous community: Social capital and public life. *American Prospect, 13,* 35-42.

Reeb, R. N., Katsuyama, R. M., Sammon, J. A., & Yoder, D. S. (1998). The Community Service Self-Efficacy Scale: Evidence of reliability, construct validity, and pragmatic utility. *Michigan Journal of Community Service Learning, 5,* 48-57.

Rodgers, R. F. (1989). Student development. In U. Delworth, G. R. Hanson, & Associates (Eds.), *Student services: A handbook for the profession* (2nd ed., pp. 117-164). San Francisco: Jossey-Bass.

Ross, L., & Boyle, M. E. (2007). Transitioning from high school service to college service-learning in a first-year seminar. *Michigan Journal of Community Service-Learning, 14*(1), 53-64.

Schuman, S. (2005). Teaching honors. *Journal of the National Collegiate Honors Council, 6*(2), 31-33.

Serow, R. C. (1990). Volunteering and values: An analysis of students' participation in community service. *Journal of Research and Development in Education, 23*(4), 198-203.

Serow, R. C., & Dreyden, J. I. (1999). Community service among college and university students: Individual and institutional relationships. *Adolescence, 25*(99), 553-567.

Shiarella, A. H., McCarthy, A. M., & Tucker, M. L. (2000). Development and construct validity of scores on the Community Service Attitudes Scale. *Educational and Psychological Measurement, 60,* 286-300.

Smidt, C. (1999). Religion and civic engagement: A comparative analysis. *Annals of the American Academy of Political and Social Science, 565,* 176-192.

Stewart, T. (2002). Outcomes from Catholic service-learning. *Academic Exchange Quarterly, 6*(4), 123-30.

Stewart, T. (2003). *Catholic schools and civic engagement: A case study of community service-learning and its impact on critical consciousness and social capital.* Unpublished doctoral dissertation, University of Southern California.

Stukas, A. A., Jr., Switzer, G. E., Dew, M. A., Goycoolea, J. M., & Simmons, R. G. (1999). Parental helping models, gender, and service-learning. *Journal of Prevention & Intervention in the Community, 18*(1/2), 5-18.

Terry, A. W. (2000). An early glimpse: Service learning from an adolescent perspective. *Journal of Secondary Gifted Education, 11*(3), 115-135.

Terry, A. W. (2003). Effects of service learning on young, gifted adolescents and their community. *Gifted Child Quarterly, 47*(4), 295-308.

Tinto, V. (1993). Principles of effective retention. *Journal of The Freshman Year Experience, 2*(1), 35-48.

Tocqueville, A. D. (1969). *Democracy in America* (J. P. Mayer, Ed., G. Lawrence, Trans.). New York: Doubleday. (Original work published in 1835).

Upcraft, M. L., & Moore, L. V. (1990). Evolving theoretical perspectives of student development. In M. J. Barr, M. L. Upcraft, and Associates (Eds.), *New futures for student affairs* (pp. 41-68). San Francisco: Jossey-Bass.

Verba, S., Schlozman, K. L., & Brady, H. (1996). *Voice and equality: Civic voluntarism in America*. Cambridge, MA: Harvard University Press.

Vogelgesang, L. J., Ikeda, E. K., Gilmartin, S. K., & Keup, J. R. (2002). Service-learning and the first-year experience: Learning from the research. In E. Zlotkowski (Ed.), *Service-learning and the first-year experience: Preparing students for personal success and civic responsibility* (pp. 15-26). Columbia, SC: University of South Carolina, National Resource Center for The First-Year Experience and Students in Transition.

Vozzola, E. C., & Long, K. (2007). But is it service? Problems of participatory democracy and justice in a service learning course. *Journal of College and Character, 2*. Retrieved August 25, 2008, from http://www.collegevalues.org/articles.cfm?a=1&id=282

Webster, N. S., & Worrell, F. C. (2008). Academically talented students' attitudes toward service in the community. *Gifted Child Quarterly, 52*(2), 170-179.

Whiteley, J. M. (1989). Character development. In M. L. Upcraft & J. N. Gardner (Eds.), *The freshman year experience* (pp. 168-180). San Francisco: Jossey-Bass.

Winchester, D. (2005, September 16). Wanted: 30,000 new teachers in Florida. *St. Petersburg Times*. Retrieved August 25, 2008, from http://www.sptimes.com/2005/09/16/State/Wanted__30_000_new_te.shtml

Wuthnow, R. (1991). *Acts of compassion: Caring for others and helping ourselves*. Princeton, NJ: Princeton University Press.

Youniss, J., & Yates, M. (1997). *Community service and social responsibility*. Chicago: The University of Chicago Press.

Zlotkowski, E. (Ed.). (2002). Service-learning and the introductory course: Lessons from across the disciplines. In *Service-learning and the first-year experience: Preparing students for personal success and civic responsibility* (pp. 27-36). Columbia, SC: University of South Carolina, National Resource Center for The First-Year Experience and Students in Transition.

Zlotkowski, E. (2004). Service-learning and the first-year student. In M. L. Upcraft, J. N. Gardner, & B. O. Barefoot (Eds.), *Challenging and supporting the first-year student: A handbook for improving the first year of college* (pp. 356-370). San Francisco: Jossey-Bass.

PART II

RESEARCH TO SUSTAIN
SERVICE-LEARNING IN K-12 EDUCATION

CHAPTER 3

PROMOTING SECONDARY STUDENTS' CHARACTER DEVELOPMENT IN SCHOOLS THROUGH SERVICE-LEARNING

Shelley H. Billig, Dan Jesse,
R. Marc Brodersen, and Michelle Grimley

This chapter provides an examination of the ways in which service-learning can be used to promote students' character development in schools. After a brief discussion of why service-learning has promise in this area, authors provide the results of a 3-year quasi-experimental study of middle and high school students in the School District of Philadelphia. Case studies of schools with the highest student gains in civic engagement and citizenship, prosocial attitudes and behaviors, and resilience and academic efficacy are presented. Discussion of the cases illustrates the components of service-learning most highly associated with outcomes and the factors that appear to be associated with sustainability.

INTRODUCTION

Service-learning in secondary schools has a long history in the United States. As early as 1907, educators wrote of the need for young people to be exposed to civic education in the schools so that they could develop a

Scholarship for Sustaining Service-Learning and Civic Engagement
pp. 57–83
Copyright © 2008 by Information Age Publishing
All rights of reproduction in any form reserved.

sense of personal responsibility for community affairs (Hepburn, 1997). Dewey (1910) exhorted that learning must be experiential. Service-learning concepts languished for several decades, until educators, policy-makers, and others became concerned about youth alienation from politics and society (Kraft, 1996).

As service-learning emerged as a more popular school-based strategy, practices appeared to be related to whether the purpose of service-learning was for the reform of education or for the reform of youth (Conrad & Hedin, 1991). Those who promoted the reform of education tended to see service-learning as a strategy for academic engagement and performance (see, e.g., Schine, 1997; Shumer & Belbas, 1996). Those who focused on the reform of youth tended to link service-learning to character development, political and civic identity, moral development, job skills training, or leadership development (see, e.g., Boyte, 1991; Keith, 1994; Rutter & Newman, 1989). Effects of service-learning for both of these purposes are relatively well documented (Billig, 2000, 2004; Conrad & Hedin, 1991).

Many recent school-based programs have begun to establish both purposes as goals for service-learning in order to locate and sustain service-learning practices in the current standards-based K-12 school environment. An early adopter in this regard was the School District of Philadelphia. In 1998, the district began to require service-learning (not just community service) as a condition for promotion from one grade span to the next and for graduation, with the rationale that the experience would help the district to both produce socially responsible citizens and increase academic achievement (Holdsman & Tuchmann, 2004; Hornbeck, 2000).

In 2002, the school district received a character education grant to help fund the service-learning activities. Leaders chose to use the funding to enhance support services for program implementation in the middle schools and high schools in areas characterized by highest economic disadvantage. The funding requirements included the need to conduct a research project to document outcomes, and a large scale quasi-experimental study was conducted. The study focused both on outcomes and on identifying program factors most closely associated with outcomes. Further, the study included in-depth case studies to tease out the differences in service-learning implementation associated with the strongest academic outcomes versus those associated with the strongest citizenship and character development outcomes and to explore factors associated with sustainability.

This chapter provides both the overall results of the study and an examination of those characteristics most closely associated with the varying outcomes. A brief literature review discussing the theoretical underpinnings for offering service-learning as a character development and academic engagement strategy is provided, followed by a description of the study and the results. Discussion of results, limitations of the study, and implications for future research follows.

The Rationale for Offering Service-Learning as a Character Development and Academic Engagement Strategy

Service-learning is an academic approach that requires students to engage in community service as a way of learning important curricular outcomes. In programs that offer service-learning as a character development approach, service-learning often has a more explicit focus on developing citizenship, civic responsibility, and a strong ethical orientation.

Several theories can be cited to explain why service-learning should serve to develop character. According to Berkowitz and Bier (2005), the purpose of character education is to help young people develop their capacities and dispositions to be socially and personally responsible, moral, ethical, and self-managed. In a summary of the research, they demonstrated that the most effective character education programs had an explicit focus on values; were well integrated into the academic curriculum; and targeted specific outcomes including building social skills and awareness, increasing students' personal awareness and self-management, problem-solving, and decision-making skills. General outcomes of character education included decline in the incidence of risky behaviors, improved academic performance, and better overall school climate. The reasons for these outcomes were that young people found more relevance in their school work and that the environment changed to nurture an "other" orientation, self-confidence, and control.

Likona and Davidson (2005) write of the dual nature of character education, suggesting that character education promotes both mastery and relational orientations. The mastery orientation helps young people develop qualities such as persistence, diligence, creativity, and self-discipline while the relational orientation promotes integrity, justice, caring, and respect.

The National Research Council (2005) suggests that settings that promote positive youth development (including character) have several features in common: they promote *physical and psychological safety,* especially those that increase positive peer group interactions and decrease confrontations; *appropriate structure,* including limit setting and clear and consistent rules with monitoring; *supportive relationships* that feature connectedness, caring, responsiveness, good communication, and support; *opportunities to belong* to support sociocultural identity formation and cultural and bicultural competence; *positive social norms,* including explicit rules for behavior and obligations for service; *support for efficacy and matter-ing*, including empowerment practices and practices that grant and enable responsibility and meaningful challenge; *opportunities for skill building* in the physical, intellectual, psychological, emotional, and social domains; and *integration of family, school, and community efforts*.

The use of service-learning to build character, ideally implemented, has all of these features and results in strong academic and civic outcomes (Billig, 2007). Effective service-learning programs have been found to have the following features (Billig & Weah, 2008):

- sufficient duration and intensity;
- close link to or integration with curriculum;
- youth voice;
- meaningful service from the point of view of the participants;
- opportunities to address diversity;
- reciprocal community partnerships;
- cognitively challenging reflection activities; and
- monitoring for progress and quality.

While the literature provides a compelling argument for why service-learning should work, there is a need for more information on exactly what K-12 service-learning looks like when it is used simultaneously to promote character development and academic performance. This study was developed to address this need, and specifically was designed to identify both overall outcomes of participation in the program and the specific characteristics of service-learning that appeared to maximize specific desired outcomes.

In addition, researchers briefly explored factors associated with sustainability. Billig (2002) developed a framework that identified six key factors associated with sustainability:

- **Policy:** codification of the importance of service-learning and/or removal of barriers to service-learning implementation;
- **Leadership/champions:** key individuals who formulated and disseminated a vision for success, promoted allegiance to purpose and established a sense of community to support implementation;
- **Incentives:** stimulants to practice including people of influence, financial and human resources, and recognition for success;
- **Revenue streams**: stable sources of support;
- **Infrastructure for support:** organizational norms, professional development, and partnerships to assist with implementation; and

- **Visibility:** tangible evidence of success that serves to heighten awareness and motivation to implement service-learning.

These variables were tested within the case studies to determine the extent to which they predicted sustainability.

Character Education Program Description

The character education program in the School District of Philadelphia was focused on middle and high schools that served large proportions of young people from economically disadvantaged families. Grants were provided to schools and individual teachers to implement service-learning with a character education focus. Teachers could opt either to work with a specific program model or develop their own approaches. The specific models from which they could choose were Earth Force, Champions of Caring, City Year, or Need in Deed. Earth Force provided professional development on topics related to recycling, integrated pest management, and other environmental concerns and gave the teachers many materials and lesson plans they could adopt. Champions of Caring provided intensive professional development and a year-long curriculum guide that included very specific approaches, lessons, activities, and materials for teachers to use with students that empowered young people to improve communities. City Year offered support by providing Corps members to help with tutoring, service planning and assistance with implementation, and lunch and after school programming that featured service-learning. Need in Deed gave teachers a curriculum called My Voice that guided them through the components of the service-learning approach and supported the teachers by helping them locate appropriate community partners for service. Most school sites participated for 3 years in the project, though some dropped out and others were added over the course of the project.

METHODOLOGY

To evaluate project outcomes, researchers asked students to complete pre-/postsurveys each year. Teachers also completed surveys in the spring to indicate the ways in which they had implemented the program and their perceptions of impact. Both teachers and students responded to items that measured students' prosocial behaviors such as caring and altruism; students' attachment to the school community; students' sense of citizenship and civic responsibility; the degree to which students valued school and experienced academic efficacy; and students' respect for self and others. Only the student survey data are presented here.

Student surveys contained 57 items and measured the outcome areas listed, along with demographics, participation in school-related activities and service, and approximate, estimated grade point average (GPA). The survey items were developed by RMC Research or adapted from a wide variety of existing scales. Response categories were either agreement/disagreement scales or frequency scales. Some items were reverse coded so that all higher scores indicated positive results. Exhibit 3.1 shows the constructs measured by the surveys and the internal reliabilities of each scale. Note that some of the measures were items only and as such, findings in these areas should be treated with caution.

Researchers also collected objective measures of both academic performance and student behaviors related to character development. In-school suspensions, out-of-school suspensions, and serious incidents were examined as independent sources of behavioral performance that are hypothesized to be affected by participation in the program.

The study employed a quasi-experimental design where participating classrooms were matched on demographic and achievement variables with nonparticipating classrooms. In some cases, the comparison site was located at the same school as the participating site, and in other cases the classrooms were matched with those from nearby schools. In all cases, the matches consisted of teachers and classrooms in the same subject matter

Exhibit 3.1. Internal Reliabilities of Presurvey Student Subscales, Fall 2005

Subscale	Number of Items	Internal Reliability Fall 2005 (N = 995)
Citizenship	2	.428
Civic engagement	3	.047
Social responsibility	3	.473
Altruism	4	.756
Caring	9	.686
Respect	4	.213
Ability to choose	1	—
Efficacy	4	.664
Persistence	2	.413
Internal locus of control	2	.309
Value of school	10	.774

(e.g., English, social studies, or biology) and had no more than 10% deviation in the percentage of nonwhite students served and the percentage of students scoring at the proficient level on the student achievement tests during the baseline year.

Data were only included in the study if the students completed both the pretest and posttest. The final sample consisted of 840 participating students and 155 comparison students, 568 of whom were middle school students and 427 of whom were high school students. Exhibit 3.2 shows the characteristics of the student sample. The sample had a strong representation of African American students and students whose grades most often were Bs and Cs. Because gender and ethnicity were so different in the participant and comparison sites, their effects were controlled statistically.

Exhibit 3.2.   Student Sample Characteristics (*N* = 995)

Characteristic	Character Education Students (N = 840)		Comparison Students (N = 155)	
	Frequency	Percentage	Frequency	Percentage
Gender				
Male	379	45.8	107	70.9
Female	449	54.2	44	29.1
Ethnicity[a]				
White	131	15.6	17	11.0
Asian	82	9.8	14	9.0
Black/African American	493	58.7	114	73.5
American Indian	36	4.3	4	2.6
Hispanic/Latino	132	15.7	15	9.7
Other	66	7.9	9	5.8
Language Spoken at Home				
English	684	84.7	136	88.3
Spanish	49	6.1	4	2.6
Korean	5	0.6	0	0.0
Chinese	12	1.5	1	0.6
Other	57	7.1	13	8.4
Grades[a]				
Mostly As	136	16.2	35	22.6
Mostly Bs	420	50.0	81	52.3
Mostly Cs	338	40.2	50	32.3
Mostly Ds	47	5.6	5	3.2
Mostly Fs	11	1.3	1	0.6

Note: [a]Percentages do not sum to 100 because respondents could select more than one answer and some students did not respond. Responses are from presurveys given in the fall of 2005. Percentages are calculated by using all valid responses.

Researchers analyzed data for changes over time using a mixed analysis of covariance (ANCOVA) model with presurvey and postsurvey repeated measures. Ethnicity and gender main effects and interactions were included to control for variance. To further adjust for preexisting differences between the groups, four additional covariates were included: (1) GPAs calculated from pre-survey student grade estimates; (2) the sum of service activities in which students reported participation (in school, with a youth organization, with a church, with family and with neighborhood); (3) the sum of clubs in which students reported participation (academic clubs, service clubs, student leadership groups, or other clubs); and 4) student age. Student survey responses were linked with teachers so that most effective pedagogical practices could be identified.

Researchers then compared the data at the classroom level to determine the distribution of student survey scores and which classrooms scored highest. Difference scores between matched treatment and comparison classrooms or schools were derived. Lists were compiled that rank ordered the classrooms with the highest difference scores for the treatment sites. These lists revealed which teachers had students who increased their scores the most on each of the survey scales.

The lists were sorted by grade span so that the resultant list showed highest scores for middle schools and for high schools. From this list, teachers were identified as potential candidates for the subsequent effective practices study. Names were shared with the project director, and several teachers were eliminated because they either were no longer at the school or were no longer participating in the grant. The final sample included five teachers who had students with high gain scores in prosocial attitudes and behaviors, civic engagement and citizenship, and valuing school/academic efficacy. Identified classrooms then became the subjects of case studies.

The case study utilized multiple methods. Focus groups were held with students in all five of the classrooms. Students were asked structured questions regarding their experiences with the character education program and their perceptions of the value of the activities. They were also asked to describe impacts in the areas being studied and for ideas for program improvement. Focus group questions also had students compare their service-learning/character education experiences with regular classroom experiences in terms of utility and value. In-depth, structured interviews were conducted with each of the teachers. In one case, evaluators discovered that two teachers—one regular classroom teacher and one special education teacher—had facilitated the project, so both teachers were interviewed together. Interviews typically lasted about an hour and included questions about motivation to participate; description of preparation, action, and reflection activities; roles of community partners; roles of the teacher and the students in implementing projects; implementation challenges; and student impacts in the areas of interest.

RESULTS

Exhibit 3 shows that most scores went down over time, but that participating students' scores decreased less than nonparticipating students in the areas of citizenship and valuing school. Scores for participating students increased slightly in civics and caring while nonparticipating student scores dropped.

Exhibit 3.3. Students' Subscale Average Scores

	Character Education				*Comparison*			
	Time	*N*	*M*	*SD*	*Time*	*N*	*M*	*SD*
Citizenship*	Presurvey	764	3.26	0.829	Presurvey	152	3.38	0.986
	Postsurvey	764	3.19	0.857	Postsurvey	152	3.10	0.999
Civic engagement**	Presurvey	774	2.87	0.696	Presurvey	152	2.98	0.801
	Postsurvey	774	2.89	0.696	Postsurvey	152	2.79	0.826
Social responsibility	Presurvey	784	2.93	0.812	Presurvey	152	3.07	0.937
	Postsurvey	784	3.06	0.784	Postsurvey	152	3.04	0.900
Altruism	Presurvey	754	3.19	0.686	Presurvey	144	3.24	0.792
	Postsurvey	754	3.12	0.714	Postsurvey	144	3.12	0.852
Caring*	Presurvey	792	2.92	0.591	Presurvey	151	2.95	0.676
	Postsurvey	792	2.93	0.591	Postsurvey	151	2.82	0.688
Respect	Presurvey	777	2.83	0.753	Presurvey	151	2.85	0.872
	Postsurvey	777	2.83	0.780	Postsurvey	151	2.72	0.909
Ability to choose between right and wrong	Presurvey	727	3.19	0.944	Presurvey	139	3.40	1.096
	Postsurvey	727	3.19	0.944	Postsurvey	139	3.40	1.120
Efficacy	Presurvey	791	3.05	0.703	Presurvey	152	3.11	0.814
	Postsurvey	791	3.04	0.731	Postsurvey	152	3.06	0.838
Persistence	Presurvey	754	2.13	0.879	Presurvey	145	2.11	0.999
	Postsurvey	754	2.11	0.851	Postsurvey	145	2.16	0.975
Internal locus of control	Presurvey	763	3.22	0.691	Presurvey	146	3.21	0.785
	Postsurvey	763	3.20	0.746	Postsurvey	146	3.14	0.870
Value of school*	Presurvey	800	3.30	0.735	Presurvey	154	3.43	0.844
	Postsurvey	800	3.26	0.764	Postsurvey	154	3.22	0.869
Aggregate**	Presurvey	808	3.00	0.426	Presurvey	155	3.08	0.486
	Postsurvey	808	2.98	0.426	Postsurvey	155	2.95	0.498

Note: $*p < .05$, $**p < .01$, group by time interaction. Means are adjusted for estimated GPA, number of service activities, number of clubs, and age. Ethnicity and gender are also included as independent variables.

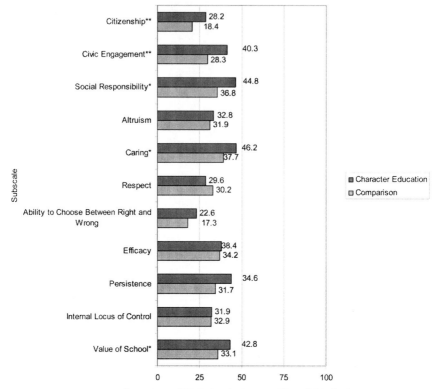

Note: *p < .05, **p < .01, one-tailed test, z test for two proportions.

Exhibit 3.4.   Percentage of student with increases from fall to spring, 2005-2006.

Exhibit 3.4 shows that in all areas, over 20% of the service-learning character education students measured showed gains over time and in all cases but two (respect and internal locus of control), higher percentages of participating students had gains than their peers.

Analysis of behavioral disciplinary measures showed that participating students were significantly less likely to have in-school or out-of school suspensions. Only 1.8% of the participating students experienced in-school suspensions, compared to 15.6% of comparison students. Similarly 21% of participating students had out-of-school suspensions compared to 36.1% of comparison students. Serious incident data (percentage of students carrying or using weapons, fighting, and other acts of violence or abuse) revealed no statistically significant differences between these two groups, though once again, there were fewer incidents among participating students.

Promising Practice Sites

As explained in the methodology section, to gain a greater understanding of the practices associated with highest gains on survey scales over time, the data were examined by classroom, and the classrooms with the highest gains on each of the subscale areas were identified. These classrooms then became the subject for brief case analyses using the methodology described. A brief description of each of the sites is presented, classified according to the area of greatest student impacts. A discussion follows, identifying common program components.

Best Practice Civic Engagement and Citizenship Sites

Two high school sites and one middle school site had the greatest gain scores on the survey for civic engagement and citizenship (and both also had relatively high difference scores for valuing school).

Site 1

The first site was a high school classroom taught by an English language arts teacher and a special education teacher. During that academic year, the class conducted a project that focused on prevention of sexually transmitted diseases (STDs). The teachers facilitated the project by following the Need in Deed process. Students brainstormed and identified multiple community issues that they could address. They took a vote and decided to learn about STDs because they knew people in the community who had contracted these diseases and wanted to know how they could help with prevention and treatment.

Need in Deed identified and sent speakers to the school. Representatives from a local nonprofit health care organization, *Health Partners*, spoke about AIDS and STDs. A law school student also visited the classroom and talked about having been a teen mother and the struggles she faced earlier in her life because she had to manage both a child and a job in addition to getting an education. Students also viewed a videotape of a student with AIDS discussing the disease and how it had affected his life. The teacher commented about student reactions to the film:

> The students said they were moved by the movie they saw. Need in Deed people still had contact with the person in the movie so they told us what happened to him.

Students conducted research on the most common STDs, requesting that fellow students complete a survey that asked them to discuss the prevalence of the disease among teens and how the diseases were contracted and treated. They identified myths and facts, discussed multiple health issues that arose from contracting the various diseases, and had conversations about the social difficulties faced by those with STDs and AIDS. They also discovered the resources available in the community to help those with STDs.

For their community action project, the students decided to sponsor a health fair. Groups of three or four students were assigned to work together to plan the event. The groups each selected a different disease and the best ways to communicate about prevention. Special education students participated in each of the groups. The students thought that the best way to inform other students and motivate them to engage in prevention activities was to show a graphic presentation of what happens to individuals when they contract either a STD or AIDS. The groups conducted more research and developed trifolds to communicate about each of the diseases, the prevention strategies, and the treatments.

Students invited younger students from the nearby feeder school to attend the health fair. They had to organize the event so that parent permission was secured and students were given appropriate information in a mature and sensitive manner. The teacher stated:

> We discussed what to do with the information and talked about what would help the community the most. We decided to host a health fair and disseminate brochures. They designed a trifold brochure with pictures. They wanted to make it fun so they came up with a scavenger hunt for other students to use to learn about STDs. The Health Partners gave prizes like pencils and sweatbands. The students from the other school, grades six through eight, came to the fair. We had to get parent permission for them to come because of the topic. It was active parent permission forms. We invited kids from other schools, too, but no one else came because it was a busy time of year.

The teachers facilitated reflection sessions after each speaker came to the class and again after the health fair. The reflection sessions helped to move the project from one phase to the next.

> They saw the effects, what could happen if you have unprotected sex. They saw how hard it was to live with a child when you are a teenager. They saw people with AIDS and other diseases. They discussed myths and figured out the truth. Over time, they started asking more personal questions.... After the health fair, they discussed how well it went and what they would do differently if they did this again. They also prepped for the showcase so that they could communicate even better. (Teacher)

Both teachers explicitly aligned the project with standards in English/language arts. The project included conducting research; analyzing cause and effect; reading the newspaper; summarizing, comparing, and contrasting; identifying problems and solutions; persuasive writing; and identifying the main idea. However, they did not tell the students it was tied to the curriculum because they believed that the students saw the project as a break from the regular classroom routine. As one teacher pointed out:

> Sometimes when students think the work is not tied to the curriculum, they get more excited about doing it. It's special, unique.

According to the teachers, several challenges were associated with the topic that the students selected. For example, when the class discussed teen pregnancy, rape, and STDs, the male students were initially reluctant to get involved. Once the project was organized, though, the male students joined in as full participants.

Finding appropriate articles to have students read independently was also a challenge. Many of the articles used medical terms and sophisticated vocabulary, so students often asked questions of community partners or other students so that they could better understand what they were reading. Obtaining parent permission for students to participate in the grant was also problematic since some parents did not think the students should be studying these topics.

At the end of the year, the teachers felt that the students had acquired knowledge about health issues and skills related to organizing and presenting information, persuasion, and writing skills. More importantly, they assumed responsibility for their own learning, ensured that the students served in special education were included and took responsibility for their roles and tasks, and tackled an issue which resulted in a significant decrease in STDs as measured by treatment incidence at a local clinic. Follow up revealed that the approach showing very graphically the consequences of the disease and the ease with which it could be prevented were the key reasons why the teens changed their behavior.

The teacher who facilitated this project reported that she intends to continue using service-learning as a key instructional strategy in her classes. She noted that each year, her students had tackled a different issue, and they nearly always could document the impact of their efforts. She believed that her ability to sustain the project was dependent upon the support of her principal, the assistance of the community partner, the visible results that had been attained and well-documented, and the resources she had to implement the program.

Site 2

The second site with high civic engagement and citizenship gain scores on the survey had students who engaged in an environmental service-learning project. Two natural resources science classes taught by the same teacher were engaged in the project during the 2005-06 school year. Two days a week as part of their classroom activities, the first period students collected the articles to recycle and the second period students sorted the items and placed them in appropriate recycling bins. Earth Force and a local park beautification group were partners in the project. Earth Force presented information about the importance of waste management and how to approach the recycling task. Students learned about pollution and its effects. The local park beautification group discussed the need to take care of the park and how important parks are to neighborhoods. These partners gave rewards to students who participated and developed environmental activities for students to engage in after school and on Saturdays. Students presented the results of their project to the community partners at a meeting during the school year.

When the school recycling project first started, the students were appalled by what they found in the trash (e.g., wallets, book bags, money, drugs). Some students did not want to do the dirty work of sorting, so they took up other tasks such as scheduling or getting supplies. Other students volunteered for any job that needed filling. Over time, about 80% of the students in the two classes decided they wanted to be involved in some sort of recycling. Some students started to volunteer with the park group and other organizations to help with cleaning the park and recycling on Saturdays.

> The teacher asked us to volunteer. At first a few students collected things, but everyone would help crush the cans. Then we decided we all should do it because we learned about global warming. We needed to be there. Everyone had a job— bottle washer, crusher, collector. We knew we were making a difference. (Student)

Originally, students wanted to participate so they could complete their service-learning requirement. After a while, students started to expand the project as they learned more about the need to recycle and about environmental concerns, saying they wanted to "save the earth." They invited others, particularly those students in special needs classes, to help them with the recycling, and they designed and wore blue shirts to signify what they were doing. They convinced their peers to be mindful of recycling of bottles and cans and of putting trash into the appropriate bins.

At some point during the year, the students were informed that they could not have trash cans or recycle bins in the hallways, so they designed a "door-to-door campaign" wherein they figured out how to collect all of the recyclables in the first 20 minutes of the school day. They designed a collection system and division of labor for teams and tweaked the system until the timing was perfect. All of the students in the class participated in the design task, with some taking leadership and management roles, and others doing what they called the "down and dirty work." Students were allowed to enforce the plan, even with adults.

> This gave them the sense that they could run something. They were given control over something important. The vice principal threw a can in the trash can once and they wrote him up on a pink slip. He never did that again. They told the teachers they had to recycle. It was fun! (Teacher)

During the year, students also developed and conducted a survey on opinions about recycling and presented to several community groups on the importance of recycling.

The teacher integrated the project into the natural resources course curriculum at appropriate times, but did not force the alignment when it seemed a bad fit. The teacher believed that the fit was best with eight of the natural resource science standards, so she had students discuss the concepts associated with recycling at that time.

> We applied the concepts when we could with the eight standards. We saw how the information applied to what we were doing and why it was important. (Teacher)

The teacher reported a noticeable change in student behavior. They engaged in more teamwork, developed more self-confidence, and took a stand by promoting and reinforcing recycling in the school. Students also spoke at various community meetings and gained confidence in their ability to convince others of the importance of saving the environment.

With a change in leadership of the school, the teacher was not convinced that she would be able to continue the project during the school day, but instead would support the project as an after school program. The teacher believed that the students benefitted greatly, but because she could not "prove" that the approach resulted in increased test scores, she was placed in a position of needing to follow the scope and sequence and pacing guide provided by her school for teaching environmental science. Students reported that as long as they could continue the program, they did not care whether it happened during or after school.

Site 3

The third site with strong increases on the civic and citizenship survey measures was a middle school classroom where students engaged in an anti-smoking campaign. Students initiated the project by conducting a survey that they developed to determine community feelings about smoking. They asked about the prevalence of smoking in the families and whether any relatives had suffered from smoking-related diseases. Students organized the project into committees so that each would have specific activities to do, such as making sure the surveys were prepared for delivery and getting the right postage on each of the surveys.

> I had to explain what the mission and the goals of the grant were. We had to go into a bit of statistics and data analysis. They brought up lessons on their own on data analysis. They got used to the vocabulary of how to conduct research, for example.... The students had to determine how to get the questions out to the community, how to best collect and analyze the data. (Teacher)

Students also conducted research on the Internet and through participation in an antismoking rally in Center City. They learned about the cost of cigarettes, the types of damage that smoking can inflict in 36 months, and policies being considered by the City of Philadelphia. Students collected brochures and information from the Cancer Center. The neighborhood community health center also provided information. One of the mayoral candidates came to speak with the students about city policies and to listen to their concerns about smoking. Students wanted to know how far smoke traveled in restaurants, so they asked some of the business owners if they could measure the distance. Once information was collected from this activity, from the surveys, and from the Internet research, students created collages on poster boards to inform the public about the dangers of smoking. Based on the research they had conducted on the various aspects of smoking, students decided on the antismoking theme they would address.

> We gave them more autonomy on that, based on their own specific research and their own personal feelings. We entered into a regional character education contest and our students actually won. They presented their collages and their poster boards. They had to talk about ... what their issues were in terms of how smoking ... affected your health and its financial and personal impacts. The themes and messages were varied. (Teacher)

Some students videotaped interviews of community members and health care workers. Students also testified at city hall and wrote a letter to the councilman who had visited their classroom, telling him what they found and how he should vote on the policy being debated. At the end of the project, students were asked to reflect on their experience and on what they had learned.

> We talked about efficacy all the time—how anything you can do can affect change. They recognized that this was a prime example, how to gather data and providing [them] to people who need it can affect change. (Teacher)

The teacher reported that the major challenges were in finding enough materials and research to use to develop questions for the survey and ensuring that the questions were clear and well designed. A few students struggled with the terminology used in the medical literature that they accessed. The students met the challenges by having discussions about the topic and looking up various definitions online. Initially, figuring out how to administer the surveys was a challenge, but students brainstormed solutions that seemed to work.

> The students thought of ways to solve problems. There were some issues that were brought up that I thought were examples of students using higher-order thinking skills. They would troubleshoot how to get the surveys out.... Many of the students had responsibilities or jobs. Students had to make sure the surveys were prepared for delivery and organize themselves to do it. (Teacher)

Teachers at this site were absolutely committed to sustaining service-learning as an in-class project in the future. They had the principal's support, students who enthusiastically looked forward to engaging in a service-learning project each year, sufficient resources, a helpful community partner, and visible results, all of which they attributed as key factors to sustainability.

Best Practice Valuing School and Academic Efficacy Site

A middle school classroom that focused on illiteracy had the strongest increases in survey items measuring value of schooling and academic efficacy. During the 2005-06 school year, when the survey results were strong, the teacher spent quite a bit of time with students discussing community issues and things that concerned them, reading different articles, and exploring multiple ideas with community partners to determine which service-learning project they would undertake. As a result of these discussions, the class decided to help others acquire literacy skills.

> I set up different scenarios for them [the students] to get their ideas of trust and honesty and to see where they stand and what they would do in certain situations. They did a lot of research at school and at home about different topics, and they ended up taking a vote on, I think, six or eight different topics. They eventually came up with illiteracy in the community and [the project] became, "What could you do to help literacy?" (Teacher)

One community partner member read a biography of Frederick Douglass. He was an inspiration to the children because he became a reader even though during his childhood he could have been killed for learning how to read. Students discussed why he was so passionate about reading and how important it was to be literate.

The partner also discussed other role models who took up the challenge of helping others to read and literacy problems in the local community. Staff from the local library helped students gather articles and read stories to them about people becoming readers under adverse circumstances.

The librarian also worked with prisoners who were learning to read so another community partner, Need in Deed, collected some letters from inmates in the program who stated that they wished they had learn how to read and regretted dropping out of school. The students studied the problem and learned the correlation between illiteracy and crimes. They shared their own stories about the problems that occur when people do not finish school and talked about the successes people have when they do complete school. They also researched both careers associated with literacy and various programs on literacy offered throughout the Philadelphia area. Several interviewed individuals who were working on literacy initiatives to find out about the work and the educational qualifications needed to obtain the jobs.

> They did well with the adults. Usually when we had partners come, I had the students develop the questions they wanted to ask beforehand. Then they would ask the questions. They got really used to one of the partners that came a lot. They would get upset if she didn't come. Some of the kids ended up applying for summer jobs with the (literacy) program. (Teacher)

The students decided to address the literacy problem by working with students from one of the local elementary feeder schools. The students made books that could be read by students at various reading levels. They discussed, for example, how to enlarge print, use pictures, and make the text understandable to kindergarteners, later readers, and fluent readers. Each student created two or three books, and the class as a whole developed over 100 books.

The students decided to sponsor a "Literacy Fun Day" at the elementary school so that the project included a big event. They planned a buddy system in which they would pair with one of the younger children, discussed how they would introduce themselves, which books to read, and how to work with young children. The librarian taught them how to read aloud in a lively way, to interest the younger children. Students engaged in role play and rehearsed the games they would play with the younger students. On Literacy Fun Day, they read poems and several big books, and they sang a literacy rap, asking the younger students to sing along. They also had the younger children read to them.

> A lot of them developed really good relationships with the younger children. Some of them wanted to follow up and keep working with the kids. A couple of my students decided they wanted to go into a field where they could work with young children. (Teacher)

Students created flyers about the importance of literacy and distributed them in the community. They sponsored an activity at the library and invited their families, friends, and neighbors. At the event, they read some of their books and poems and shared what they learned, with every student presenting information in different way.

The teacher closely aligned the service-learning activities with the curriculum. She addressed multiple reading/language arts standards within the project and intentionally reinforced the connection within her classroom activities.

> With the skills, I tried to pull out articles and discuss main ideas and context clues.... A lot of the examples I would use would have to do with illiteracy in the community. Not everything.... I allowed the students to bring in their own articles, too. (Teacher)

According to the teacher, students made great gains in developing positive character traits including treating each other with respect and learning to work well together in teams. Students took responsibility for their work and became civically engaged, expressing a desire to help others in the community.

> I found that students that wouldn't normally sit with others would. Those that would normally argue would sit together and share, even if they didn't have to. They chose to work together. This group was supposed to be a group of problem kids, but it didn't show when they worked on their service-learning.... I didn't know until after the fact that these kids were known for having behavior issues. By the middle of the year, one student stopped using curse words. Other kids actually noticed this. With another, his thing was teasing other kids. By the end, he was not teasing, though he had his moments. By the end, he had improved so much. (Teacher)

Students learned facts about illiteracy and crime, jobs that related to literacy, and developmental processes in children who were learning to read. The teacher believed that the students read better at the end of the class because each student was able to succeed at something related to literacy.

In some way, whatever they were good at, it ended up being touched on. Every time we did the service-learning activities, some of them would just light up. It really made a difference. I involved a lot of hands-on activities and they enjoyed it, no matter what their expertise was. (Teacher)

The teacher at this site was strongly committed to the practice of service-learning as a key teaching and learning strategy. She believed that one of the functions of schooling was to help young people see their place in society, to experience success, and to see that they could make a difference. She said that her principal was supportive of her work and came to see the students present during showcases and other public events. She also believed that having a strong community partner was critical to sustainability, and mentioned that the professional development she received helped her to become more confident and competent in facilitating service-learning experiences.

Best Practice Prosocial Behavior Site

The high school site with the largest gains in measures of prosocial behaviors, including altruism, caring, and respect for self and others, engaged students in a global citizenship project that included fundraising and promoting policy awareness of the needs of children in Northern Uganda. The teacher said that she got the idea from attending service-learning workshops during the previous school year, and, as she shared the idea with students and other teachers, the excitement about her idea built. The teacher selected northern Uganda as the place to study, and the class organized a series of information-gathering activities to understand the needs of Ugandan children.

Students conducted research on Uganda and partnered with an organization that works in Gulu, the second largest town in Uganda. Students learned that Acholi children had to walk each night from their homes into town because if they stayed in any other area, they were subject to violence or abduction by a rebel paramilitary group. Up to 40,000 children participated in this walk each night and averaged only about four hours of sleep since they needed to return at sunrise. In addition, these Ugandan children lacked medical care, clean water, and food.

The class invited experts to their school to discuss the issues, and the experts brought pictures and booklets with information. A journalist from the local newspaper also provided the students with information and discussed Ugandan issues with them. The class discovered that there were organizations that raised funds through GuluWalks, paralleling the walks that Ugandan children took each day. Students conducted research on the Internet to learn more about the country and engaged in multiple dialogues about what they could do. The class decided to focus on raising awareness and funds to help the Ugandan children and to encourage politicians to become more accountable for addressing the needs of the Ugandan children.

To raise awareness, the students surveyed other students in the school to assess their knowledge of Uganda and its needs, and then conducted a "street survey," interviewing passersby about their knowledge of Uganda and whether they were concerned about the issues there. They compared the violence in Philadelphia with the violence in Uganda and solicited opinions about which was worse. Students videotaped the respondents to the street survey and discussed what they found. To raise funds, students designed and executed multiple projects such as collecting toiletries and blankets from nearby hotels and residents and organizing their own Gulu-Walk.

> They researched and had to understand the political process. Until you dive deeply into politics, talk to politicians, you do not understand it. It is not just black and white issues. There are other factors which motivate politicians to do things. Money is involved, political power is involved. There are many things that make things happen in government. So students had to understand how politicians are elected and their civic responsibility as citizens. (Teacher)

The teacher clearly expressed the need to fit the project into the curriculum. She worked to ensure that the project fit into the structure that already existed and she said she worked diligently on a daily basis to ensure alignment with lesson plan objectives.

> The curriculum has standards we must meet, but there is leeway in how we meet them. For example, there is measurement in a math standard, but you can focus on the service-learning project as a way to teach it, like having students calculate transportation and mileage in northern Uganda. The technology class could (conduct) research on the Internet. (Teacher)

The teacher believed that the students learned how to work better in teams and to have a greater understanding and appreciation of living in America.

> It's a normal growth process. When you allow the opportunity for students to work as a team, regardless of the problems, in the end, growth will have taken place, and normally does so long as there are guidelines and supervision. They will learn teamwork, how to get along without being aggressive … you can agree to disagree, but you cannot be disagreeable.… The students take for granted what they have in America. They assume that what they have in America is [their] right. Regardless of how much reading they do, they can't understand the struggle of their predecessors to appreciate

what they have, their right to a free education. So when they engage in activities that show them individuals who do not have [these rights], they appreciate it. (Teacher)

This teacher was a service-learning enthusiast, but did not continue its practice into the next year. She had been reassigned to teach different courses (computer courses rather than social studies) and could not see how to implement the same type of project within this subject matter. The teacher said that she had "grown her own" service-learning and did not have a community partner to depend on to assist her with project planning, and that she had run out of ideas. On the other hand, she supported other teachers who were engaged in service-learning by providing them with materials and resources that she had acquired when she was implementing her project.

DISCUSSION

The survey data revealed that service-learning had statistically significant effects on middle and high school students in terms of development of several aspects of character, including citizenship and civic engagement; altruism, caring, and respect for self and others; and valuing school and academic efficacy. Several of the projects identified as most effective utilized an approach whereby students brainstormed social, environmental, or health issues of concern to them, came to consensus on a topic that the class would collectively investigate, and conducted research on the topic, using the Internet to find research studies to understand issues, conducting surveys in the community to document incidence, and collecting information about the issue from community organizations. This approach emphasized youth voice and meaningfulness and was used for the projects that addressed illiteracy, sexually transmitted diseases, and smoking for the group with the highest gains in citizenship and civic engagement. The other two projects, recycling and the Uganda project, did not have as much student choice and voice, but they were considered by the students to have great relevance and meaning. These variables were found in the character education and service-learning literature to be among the practices associated with strong outcomes and with the most recent literature on the "quality" variables associated with civic outcomes in service-learning (Billig & Weah, 2008).

Most of the teachers invited speakers from the community to give the students more information about the issue and about some community-based solutions being implemented. Many of the speakers made the issues come alive for students by presenting personal stories. These activities tended to spur both the mastery set and the relational set discussed by Lickona and Davidson (2005) as being critical to the development of character.

Partners played a large role in the success of several of the projects by providing the speakers, identifying research, and helping teachers to devise community activities. Teachers also received professional development and coaching from the community partners. While the students may not have been as directly affected by this as the teachers, it is clear that the support provided by the partners assisted the teachers with project implementation.

Projects normally lasted for several months and teachers typically thought that this amount of time was optimal. All of the projects had investigation, preparation, action, and demonstration components. Some used a variety of reflection and celebration activities, but several did not. The teachers who used reflection activities that promoted deeper thinking by asking students to engage in synthesis, perspective taking, and linking experiences to larger societal issues tended to be the ones with students who could better articulate the benefits of the program. Most of the projects featured strong alignment with district standards, and teachers generally reported that the alignment was not difficult to accomplish.

Teachers also reported that there were very few challenges associated with implementation. Most of the challenges that were identified had to do with students working together well. Typically this challenge was met with strong facilitation by the teacher or explicit discussion of the need for everyone to take responsibility for the completion of a project.

These findings indicate that the best practice sites were generally well aligned with the standards for effective K-12 service-learning (Billig & Weah, 2008). The duration and intensity were sufficient; the link to curriculum was generally strong; and all of the issues were considered meaningful and relevant for the students. There was strong progress monitoring, and the community partnerships that were formed were generally characterized by frequent communication and reciprocity. Only three of the sites had significant youth voice, though, and only two had strong ties to diversity issues, and reflection was strong in only one of the sites.

As a group, the cases also had most of the features identified by the National Research Council (2003) as being those that foster positive youth development. In each of the cases, teachers created an environment where students felt safe to discuss issues (STDs, global warming, international food shortages, the hazards of smoking, and illiteracy) and where positive peer group interactions with a strong task orientation were expected so that students could disseminate information and address the issue of concern. Teachers used normal classroom procedures to reinforce rules and establish appropriate structures. The teachers and the community partners with whom the students worked provided strong support for the students. These adult-student relationships were characterized by connectedness, caring, responsiveness, and good communication, thereby providing students with positive role models of good character and with information support.

Students clearly had opportunities to develop a sense of group belonging as they engaged in research, brainstorming on how to address the community issues of concern and in tasks that they performed to work with the community or disseminate information on how to solve problems. In the classrooms where traditional students and students with disabilities were working together—the classrooms addressing illiteracy, and the classroom working on Ugandan issues—students had opportunities to develop cultural and bicultural competence.

In all cases, teachers provided explicit rules for behavior and promoted an ethic of service. Support for efficacy and mattering were evident in the responsibilities and meaningful challenges imposed and taken by the students. Teachers offered multiple opportunities for skill building, primarily in the intellectual, social, and emotional domains. Finally, there was clear integration of school and community efforts.

In each case, strong character development outcomes were reported by both teachers and students. Taking responsibility for oneself and others was an outcome expressed in nearly every case study. Students developed knowledge of community issues, empathy and sympathy, and skills in project organization and teamwork. Students reported that they cared more about specific community issues and that they wanted to help solve community problems. They felt a sense of efficacy and were more likely to persist in completing projects and in trying to influence others to take action on issues of concern.

Academic outcomes tended to take the form of increasing skills in communication, both in terms of oral communications and writing and the development of research skills, specifically in finding information on the Internet about a topic of interest. Some students learned more about content in social studies or environmental science, but the stronger outcomes were in process skills.

Exploration of sustainability revealed that many of the factors associated in the sustainability framework (Billig, 2002) appeared to be predictors of sustaining service-learning in these cases. Principal support for these teachers appeared to have the greatest weight in determining whether the practice of service-learning was sustained, though it was also clear that strong partnerships, resources, and tangible results contributed strongly to these efforts. Policy was not mentioned at all, but that could be because the school district has had a long-standing policy of support.

None of the teachers mentioned revenue streams either, apparently because funding was simply not an issue since additional costs were not incurred as a result of implementing service-learning or perhaps because all of the teachers received a small stipend from the character education grant to conduct their work.

It should be noted that two of the teachers were unable to continue their service-learning practice within their traditional classrooms. In one case, the teacher continued her work after school, but said that the lack of leadership support inhibited her from sustaining service-learning as an in-class practice. In the other case, the teacher had a new assignment and because she did not avail herself of the available community partnerships and professional development, she could not see a way to continue. These cases make clear that the leadership/champion factor and the support networks are of key importance.

This study, then, begins to illuminate the ways in which service-learning can and has served as an important strategy for the promotion and sustainability of character development programming. The case studies provide a snapshot of the ways in which several teachers were able to produce strong outcomes.

STUDY LIMITATIONS AND
IMPLICATIONS FOR FUTURE RESEARCH

The study has several limitations that must be taken into consideration. First, findings showed a decline in overall survey scores over time. While this may be typical for secondary school surveys conducted in the fall and spring, showing a smaller decline instead of a larger gain is problematic. While this study addressed this issue by examining percentages of students who made gains, further study is needed to understand why more students did not increase their scores. Second, the case studies were retrospective in nature rather than occurring during the survey administration period. Teachers, then, were asked to remember and reconstruct activities and the students who were in the focus groups were not the ones who had gains on the surveys, even though they had the same teachers as the students who did make gains.

Future research should continue to explore both the specific types of character development impacts that participation in service-learning has and the implementation variables associated with impact. The data here indicate that there may be differences between practices that promote citizenship and civic engagement and those that promote prosocial behaviors. The academic and civic outcomes in this study tended to cluster, though the case study where students directly addressed academic concerns (illiteracy) had the greatest academic outcomes. The ways in which the mastery and relational sets interact within service-learning are not well known and clearly deserve more attention. Finally, because the study had overrepresentation of students from high poverty backgrounds and communities of color, it is important to replicate the study with other student subpopulations to determine the extent to which findings can be generalized.

The issue of sustainability also deserves additional attention. This study suggests that while all of the factors within the sustainability framework are important, some, including leadership and partnerships, appear to be better predictors of sustainability than others. In particular, the case studies here suggest that there is a hierarchy among the factors in the framework that could be tested within other studies. More research is needed to test this hypothesis and to understand how sustainability and quality interact.

REFERENCES

Berkowitz, M., & Bier, M. (2005). *What works in character education: A report for policy makers and opinion leaders.* Washington, DC: Character Education Partnership.

Billig, S. H. (2000, May). Research on K–12 school-based service-learning: The evidence builds. *Phi Delta Kappan, 81*(9), 658–664.

Billig, S. H. (2002). Adoption, implementation, and sustainability of K-12 service-learning. In A. Furco & S. H. Billig (Eds.), *Service-learning: The essence of the pedagogy* (pp. 245-267). Greenwich, CT: Information Age.

Billig, S. H. (2004). Heads, hearts, hands: The research on K–12 service-learning. In J. Kielsmeier, M. Neal, & M. McKinnon (Eds.), *Growing to greatness: The state of service-learning project* (pp. 12–25). St. Paul, MN: National Youth Leadership Council.

Billig, S. H. (2007). Unpacking what works in service-learning: Promising research-based practices to improve student outcomes. In J. C. Kielsmeier, M. Neal, & N. Schultz (Eds.), *Growing to greatness 2007: The state of service-learning* (pp. 18–28). St. Paul, MN: National Youth Leadership Council.

Billig, S. H., & Weah, W. (2008). K–12 service-learning standards for quality practice. In J. C. Kielsmeier, M. Neal, N. Schultz, & T. J. Leeper (Eds.), *Growing to greatness 2008: The state of service-learning* project (pp. 8–15). St. Paul, MN: National Youth Leadership Council.

Boyte, H. C. (1991, June). Community service and civic education. *Phi Delta Kappan, 72*(10), 765–767.

Conrad, D., & Hedin, D. (1991, June). School-based community service: What we know from research and theory. *Phi Delta Kappan, 72*(10), 743–749.

Dewey, J. D. (1910). *How we think.* Boston: Heath

Hepburn, M. A. (1997, Summer). Service learning in civic education: A concept with long, sturdy roots. *Theory into Practice, 36*(3), 136–142.

Holdsman, K., & Tuchmann, D. (2004, December 9). The Philadelphia story: A Guide to service-learning system building. *District Lessons, 2,* 1–41.

Hornbeck, D. (2000, May). Service-learning and reform in the Philadelphia public schools. *Phi Delta Kappan, 81*(9), 665.

Keith, N. Z. (1994, April). *Diversity, equity and community in educational reform.* Paper presented at the Annual Meeting of the American Educational Research Association, New Orleans, LA.

Kraft, R. J. (1996). Service learning: An introduction to its theory, practice, and effects. *Education and Urban Society, 28,* 131–159.

Lickona, T., & Davidson, M. (2005). *Smart and good high schools: Integrating excellence and ethics for success in school, work, and beyond.* Cortland, NY: Center for the 4th and 5th Rs (Respect and Responsibility)/Washington, DC: Character Education Partnership.

National Research Council. (1999). *How people learn: Brain, mind, experience, and school.* Washington, DC: National Academy Press.

National Research Council. (2003). *Engaging schools: Fostering high school students' motivation to learn.* Washington, DC: National Academy Press.

Rutter, R., & Newman, F. (1989). The potential of community service to enhance civic responsibility. *Social Education, 53*(6), 371–374.

Schine, J. (1997). School-based service: Reconnecting schools, communities, and youth at the margin. *Theory into Practice, 36*(3), 170–175.

Shumer, R., & Belbas, B. (1996). What we know about service-learning. *Education and Urban Society, 28*(2), 208–223.

CHAPTER 4

SUSTAINABILITY OF SERVICE-LEARNING

What Do K-12 Teachers Say?

Marjori Maddox Krebs

The purpose of this chapter is to compare the model of sustainability of service-learning created by Billig (2001) to Krebs' findings (2006) which, in part, investigated K-12 teacher beliefs regarding sustainability. This comparison illustrates clear connections between the teacher beliefs regarding sustainability (Krebs, 2006) and the sustainability model presented by Billig. Billig conducted case studies in New Hampshire and included in her results 8 key factors that led to the sustainability of service-learning initiatives: (a) strong leadership; (b) cultural norms; (c) organizational expectations; (d) incentives; (e) visibility; (f) availability of funding resources; (g) the production of measurable impacts; and (h) supportive policies on the national, state, or local levels. Krebs (2006) described the essence of the service-learning experience for K-12 teachers in Ohio, derived through in-depth interviews with seven teachers. Results showed that teachers valued their experiences in implementing and sustaining service-learning projects in their classrooms because (a) of the connections that were made with various people and areas of the curriculum, (b) service-learning fit with their teaching philosophies

Scholarship for Sustaining Service-Learning and Civic Engagement
pp. 85–109

and styles, and (c) their participation resonated in their hearts as they worked to make the world a better place.

INTRODUCTION

Shad was a bright student achieving much below his potential in my high school American humanities class. He visited a nursing home each week, where he typically played euchre and other card games with three men over the age of 75. This social time was an opportunity for Shad and his classmates to learn about events in U.S. history from those who lived them. One morning, Shad was in the hallway just as the first bell was about to ring. As he passed by he called out, "Hey, Mrs. Krebs! I was about to cut school today, but then I remembered, 'Hey, it's service-learning day.' I just knew I had to be here." That exchange was an epiphany. Shad made that comment over 10 years ago, yet I recall it as if it were yesterday.

When teachers connect academic content to meaningful service through service-learning, students like Shad find new motivation for school attendance and academic achievement. It is important to determine what factors assist teachers in sustaining such projects so more students can benefit, especially in the standards-driven, test-centralized world in which we teach today.

During my first year as a high school social studies teacher, two district-level administrators introduced me to the concept of service-learning by inviting me to participate in a local professional development workshop. I have implemented service-learning with my students ever since, from my high school social studies students to my college-level pre-service teachers. I know that without the support and encouragement from key district-level and building-level administrators, I would never have implemented such a meaningful pedagogy with my students. Even though I have been successful in my implementation of service-learning, I have been challenged at times to sustain such projects. My experiences led me to wonder what general factors are important to sustain service-learning, and whether or not my experiences were unique or could be generalized.

This chapter provides the results of an exploratory study examining the factors related to sustainability. The chapter starts with a brief literature review, focusing on the framework that was tested through the study. The methodology used to collect data is then delineated, followed by an in-depth presentation of results. The last section provides conclusions and some recommendations for further investigation.

RESEARCH ON SUSTAINABILITY

Sustainability of service-learning refers to the continuation of a program over time, with long-term partnerships, supportive stakeholders, and secure funding sources. Little research has been conducted on sustainability of service-learning before this decade (Billig, 2001). Previously, studies by Melchior (1999) for the Corporation for National and Community Service have been conducted.

Melchior (1999) studied 17 middle schools and high schools across the country that received Learn and Serve America grant funds. He found issues related to sustainability: only small groups of teachers were involved in implementing service-learning projects, and few of those teachers had participated in any formal professional development on the subject. In addition, there were several barriers to implementing service-learning as part of institutional change. Those barriers included lack of funding, a district focus on other areas of professional development, overriding concerns for meeting new content standards, lack of teacher planning time, logistical problems within school schedules, and a greater focus on community service rather than service-learning.

Essential to service-learning sustainability is the philosophical belief in the integration of service-learning into the regular school curriculum and the linking of service-learning to educational standards. District leaders must support program sequencing to sustain the progression of implementation of service-learning activities for students each year and provide appropriate professional development for such sequencing (Kramer, 2000). In his case study (2003) of a suburban high school in the northeastern United States, Pontbriand found that the excitement generated by the students who participated in service-learning projects in elementary schools resulted in both student and parent pressure for teachers to continue to implement service-learning in middle school and high school.

Billig and Klute (2002) concluded that sustainability of service-learning requires the attention of fundraising, policy development, the creation of support networks, opportunities for participant sharing and reflection, and advanced professional development opportunities. Pontbriand (2003) supported these findings, reporting that sustainability of service-learning requires "high system-level support" (p. 110) with a commitment from district leaders, curricular integration, and support and assistance for teachers. For service-learning to be supported at the district level, it also must be an integral part of the district's strategic plan (Ammon, Furco, Chi, & Middaugh, 2002; Billig & Klute, 2002; Kramer, 2000). That plan should clearly outline how service-learning functions in conjunction with the overall goals of the district.

Financial support is a critical factor in success. A key part of administrative leadership is providing funding in addition to available grant dollars to enable the continuation of the program after grants have been depleted (Ammon et al., 2002).

Service-learning is also more likely to be sustained when district leadership provides a key staff member or members whose responsibility it is to create and promote service-learning in the schools and in the community. The designated permanent staff member administers the service-learning program and assists in teacher training and recruitment, as well as locates and fosters community partnerships (Ammon et al., 2002; Billig & Klute, 2002). The service-learning coordinator holds the key position linked to sustainability and should be a professional with philosophical, personal, and financial support (Melchior, 1999). This partnership coordinator should have a continual budget line and a manageable number of responsibilities. Finding one person who is capable of providing leadership, securing funding, networking with key stakeholders in the community, and providing professional development and support to teachers and other school staff can be a difficult task (Ammon et al., 2002).

As part of the funding requirements, the administration must make a financial commitment to provide introductory and advanced professional development opportunities for teachers to implement quality service-learning experiences for their students (Ammon et al., 2002; Billig & Klute, 2002; Pontbriand, 2003). Ammon et al. conducted a study of 28 schools participating in the CalServe Initiative that received grants providing seed money to support new or expanding service-learning partnerships. In this study, the majority of the service-learning partnerships emphasized expanding the quantity of service-learning projects over improving their quality. Participants generally believed that when working toward sustainability, the emphasis was on getting more teachers and administrators involved in service-learning. The authors warn, however, that having numerous service-learning activities that are not of high quality could actually hamper sustainability efforts. These researchers suggest a balance of emphasis on both quantity and quality of service-learning activities, thereby allowing school districts to focus their energies and resources on clear and realistic implementation standards, leading to better sustainability of their service-learning partnerships over time.

Effective integration of quality service-learning into the curriculum requires training in service-learning for teachers new to the district and advanced training for teachers who are experienced in implementing service-learning projects (Billig & Klute, 2002; Kramer, 2000; Rada, n.d.). Kramer suggests that even though training teachers to embrace a new methodology takes time, the return on the investment can be unlimited if new projects and ideas with curricular connections continue to evolve. "In theory, once all of the elements of a service-learning system are established, they should continue to function with little effort" (pp. 20-21). When service-learning is self-regulating and maintains itself, functioning efficiently and growing throughout the district, it has been institutionalized (Kramer, 2000).

In addition to a strategic plan including a vision for the district, another key component in sustainability is the role of community partners as part of the district's vision (Ammon et al., 2002; Billig & Klute, 2002; Pontbriand, 2003; Rada, n.d.). According to school superintendent Rada (n.d.), district administrators should provide leadership for establishing and maintaining community partnerships by providing opportunities for collaboration between teachers and community members. Administrators should serve as role models, strengthening ties to the community and promoting shared ownership of the outcomes with staff throughout the school district and with the community that it serves (Ammon et al., 2002; Pontbriand, 2003).

Service-learning programs have the unique ability to link schools and their communities, increasing the likelihood of sustainability and institutionalization of service-learning (Pontbriand, 2003). For sustainability to be taken seriously as a district issue, district administrators must focus on securing and retaining key stakeholders who can move the district's service-learning initiatives forward (Ammon et al., 2002).

THREATS TO SUSTAINABILITY

Even when service-learning is an integral part of a district's strategic plan and vision for the future, and strong community partnerships are in place, there are still threats that could dampen the success of service-learning sustainability. These threats include the vulnerability of continued funding after initiating grants have expired and the difficulty of adopting schedules to allow for varied, flexible use of time (Pontbriand, 2003). In addition, the lack of consistent building leadership and administrative support, along with the infusion of many new staff members unfamiliar with service-learning, can threaten sustainability (Ammon et al., 2002). The perception that academic gains through service-learning can lack rigor if improperly coordinated is also a threat to continuation of the practice. Finally, the lack of continuity of personnel and programming can affect all levels of service-learning partnerships (Pontbriand, 2003). This lack of continuity can be caused by high turnover of various categories of stakeholders: partnership coordinators, administrators, teachers involved in implementing service-learning, program evaluators, community organization leaders, and others (Ammon et al., 2002).

TESTING THE SUSTAINABILITY FRAMEWORK

In a 2001 study considering sustainability of service-learning, Billig investigated the concept of sustainability by conducting case studies at several schools and school districts in New Hampshire that had received state grant funds for implementing service-learning initiatives. One section of the findings created a framework of key factors necessary for teachers to sustain service-learning projects. This study investigated the extent to which the framework presented in the study was useful in explaining sustainability in other sites.

The purpose of this chapter is to compare this new framework of sustainability created by Billig (2001) to the findings of Krebs (2006) who reported what central and northwest Ohio teachers said about their experiences implementing and sustaining service-learning projects.

Billig (2001) conducted case studies in eight schools and three districts in New Hampshire. These sites had received state grants to implement service-learning as part of their educational reform efforts. Researchers conducted site visits; observed service-learning activities; conducted focus groups with teachers, students, and community members as participants; and interviewed principals and service-learning coordinators. Data were collected for each year of the study from more than 100 participants at the 11 sites. Principals, teachers, and community members at several sites completed self-assessments of the implementation of and support for service-learning in their schools and districts. The independent scores were reconciled in group sessions and single ratings were agreed upon for each item.

Four years later, after the initial 3 years of state grant funding had expired, researchers investigated whether the service-learning was still being practiced at the sites. Those still participating in service-learning were determined as being *sustained*. Service-learning initiatives at two of the sites had either diminished in size and scope or had an unpredictable future. Data from the remaining nine case studies were reanalyzed, sorted into factors, and further refined, creating new categories, then reorganized again until the final categorization led to a new framework for service-learning sustainability.

As a result, Billig (2001) reported eight key factors of sustainability for service-learning initiatives: (a) *strong leadership;* (b) *cultural norms;* (c) *organizational expectations;* (d) *incentives;* (e) *visibility;* (f) *availability of funding resources;* (g) *the production of measurable impacts on student achievement or other valued outcomes such as character education, citizenship, or workplace skills;* and (h) *supportive policies on the national, state, or local levels for resources, professional development opportunities, and quality program design.* Each of these factors will be explained in greater detail when compared to teacher comments in each area.

The purpose of the Krebs (2006) phenomenological study was to describe the essence of the service-learning experience for K-12 teachers in central and northwest Ohio. In phenomenology, researchers study *lived experiences* and conduct studies with individuals to explore a particular concept or *phenomenon*. Lived experiences are events or experiences that have occurred in people's lives (Creswell, 1998; Moustakas, 1994; van Manen, 1990).

Phenomenology is particularly appropriate for the study of service-learning because it is a *human* science rather than a natural science. The researcher strives to structure meaning in the human, lived world, as opposed to the natural world of objects that do not have experiences. Phenomenology is a "ministering of thoughtfulness" (van Manen, 1990, p. 12) in the study of everyday practical occurrences, particularly in the lives of parents, teachers, psychologists, and school administrators. Service-learning pedagogy is a complex structure, involving various stages and phases, along with definite personal influences from both students and teachers. Using phenomenology to study service-learning is particularly appropriate because it is an attempt to

> construct a full interpretive description of some aspect of the lifeworld, and yet to remain aware that lived life is always more complex than any explication of meaning can reveal.... Phenomenological human science is interested in the human world as we find it in all its variegated aspects. (van Manen, 1990, p. 18)

By focusing on a phenomenon, describing it just as it seems, and then continuing to focus and look, the researcher incorporates the many varied dimensions of the phenomenon. According to Moustakas (1994),

> We look and describe, we look again and describe, until there is a sense of having fulfilled our intention, of having arrived at a breaking off point, of having a sense of completion or closure, of really knowing what is there before us. (pp. 73-74)

By recording the experiences of others, in essence, *borrowing* them, researchers gain experience and knowledge (van Manen, 1990).

METHODOLOGY

This study sought to explore the essence and meaning of the service-learning experience from the K-12 teacher's perspective, specifically focusing on the motivations to initiate service-learning. Phenomenology was the logical research method to employ. This researcher investigated teacher thinking and practice by conducting lengthy, in-depth interviews with six K-12 teachers in central and northwest Ohio who had implemented service-learning in their classrooms within 24 months prior to the study. These teachers taught in a combination of urban, rural, and suburban districts, spanning Grades 3-11.

The researcher interviewed each participant, transcribed each interview, and followed the Stevick-Colaizzi-Keen Method of Analysis of Phenomenological Data for data analysis. This analysis involves considering each individual statement made by each of the participants, listing each non-repetitive statement, clustering those statements into themes, and synthesizing the themes into descriptions of the textures of the experience (Moustakas, 1994). Through this method, three major themes emerged to describe the essence of implementing and sustaining service-learning from the K-12 teacher's perspective: Connections, Resonation in the Heart of the Teacher, and The Right Fit with a Teacher's Philosophy and Teaching Style.

- *Connections* explains the importance of creating, maintaining, extending, and nurturing links between teachers and their students, between teachers and other teachers, between teachers and parents, among different areas of the curriculum, and between teachers and members of the community-at-large.
- *Resonation in the Heart of the Teacher* involves a deep, personal belief about the importance of making a positive difference in the world, and teaching this belief to students.
- *The Right Fit with Teaching Philosophy and Teaching Style* explains the importance of creating a well-balanced, harmonious relationship between service-learning and a teacher's philosophy about teaching being centered on the students themselves, not just the content, and a teacher's experiential teaching style.

These three themes have clear connections to the sustainability framework presented by Billig (2001). In order to investigate these key factors of sustainability, the researcher compared the results of this phenomenological study on the essence of the service-learning experience from the K-12 teacher's perspective to the eight factors of sustainability identified by Billig. The teachers in Krebs' study (2006) were not interviewed according to these eight factors specifically, but their comments on support and sustainability were gleaned from responses to other interview questions on implementation and sustainability of service-learning.

Interviews

Krebs (2006) interviewed six teachers in sessions lasting from 90-120 minutes. In addition, as appropriate in phenomenological research, the researcher also participated as an interviewee, bringing the total number of participants to seven; however, the researcher's comments are not included in data analyses. The following is information about each of the other teachers involved as participants and brief descriptions of their service-learning projects. All names are pseudonyms but first names are being used to reflect the nature of the methodology.

Teacher 1: Jill is a middle school teacher of Family and Consumer Sciences and has taught for 30 years in a suburban school district in central Ohio. Her students plan, implement, and reflect on service-learning projects of their own individual design, implemented to meet core curriculum standards.

Teacher 2: Nancy is a fifth grade teacher in a suburban district in central Ohio and has taught for 25 years. Her fifth graders participate in a Grandpals Project where they visit their adopted Grandpals at a local retirement center once a month, participating in various projects with their Grandpals on each visit. These projects range from in-depth interviews, to reading, to music and art projects—all meeting core curriculum standards.

Teacher 3: Andy has taught for 4 years and currently teaches sixth grade in an intermediate school in a suburban district in central Ohio, and has former experience in an inner city middle school in northwest Ohio. Andy teaches social studies, math, and literacy and has facilitated several service-learning projects with his students at both schools. His most recent project was a student-led assembly held for the public to raise funds for schools in South Africa, featuring songs, dances, and readings of the words of Nelson Mandela. He also organized a Civil War Day for the community surrounding his school, where the students sang, danced, and worked with re-enactors to recreate the setting of the time.

Teacher 4: Bonnie teaches third and fourth graders in a suburban school district in central Ohio, with 15 years of teaching experience. Her major projects include content-centered, student-created fundraising projects for service organizations of the students' choosing.

Teacher 5: Kim is an American history teacher in a suburban middle school in central Ohio and has taught for 30 years. Her largest continuous project is feeding homeless men in the downtown area through a partnership with a homeless shelter.

Teacher 6: Erin has taught social studies for 5 years in a rural high school in northwest Ohio. Her students completed a project where they taught concepts of the U.S. Constitution and Bill of Rights to students in the special needs class down the hallway.

RESULTS

In her service-learning sustainability framework, Billig (2001) identified eight key factors that are important for sustaining service-learning in schools and districts. In the sections that follow, each of Billig's key factors is stated, followed by relevant teacher comments and analyses regarding each of these factors.

Strong Leadership

> Sustained sites had strong leadership that stimulated the development of a shared vision, encouraged action and allegiance to the purpose of the project, engendered a sense of community within the project, and provided continuity and growth through development and implementation of systematic succession plans. (Billig, 2001, p. 263)

Strong leadership was indeed the most important factor of sustainability in the Krebs (2006) study. The teachers interviewed as a part of this study particularly focused on the personal contact and interest of administrators, indicating the importance of strong leadership at all levels. They spoke about the positive influence of district leaders, building-level principals, teachers as leaders and also community partner leaders in the sustainability of their service-learning projects.

District Level Leadership

For students to experience the benefits of service-learning at every grade level, K-12, the teachers strongly concurred that district leaders should promote a vision of a continuous, developmentally appropriate K-12 service-learning program. As Nancy described,

> It [service-learning activities in elementary school] builds a foundation, and gives them the scaffolding for experiences later.

Bonnie also was a true proponent of K-12 service-learning programs as a district focus:

> It is a valuable experience. I can't imagine why it wouldn't become a part of school at every level. Every level. And the older you get the more you can do and the more elaborate, the more meaningful, the more effective it can be.

Kim cited strong leadership from the administration as her number one level of support for incorporating service-learning into her classroom. The superintendent spent time with her students at the Open Shelter, even participating in sorting hundreds of shoes in the donation room. The director of the district's Career Education Department was a strong supporter, along with the other teachers in Kim's building:

> The number one support I had was the administration. In this building, I can say the support was tremendous. The higher administration in the district, the superintendent ... found several times out of his busy schedule to join us at the Open Shelter and worked with us.... I will never forget that man in his nice pants and tie ... in the floor with the kids when they were matching shoes and sizes.

Building Level Leadership

Nancy identified her principal's support as the most critical element in implementing and sustaining her Grandpals Project.

> I don't think that I would have been able to do this program without his support and his rubber stamp.

Her principal occasionally accompanied the students to the retirement center to conduct activities with their Grandpals and talked individually with the students about their experiences.

Teacher Leadership

Teachers also gave important examples of strong teacher leadership at the building level. During her U.S. Constitution project, Erin found support and partnership from the special needs teacher with whom she planned and implemented her project. Neither her principal nor any other school district administrators were involved with or even aware of the project. Assuming responsibility as a teacher leader herself, she put photographs of the students working together in the school district newsletter along with an article explaining the project. Through this, she hoped to create greater awareness of the project and of service-learning in general.

As a teacher leader herself, Kim was able to gain the support of almost all other teachers in her building. Because of her leadership, all the eighth grade teams got involved in the homeless shelter project. As other teachers began to plan their service projects, they used Kim as a resource, asking questions about funding, transportation, parent involvement, and other planning and implementation details.

Community Leadership

Along with district, building, and teacher leadership, strong leadership is also important at the community sites. Kim's biggest roadblock came during the planning stages of the project in searching for a community partner. She found it very difficult to find a community agency that was willing to work with eighth grade students. It was the leadership of the head of the community organization, the director of the homeless shelter, who took on both the risk and the responsibility by giving official permission for the students to participate, even though they were under the age of 16. Kim had called down a long list of organizations and received negative responses. The homeless shelter was the last name on the list.

> They were afraid to work with young children.... The only person that came through was [the director of the homeless shelter] and the reason why is that he was a graduate of [this district's high school] and he'd listen to my idea of what I wanted to do, why I wanted to do it.

The teachers in this study (Krebs, 2006) unanimously cited administrative support as a significant factor in their motivation and success in implementing and sustaining service-learning projects in their classrooms. Administrators help sustain service-learning by providing positive feedback through sponsoring professional development opportunities, or by lending philosophical support for experiential learning, providing flexibility in schedules, and giving funding for projects and the materials necessary to support those projects.

By implementing a K-12 program, the administration helps create a district culture with service-learning at its core. Students come to expect to play a valuable role in making a difference in their communities every year. District leaders help community partners see the benefits of service-learning not only for the students, but also for the community. Having personal connections with one or more administrators greatly benefits teachers who are implementing service-learning, and those relationships encourage the teachers to sustain their projects.

Cultural Norms and Organizational Expectations

> Sustained sites had strong norms and organizational expectations that simultaneously stressed human interdependence and autonomy, two-way communication systems, appropriate human and fiscal management, feedback loops for identifying and understanding needs and ways to improve continuously, enduring partnerships that featured mutual high regard and reciprocity, mechanisms for problem solving, and strategies for professional growth. (Billig, 2001, p. 264)

Teachers in Krebs's (2006) study agreed that when service-learning is part of the cultural norms and expectations of a school and district, there is a greater opportunity for sustainability of such projects. There are many facets to the concept of school culture. Teachers cited specific cultural norms and expectations that were important for sustainability, specifically noting time for professional development opportunities, flexible scheduling and usage of time, and communication and transportation. When these issues were not resolved, they most often led to roadblocks to sustainability. Once again, the teachers cited the importance of strong leadership to assist in creating these cultural norms and organizational expectations to establish service-learning as part of the district culture.

Jill summarized the importance of strong leadership in all aspects of cultural norms of a district in its support of teachers implementing and sustaining service-learning projects:

> We [teachers who were implementing service-learning] didn't have to fight the battles and become exhausted by fighting the battles to be able to take kids places liability-wise; they [district and building administrators] helped us with that, utilized class time to tie it in, helped find places to go and things to do. There were people at the Board Office who would do that for us. To do the big grant writing, to get us involved in the consortium, to provide course work, to develop courses for us to help us work on our masters' programs. Get dollars to help us move ahead in the pay scheme of things in the district. I don't think I had to fight a single battle with an administrator and very few with classroom teachers because they knew that it was a big focus in our district. I can't tell you. That was huge.

Providing opportunities for professional development works to create the expectation that service-learning is an important part of district cultural norms and expectations.

Providing time and flexible scheduling is an important cultural norm and expectation that helps sustain service projects. Teachers need flexibility in the school day schedule to incorporate service-learning projects. Some students at the high school and middle school levels may need to miss other classes in order to have time for trips to community sites. At the elementary level, teachers needed support for changing schedules with art, music, and physical education teachers.

When service-learning is part of the culture, school and district leaders not only show their support philosophically, but also logistically. It is the support of basic elements such as time, flexibility, communication and transportation that can help teachers sustain their projects. District and building leaders are key players in creating a culture of service-learning. When this culture exists, teachers can avoid roadblocks by having cultural norms and organizational expectations in place to assist in sustaining service-learning projects.

Incentives

> Sustained sites had incentives to draw people to service-learning and encourage them to continue practice, generally through a combination of the positive interdependence and peer influence, creation of social potency ("I can make a difference"), self-efficacy and organizational efficacy, the ability to see the results, and feelings of satisfaction with the efforts. (Billig, 2001, pp. 264-265)

Incentives, both internal and external, were of extreme importance to the teachers in the Krebs (2006) study in order for them to sustain their service-learning projects. When administrators reward teacher behavior with positive personal comments, increased funding, and/or paid visits to conferences, teachers are even more motivated to continue their projects.

Nancy expressed appreciation for the positive comments she receives from administrators in the district and explained that those comments helped her to sustain her Grandpals project.

> They seemed to sense and recognize that this was the whole [service-learning program] deal; this was what it should look like, and they kept telling me that—rewarding me with perks and trips and you know, so that was great.... People were saying, "You're doing a great thing, here's some money. Keep doing it."

Nancy noted,

> I think, if you just taught your normal day and your normal subjects and did your normal thing, you wouldn't be giving these kids the opportunity to really shine in ways that some of them can't shine. When you go over there and you see the little "trouble-maker"—so to speak—who is playing cards and carrying on a conversation with a man who has Alzheimer's, or having a chess game with one of the residents, and it just touches your heart. It touches the resident's heart. It is like a magic that happens between them and you think, "How could I not do this?"

These teachers also recognized the importance of district and building leaders connecting with the students themselves as meaningful incentives for sustainability. The physical presence of an administrator during a project served as a tremendous incentive for both teachers and students. Teachers truly believed they had district support when administrators came to their classes and their service sites. In addition, this was powerful role modeling for students.

It was also important for administrators to listen to the students as they reflected on their experiences. A district administrator took time to come out and interview Nancy's students, and Nancy recalls,

> It was great because he sits there and takes notes, you know, and he always wears a tie and asks them for their opinion. And here's an adult that they assume is an important person because of his demeanor and he is telling them that they just do wonderful stuff and it is really neat because that just reinforces that they are doing something special. And they are.... So having an audience to share this with validates what they are doing.

Teachers, too, create their own personal incentives through their own sense of efficacy and personal beliefs that they are making a difference. Seeing this belief in action through their students can reignite their passion for teaching.

Visibility

> Sustained sites were characterized by visibility so that individuals could easily learn about the service-learning project, understand its purpose and benefits, and support activities. (Billig, 2001, p. 265)

The teachers interviewed (Krebs, 2006) agreed that visibility in the community is another key component to sustainability. District leaders forged the way for teachers to make community connections by speaking with community members about the concept of service-learning and opening the doors for teachers to implement projects. By serving as liaisons, district leaders increased visibility for service-learning by communicating to businesses and local agencies the capabilities of students.

Kim discussed the difficulty of the cold-call from the teacher to a community agency:

> After all, you are two strangers who are coming together with an idea. You are ... about to invade their organization, their world, depending on what grade level of kids you are going with. People out in the business world are not accustomed to children. They are very, very hesitant about giving kids chances, and you've got to give kids chances. The business world is very difficult. They just don't look at things in a humanistic way. It's black and white. You know, we are teachers; we look at it globally.

Teachers sometimes must take the lead when it comes to creating media visibility. In terms of media visibility for Andy, the message being sent out from his central administration office clearly indicated the need for visibility of the schools through the media so the community could recognize positive things going on in the district. He reported,

> This [service-learning] is it. This is what you need to do. Get them [the students] out in the community. Do some of these projects not behind closed doors but maybe out where people can see what they are doing.

Availability of Financial Resources

> Sustained sites had sufficient funds, generally from multiple sources. (Billig, 2001, p. 265).

Teachers interviewed (Krebs, 2006) responded strongly regarding the need for financial resources, especially those funds available to provide transportation and supporting materials. They also used creative ways to obtain funding so their projects could be sustained. They worked with parent organizations, wrote grants, and worked with district administrators to obtain funding from state and national career education and service-learning resources.

Nancy identified funding as a necessary, critical, and even *paramount* form of support. For her Grandpals project, transportation was required for the students to visit their Grandpals each month, so funding for buses was crucial. She went to great lengths to continue the funding for this program, including writing grants, campaigning for exceptions to the "one field trip per classroom per year" rule, and obtaining a $650 donation from the retirement center itself for transportation. This money was donated directly to her district's board of education and then earmarked specifically for her service-learning transportation costs. This complex budgetary arrangement necessitated a great deal of support from the principal, the treasurer, and administrators at the retirement center, to name a few.

> Without hesitation, Jill named the lack of transportation funding as a major roadblock: "That has always been my one remaining struggle and I still think that every school should have a van with a licensed driver."

However Jill, with encouragement from her building principal, even turned this hardship into a positive by asking other teachers to help drive students to service sites after school. Through their involvement by transporting students, the teachers have begun to understand what she is trying to accomplish in her class; they see the important service the students are providing, so "in a round-about way, it was a good thing," as it helped to solve a financial roadblock and increased support from other teachers at the same time.

Bonnie indicated funding was also the most critical area of support to sustain her project. She believed that her projects could still have been completed without funding, but there would have been questions about paying for buses and field trips that make the service-learning experience more meaningful. She received Learn-and-Serve federal grant funds from the Corporation for National and Community Service to implement her projects. Bonnie also received monetary support from the Career Education Department in her district. She also mentioned the importance of financial support from individual families interested in being involved with the projects.

Kim received the funding for her homeless project from Career Education funds from the district. She was able to purchase cooking utensils for meal preparation and bus passes for students to take city buses downtown to the homeless shelter. School parent-teacher organization funds and other grants were available to support her project.

Andy received financial support through grant-writing and from the school's parent organization, but when funds were not readily available, Andy found ways to make the project work despite the lack of funding, which goes against one of the arguments in the framework. For example, for the Civil War Celebration, his students wrote letters to different agencies and school business partners requesting donated items. Andy recognized his district's current financial constraints:

> I know things are so tight around here. I don't want to go out and say this or that. It just seems like, "Don't talk about money. Just try to make it happen without."

And he did.

To fund various projects, district administrators provided monies for bus tickets downtown, transportation, conference attendance costs, professional development time, and materials. Most teachers said they could find ways to complete projects if funding was cut, but teachers definitely appreciated the financial support they received. Bonnie named money as the "bottom line with everything."

Producing Measurable Impacts

> Service-learning will be sustained only if it produces measurable impacts on student achievement or if it is attached to other valued outcomes such as building character, citizenship, or workplace skills. (Billig, 2001, p. 266)

The teachers in the Krebs (2006) study realized the importance of connecting content standards to service, but did not strongly indicate the importance of measurable impacts as an important factor for sustainability. Teachers did understand that a critical element in sustainability is the necessity of relating their service-learning activities to the standards, but were not as concerned with providing quantitative data to support their work in service-learning. According to Andy,

> Relating to the curriculum ... if you want to get permission to do things that is always the first thing they are asking, "Is it related to the standards?" Integrating with as many subjects as possible, you get that thematic aspect, making sure it has a kind of a sense of responsibility, civic responsibility, where the kids are doing something for the community.

Andy found that it was easier to get administrative support when he clearly showed connections to the curriculum and content standards. He expressed regret, however, because he had not compiled more academic data in support of service-learning to show administrators the measurable impacts service-learning has had on his students' achievement of those curricular standards.

Bonnie indicated that standardized testing had become somewhat of a roadblock to adopting service-learning as a teaching practice because of the level of accountability necessary, especially for young teachers. Bonnie sees these teachers worrying about getting all the information and curriculum taught within the school year, yet because of her positive service-learning experiences over time, she is quite comfortable meeting the standards through her service-learning projects.

> For me that's not an issue, but for a new teacher, I could understand where there might be a reluctance to bite off something. That might seem overwhelming or too time-consuming.

The teachers in this study (Krebs, 2006) recognized the integral role curricular concepts play in service-learning, but did not seem as concerned with producing measurable impacts. Part of the reason for this lack of concern for measurable impacts could be the collective long-term successes of their projects, strong leadership, and cultural norms created by their projects. Thus they may not be driven by measurable impacts as a key element in their sustainability. In addition, these teachers have implemented and sustained their service-learning projects over time. They have seen the positive impact participation in service-learning has had on their students. Therefore, they may not be as concerned with measuring those impacts as district or building leaders may be.

Requiring Supportive Policies

> It [sustaining service-learning] will require supportive policies on the national, state, or local levels to ensure that appropriate resources are allocated, professional development can be acquired, and quality program design are continued. (Billig, 2001, p. 266)

The teachers interviewed (Krebs, 2006) indicated the importance of local policies over those policies at the state or national levels. They especially indicated the importance of local policies that provided resources that supported participation in professional development. For example, administrators invited Nancy and her students to numerous conferences and in-services to share their Grandpals experiences.

Yet once again, the importance of strong leadership emerges, especially in the creation of local policies and priorities set by district leaders to provide the opportunities for such professional development to sustain teachers in their service-learning efforts. These local policies also help create cultural norms and organizational expectations that lead to even greater sustainability of service-learning in a district.

IMPLICATIONS FOR SUSTAINABILITY— THE NEED FOR STRONG LEADERSHIP

As indicated in the above comparison, the comments of teachers participating in the Krebs study (2006) supported the sustainability framework identified by Billig (2001). The importance of strong leadership, a key component of the Billig framework, is inherent in all the implications for administrators and their roles in the sustainability of service-learning and may be the key indicator associated with each factor.

When comparing the Billig (2001) sustainability framework to the comments from teachers made in the Krebs (2006) study, many implications surface.

Suggestions for Cultural Norms and Organizational Expectations

It is evident through this comparison that strong leaders can provide valuable assistance in establishing norms and cultural expectations in a district. To that end, the teachers in this study (Krebs, 2006) offered suggestions for leaders in this area involving time, collaboration opportunities, mentoring of new teachers in service-learning, providing teachers with information from national studies, and providing a personal touch in recruiting teachers to learn more about service-learning and giving them personal support.

These teachers suggested that in order to include service-learning as a cultural norm, it is beneficial for leaders to organize purposeful collaboration opportunities so that teachers implementing service-learning can effectively coordinate with, mentor, and motivate other teachers to participate. Such an approach uses the expertise of teachers in the district to teach others formally through in-services and conferences, and informally through teaming, by putting service-learning teacher leaders in informal leadership positions to influence other teachers. Organizing round-table dialogues among teachers in a district or between two or more districts provides teachers with valuable opportunities to learn from each other to create cultural norms and organizational expectations that involve service-learning.

Administrators can also increase sustainability by providing time as a cultural norm for a district. Teachers need time. They also need to be compensated for the time they work outside their regular school day. Administrators can provide time for teachers to do the planning required for service-learning implementation. This time can be in the form of professional development days during the school year, scheduling team teachers with common planning time throughout the school year, and providing cross-grade level and cross-district opportunities for teachers to communicate.

As an organizational expectation, district leaders should formally communicate district administrator responsibilities to all new teacher hires in the district. New teachers will especially benefit from knowing whom to contact at the district office for support for service-learning. When one district administrator's responsibilities are shifted to another administrator, that change should be clearly and formally communicated to all teachers.

Suggestions for Incentives

In terms of incentives, personal recognition and support for teachers who are implementing service-learning are extremely important. Public recognition of great effort and accomplishment not only encourages those teachers and students who are being recognized to continue to sustain their projects, but also motivates others to get involved. Administrators need to recognize teachers for their extra work, extra effort, and extra time used to provide service-learning opportunities for their students. They also need to publicly recognize outstanding community partners for their contributions. Students, too, should be recognized for their participation in service-learning. Through student and community recognition, districts are afforded another opportunity to get more parents involved and connected with schools. Year-end demonstrations/celebrations are excellent opportunities to recognize accomplishments and make a powerful statement regarding the meaning of service-learning for teachers, students, parents, and community. A simple hand-written note of appreciation for a job-well-done is a powerful tool for the sustainability cause.

To increase teacher participation in service-learning, leaders can clearly, eagerly, and personally promote professional development opportunities such as workshops and graduate courses on service-learning being offered in and around the district. When administrators personally invite and recruit teachers to attend conferences and other professional development workshops, teachers are more likely to be motivated to participate. District leaders can provide experiential, hands-on professional development for teachers. Once teachers have personally experienced service-learning for themselves, they are much more likely to implement it. The summer provides an excellent opportunity for in-depth, experiential professional development opportunities for teachers. Administrators can assist in organizing these events, especially by providing opportunities for university graduate credit for participants. As more teachers are motivated to participate, service-learning plays a greater role as part of the district culture and then becomes an organizational expectation.

Suggestions for Visibility

Included in teacher suggestions regarding visibility and the media is the importance of creating a district-generated service-learning agency contact bank to list service agencies and contact persons to be utilized by elementary, middle, and high school students and teachers. District administrators can lead the way in contacting various agencies, educating them about the importance of service-learning both for academic and civic growth in students, and then providing this contact information to teachers. In this way, the administrators have already cleared the way for teachers to contact these organizations to form partnerships.

In addition, the creation of a district service council would help sustain service-learning initiatives by increasing visibility, and would also assist in establishing and maintaining connections between the school district and the community. Inviting parents to serve on this council is important because they have a great deal of influence and significant connections in the community. Most often parents *are* the influence and connections to the community. Including students on such a council would bring student voice and opinion to district-level service-learning discussions. In this role, students could practice the leadership, communication, and problem-solving skills they are learning in their service-learning programs.

Administrators can also increase visibility of service-learning initiatives by publicizing service-learning events and promoting public relations opportunities. A district leader can serve as a liaison between the teachers and the media by alerting the media to cover special service-learning events.

Suggestions for Funding

It is critical and imperative in order to sustain service-learning initiatives that district leaders must provide consistent and sustained funding for service-learning projects once seed money grants have expired. This funding can take on a variety of forms, from creating specific budget line-items to securing gifts-in-kind from the community. It is sometimes necessary for administrators to be creative in funding lines in district budgets. They can work with teachers to think creatively about how to fund projects and find local business partners who can help finance projects in return for public relations opportunities. Community service clubs are excellent partners for service and strong relationships can develop when students share what they have learned with these adult organizations.

Of utmost importance for sustainability would be forging partnerships with businesses that can provide or fund transportation for service-learning activities. Funding and helping arrange for student transportation is one of the most difficult and frustrating roadblocks for teachers to overcome when working to implement service-learning in their classrooms.

Administrators can also connect with university faculty to provide travel and continuing education opportunities for teachers while they learn about service-learning techniques and strategies. Funding opportunities may also arise from these partnerships between K-12 and higher education.

Suggestions for Measurable Impacts

Administrative support for measuring academic achievement resulting from service-learning experiences is a key component of future success and sustainability of service-learning. Administrators can help teachers identify and implement research methods to determine just what academic benefits students are receiving from participation in service-learning. Designing such assessments is time-consuming, and for accuracy and reliability, requires expertise in the areas of research and assessment.

Administrators could collaborate with university faculty to facilitate this type of measurement. These assessments would also serve the district well in public relations efforts to express student academic achievement to the community, while at the same time providing documented evidence of the benefits of service-learning to assist teachers in sustaining their projects. In addition, this data would be compelling for future service-learning grant applications.

Administrators can also take the lead in helping to identify possible curricular connections between standards and service-learning and making suggestions to teachers. Linking administrators who oversee service-learning to those who coordinate the district's curricular programs would set a tone for the district, indicating that definite academic goals can be met through service-learning. Administrators and teachers can work together to find and communicate those academic connections, and to provide opportunities for teachers to come together to create the links between service and curriculum.

Suggestions for Supportive Policies

The teachers in this study agreed that supportive policies certainly make sustaining service-learning projects easier, especially at the local level. Again, the teachers point to the importance of strong leadership to inform policymakers of the importance of service-learning and to gain their support to help sustain their projects.

In addition, many states' policies require formal mentor-mentee relationships for first-year teachers. When administrators recruit and assign mentors, they can use this policy to expand the use of service-learning by consciously recruiting teachers who have implemented service-learning, so those mentor teachers can positively influence younger teachers and can model the infusion of service-learning in the classroom for novice teachers.

In addition to policies at all levels, administrators need to stay abreast of legislative service-learning initiatives and funding resources at the state and national levels. Administrators need to communicate with senators and representatives at the state and national levels regarding the need for service-learning funding. It is also important to remind teachers of the power of their voices. Facilitating letter-writing campaigns that could be accessible through the Internet is one easy way to help teachers speak up in state and national government regarding favorable service-learning policies.

Administrators can also take the lead in being attentive to cutting-edge service-learning reports and exemplary programs that are promoted through national and state service-learning organizations such as Learn and Serve America. When they learn about helpful, important information, it should be an organizational expectation for that information to be passed along to their teachers and to influence policy-making at all levels.

CONCLUSIONS

Service-learning is a classroom-based, student-centered activity, but in order for teachers to be successful in this endeavor, district leaders must take responsibility for various facets of the program. From the K-12 teacher's perspective, sustainability of service-learning requires strong leadership, especially at the district and building levels. This leadership is pervasive in all the key factors of sustainability identified in the Billig (2001) framework. This comparison seems to indicate that several of these key factors of sustainability are particularly important from the K-12 teacher's perspective: strong leadership; cultural norms; and organizational expectations, incentives, and financial resources.

It is important for district leaders to maintain personal connections with teachers and the service-learning activities they are implementing in their classrooms, all the while keeping a close eye on district cultural processes, funding, and state and national policies. All the components of the Billig (2001) framework are important pieces to the sustainability puzzle, from cultural norms to national policies. From a teacher's perspective, strong leadership seems to be the glue to hold that service-learning sustainability puzzle together. One of the limitations of comparing the Krebs (2006) study to the Billig framework is that Krebs did not use the Billig framework to formulate specific questions regarding sustainability. Beneficial to the sustainability literature would be a mixed-methods study on sustainability designed with the elements of the Billig study in mind. Certainly a larger pool of participants would further clarify important issues of service-learning sustainability from the K-12 teacher's perspective. Further research is also necessary to determine what strategies administrators and teachers can implement within these key areas to continue to sustain service-learning and to further examine the role of teacher leadership as a key to sustainability.

REFERENCES

Ammon, M. S., Furco, A., Chi, B., & Middaugh, E. (2002). *Service-learning in California: A profile of the CalServe service-learning partnerships (1997-2000)*. Berkley,

CA: Service-Learning Research & Development Center. Retrieved April 27, 2005, from http://servicelearning.org/resources/hot_topics/sustain/index

Billig, S. H. (2001). Adoption, implementation, and sustainability of K-12 service-learning. In A. Furco & S. H. Billig (Eds.), *Service-learning: The essence of pedagogy*. Greenwich, CT: Information Age.

Billig, S. H., & Klute, M. M. (2002). *W. K. Kellogg Foundation retrospective of K-12 service projects, 1990-2000*. Denver, CO: RMC Research Corporation.

Creswell, J. W. (1998). *Qualitative inquiry and research design: Choosing among five traditions*. Thousand Oaks, CA: SAGE.

Kramer, M. (2000). *Make it last forever: The institutionalization of service-learning in America*. Washington, DC: Corporation for National Service.

Krebs, M. M. (2006). *Service-learning: Motivations for K-12 teachers*. Unpublished doctoral dissertation, Bowling Green State University. (ERIC Document Reproduction Service No. ED 498642)

Melchior, A. (1999). *Summary report: National evaluation of learn and serve America*. Lithium, MA: Brandeis University.

Moustakas, C. (1994). *Phenomenological research methods*. Thousand Oaks, CA: SAGE.

Pontbriand, B. J. (2003). The sustaining factors of service-learning at a national leader school: A case study. In S. H. Billing & J. Eyler (Eds.), *Deconstructing service-learning: Research exploring context, participation, and impacts*. Greenwich, CT: Information Age.

Rada, R. (n.d.). Tying service-learning to school reform. *Talk it up: Advocating for service- learning*, 7. Retrieved June 5, 2005, from http://www.service-learningpartnerships.org/site/DocServer/TalkItUp07.pdf?docID=173

van Manen, M. (1990). *Researching lived experience: Human science for an action sensitive pedagogy*. Albany: University of New York Press.

PART III

SUSTAINING FACULTY ENGAGEMENT IN SERVICE-LEARNING AND COMMUNITY ENGAGEMENT

CHAPTER 5

SERVICE-LEARNING RESEARCH AS A FEEDBACK LOOP FOR FACULTY DEVELOPMENT

**Shelley Henderson, Megan Fair,
Paul Sather, and Barbara Dewey**

The University of Nebraska at Omaha service-learning research on student outcomes has had a serendipitous impact on both the classroom implementation of service-learning and interaction with community partners. The institutional response included reinforcement of the benefits of applied learning and community engagement throughout the campus, furthering faculty development, creating service-learning objectives that apply across disciplines, and increasing dialogue with community partners. The analysis provided here indicates that an institution's response to service-learning research findings can create a campus culture that encourages and supports service-learning faculty in their quest to improve student experiences. Implications on staff development for the university's P-16 initiative are also discussed.

Scholarship for Sustaining Service-Learning and Civic Engagement
pp. 113–137
Copyright © 2008 by Information Age Publishing
All rights of reproduction in any form reserved.

INTRODUCTION

Past research shows that service-learning provides students with practical experiences that benefit learning and strengthen moral and civic values (Zlotkowski, 1996). Furthermore, service-learning increases students' devotion to school, prepares them to continue to contribute to their communities, and enhances social and emotional development (Strage, 2004). However, there is still a need for additional service-learning research. For example, Stanton (2000) calls for "a more empirically-based approach to practice and a more practical approach to research." Stanton suggests that this research direction will enable service-learning faculty to document outcomes and highlight the most effective methods for achieving those outcomes. This, in turn, can increase the capacity and motivation of faculty in implementing commendable service-learning projects and courses.

REVIEW OF LITERATURE

Service-Learning Student Research

When investigators weigh the benefits of service-learning, they also measure the success of faculty, community partners, and institutions as a whole (Chadwick & Pawlowski, 2007). In addition, collecting service-learning data from students allows institutions to reduce problems that may arise and make decisions about service-learning practices utilizing statistical evidence. Assessment is an important contribution to the service-learning process because it provides feedback to allow for change at the institutional level that will strengthen and develop programs (Chadwick & Pawlowski, 2007). For example, when evidence shows that service-learning works in a teacher education college it can lead to conclusions that service-learning could be just as effective in other programs across the university. Service-learning can be represented in all disciplines, not only those that represent social sciences or education. Additionally, Chadwick and Pawlowski found that when faculty development through service-learning was implemented on one Midwestern campus, faculty members rated these activities positively (e.g., workshops to define service-learning concepts, special topics pertaining to justice, diversity, syllabi structure, having student liaisons, etc.), and this led to more service-learning courses. Administrators began to pay more attention to service-learning activities, and through pre- and postsurveys, faculty members were able to learn the strengths and weaknesses of their service-learning courses and adjust them accordingly. Overall, developing and improving service-learning through evidence-based feedback allows students' education to improve while increasing faculty interest, skills and institutional success.

Service-Learning Faculty Development Research

Service-learning expands through the effort of faculty and the support of administrations. Zlotkowski (1998) stated that successful service-learning requires a combination of pedagogical strategies, development of specific values, creation of a supportive academic culture, and direct work with community partners. To this focus on effective practice, Bacon and Sather (2001) attributed faculty endorsement of service-learning:

> Faculty who develop service-learning projects often become immediate advocates, noting that students in these courses become deeply involved in their work, actively curious about the relationship between course content and its "real-world" application, sensitive to social problems and community issues and committed to making a difference. (p. 1)

The faculty's role is to help students achieve academic success as well as further their own professional development. When university faculty members consider the demonstrated outcomes of this pedagogy, service-learning will become more successful, and professional expertise will increase (Zlotkowski, 1998). Service-learning provides a feedback loop for faculty development and both processes benefit from the exchange.

Faculty members play a key role in keeping service-learning alive. They are the critical human resource able to implement these activities and demonstrate to administrators that the practice produces effective learning and civic outcomes (Zlotkowski, 1996). The purpose of faculty development is to increase teaching strengths and skills in order to improve student learning (Bligh, 2005). Successful faculty development practices include knowing students' learning needs, being sensitive to active listening techniques, and using teaching methods that encourage collaboration. These principles align well with the pedagogy because service-learning also requires an understanding of needs, effective reflection techniques, and a strong collaboration among students, teachers, and community partners.

Faculty members are a key factor in the development and sustentation of service-learning; therefore, it is essential to support their efforts in creating effective service-learning courses. Furco (2002) found that faculty involvement is the most important drive in the advancement of service-learning. When faculty members are involved in service-learning, they are providing the highest quality circumstances for students to learn the content of the class and expand a sense of responsibility to serve their communities (Pickeral, 1996). In addition, faculty development is derived from professional interactions that encourage discussion and examination of service-learning, support, and development of plans for action (Pickeral, 1996). Through individual interactions with mentors, faculty can learn the strengths and areas for improvement of their service-learning courses. Surveying service-learning courses and providing evidence-based feedback is one method of faculty support. It is crucial to assess the needs of faculty through surveys, focus groups, and interviews to demonstrate the beneficial aspects of service-learning courses (Scepansky, 2004). University faculty plays an essential role in service-learning through research and teaching.

In order to be spread across the university, service-learning must be supported by faculty and administrators. When faculty and institutions combine efforts, the work improves the development of service-learning on a campus (Furco, 2002). Kahne, Westheimer, and Rogers (2000) suggested the need to look at the relationship between the civic goals of higher education institutions and the design, implementation, and impact of curriculum intended to further this mission. Effective faculty development not only improves teaching, but also student learning and institutional performance; the success of the faculty reflects upon the success of the entire university (Bligh, 2005). Furco (2001) explained that in order to establish support for service-learning at research universities, faculty must understand how service-learning will benefit their research goals and connect to their current interests. Faculty involvement in service-learning is essential to the expansion of these classes across colleges and universities.

Community Partner Inclusion Research

The service-learning experience is not only beneficial to students and universities; community partners also reap benefits. However, it is important that community agencies be involved in all of the service-learning processes, not just playing the role of a variable in research. Cruz and Giles (2000) described the need for more research studies to examine the partnership between universities and communities. Specifically, service-learning researchers should view community agencies as partners and take their input into consideration. An action research approach can increase attention to the needs of the community, defining goals using the community's voice, and dedication to changing the injustices within the community (Petras & Porpora, 1993). When community agencies have a voice in the planning and implementation of the service-learning project, they perceive benefits from the experience (Miron & Moely, 2006). Community partners need to play a key role when discussing and defining research plans as well as assisting faculty in the teaching process (Sather, Carlson, & Weitz, 2007). Community partners benefit from service-learning when they are involved in the teaching and research process as partners and not subjects, and they have a voice in the development of the projects.

The purpose of this research study was to develop a systematic evaluation of service-learning to fill the gaps from previous research and develop a "culture of evidence" (Ramaley, 1996, as cited in Gelmon, Holland, Driscoll, Spring, & Kerrigan, 2001, p. viii) to support the institutionalization of the pedagogy at the University of Nebraska at Omaha (UNO). The focus of the project was to measure the impact of service-learning on students and utilize the data as a feedback loop for faculty development.

MODE OF INQUIRY

Background

UNO is a metropolitan university located in the largest city in Nebraska, population 430,000. There are 15,000 students, 500 faculty, and six colleges. The Service-Learning Academy (SLA), established in 1998, launched seven service-learning classes involving 133 students. In the 2005-2006 academic year, there were 104 service-learning courses taught, involving 1,860 students whose combined service hours were worth approximately $872,400 to local nonprofits (Service-Learning Academy, 2006). In 8 years the number of courses taught, the number of students completing the service-learning courses, and the in-kind contributions to the community have increased over 1200% (twelvefold).

Participants

Participants were recruited through classes as faculty agreed to participate in the research project. Six-hundred and seventy students completed the survey during the spring and fall 2006 and spring 2007 semesters. The sample included almost 80% upperclassmen and graduate students with 83% attending school full-time. The participants were 67% female, and European-Americans represented a large majority of the participants (82%), (5% African American, 5% Hispanic, 2% Asian-American/Pacific Islands, 2% American Indian/Alaskan Native, and 3% other). Only 50 of the total students did not work at all, and 73% worked more than 20 hours per week.

Method

Measuring the impact of service-learning on students was the focus of the initial research project. The approach taken to develop the assessment tool involved researching best practices; holding three focus groups with students, faculty, and community partners; and compiling a research tool utilizing established instruments.

The purpose of the focus groups was to build stakeholder commitment and interest, to be respectful of those doing the work, and to recommend theories and an assessment strategy to the SLA and the Office of Academic and Student Affairs at UNO. Community partners also provided feedback for improving partnerships during service-learning projects (e.g., involve the same faculty semester to semester and set goals and objectives). This study utilized focus groups for feedback pertaining to the improvement of service-learning in college courses; the purpose of the study was to examine students' evaluation of their service-learning experiences. Overall, the feedback from the focus groups was positive about participating with the UNO SLA.

After examining multiple methods, the focus groups preferred a pre- and postsurvey so that comparisons could be made for key variables within one class. The focus groups also suggested that there be a longitudinal study one year after participating students graduated. The survey method was chosen because it is an efficient way to collect data from large numbers of students. Other factors included the ease of analysis, the ability to compare different courses and types of service-learning, and different populations of students. It was acknowledged that one of the weaknesses of surveys is that stories of success, struggles, and growth are limited. The focus groups felt that UNO faculty require formal reflection throughout the semester so that this weakness was countered.

Existing surveys (Driscoll et al., 1998; Gelmon et al., 2001; Notre Dame, 1999; University of Nebraska at Omaha [UNO], 2005) were reviewed and questions chosen to evaluate the theories identified by the focus groups. Rather than developing new scales, existing scales were used, which saved time, relied on professional expertise, and offered the potential to access comparison data (Bringle, Phillips, & Hudson, 2004). The UNO Service-Learning Academy Survey was primarily adapted from a similar Portland State survey. Portland State is a peer institution of UNO, having a similar number of students and metropolitan setting. The survey questions utilized a 5-point Likert scale or a simple agree/disagree response, seeking a level of agreement with statements that assess the impact of the service-learning experience on students in the areas of future plans, perceptions and attitudes about community involvement, expectations about the course, and personal civic engagement activities. An example of the fall 2007 postsurvey is represented in Appendix A.

Procedures

Students were recruited for this study through faculty permission to survey their classes. Professors informed their students of the research project and staff from the SLA physically administered the survey to each participating class during the first (presurvey) and last (postsurvey) weeks of the semester. All of the students were provided with information about the purpose of the survey and reminded that their participation was voluntary. Students were given an informed consent statement and survey that were approved by the Institutional Review Board. Faculty names and class enrollment lists were the only identifiers. There was no connection between individual students and their survey responses. Class lists were retained so that students who participated in the study while attending UNO could be located one year after graduation or departure from the university. Retaining the data by class enables research comparisons to be done between sections of the same course, among disciplines, and between years in school and one year after departure.

LIMITATIONS OF THE STUDY

There is some bias built into the study. Participants are not randomly selected as faculty chose to have their classes participate in the SLA Student Survey. Classes tended to be more social sciences and less information technology, engineering, and business, which attract more women than men. Most participating courses were upper level or graduate.

INITIAL STUDENT RESEARCH FINDINGS

Student results have shown mostly insignificant shifts from the beginning to the end of a semester. This was not unexpected and affirms the need for longitudinal follow-up, which is planned (Driscoll et al., 1998).

When spring 2006 results were analyzed, we found surprising results. There were five survey items, related to how students perceived the community experience to have helped them understand and apply the course

Exhibit 5.1.   Spring 2006 Results Related to Course Content and the Service-Learning Activity

Statement From the Survey (N = 187)	Agree	Disagree
The community work I did helped me to better understand the lectures in the course.	75%	25%
The objectives of this course related to the community work.	90%	10%
The community work was *not* related to the materials in the course.	26%	74%
I had the opportunity in this course to periodically discuss my community work and its relationship to the course content.	71%	29%
The community participation aspect of this course helped me to see how the subject matter I learned is used in everyday life.	89%	11%

Exhibit 5.2.   Spring 2006 Results Related to Small Group Work

Statement From the Survey (N = 187)	Agree	Disagree	No Response
Small group dynamics were detrimental to learning.	51%	49%	0%
Working in small groups is dysfunctional.	13%	81%	6%

content, which students' responses the SLA and service-learning faculty found unsatisfactory. These statements are represented in Exhibit 5.1. Although a majority of students agreed that the community work helped them understand lectures better, service-learning faculty felt that there was room for improvement in the classroom. Related to this, faculty felt that *all* students should be making the connection between the course objectives and community work. Even though 90% agreed that the objectives were related, apparently when the students actually did the community project more students felt that there was not a connection to the course materials. This gap concerned the service-learning faculty. They also felt that students needed more opportunities to discuss the relationship between course content and their work in the community. Finally, faculty determined that there was a need to clarify the everyday usefulness of their community participation.

At UNO, new service-learning faculty are taught that organizing students into small groups is an effective method for conducting service-learning projects. Two survey statements addressed small group work and are shown in Exhibit 5.2. Because of these results, service-learning faculty concluded that this indicated a problem in the implementation of small group work. It seemed that students were indicating that small group work made learning more difficult but that the groups functioned well.

Service-learning faculty understood that this feedback highlighted inconsistencies in the implementation of the service-learning pedagogy: faculty development was needed.

INSTITUTIONAL RESPONSE TO STUDENT FINDINGS

Response of the Service-Learning Academy, Faculty, and Community Partners

The SLA and involved faculty responded to these findings by presenting the results for discussion in various settings, including a local pub, brown bag lunches, and in meetings with administrators in the Office of Academic and Student Affairs. Faculty established the Service-Learning and Assessment Teaching Circle to continue the analysis of results and to provide peer feedback. Teaching circles are defined as "small groups of faculty members (typically five to seven) who make a commitment to work together over a period of time to address topics, questions, and concerns related to their teaching and students' learning" (University of Nebraska at Omaha Center for Faculty Development, 2007). This teaching circle identified the need to develop specific service-learning goals and objectives applicable across disciplines, which was completed. The teaching circle also developed a midsemester community partner minisurvey to provide the opportunity to correct problems during the project. SLA staff met individually with faculty to review findings from their classes, and the Service-Learning 101 introduction for new faculty was revised with increased emphasis on connecting course content to the community work, small group management, and developing and maintaining an effective relationship with community partners.

Increased dialogue with community partners identified the desire for a better understanding of service-learning and how to partner with the university. A Service-Learning 101 orientation for community partners was created to provide partners with an understanding of the semester cycle and what is realistic for a project; the roles and responsibilities of community partner, faculty partner, student and SLA; and to empower the community partner to ask for what they need to ensure that the project is worth the time invested. A community partner checklist was developed to serve as a guide for the partnership as well as an evaluation tool. Four

Community Partner 101 trainings were held and four additional focus group feedback sessions occurred.

Response of UNO Administration

The UNO institutional culture supports service. The UNO strategic plan (Strategic Planning Steering Committee, 1997) consists of three goals: student focus, academic excellence, and community engagement. The mission, vision, and value statements affirm working together to develop creative relationships with the community. Administrative and academic leadership supports civic engagement by publicly promoting service/civic engagement, providing fiscal support, personally participating in service/civic engagement activities, and serving on community boards. UNO definitely views the service-learning pedagogy as part of its strategy to link the resources of the metropolitan university with the needs of the community.

The administration decided to create a campus culture by raising awareness of service-learning throughout UNO and the University of Nebraska system through providing opportunities to present at the faculty senate and to the board of regents. The administration funded minigrants for service-learning projects and faculty and established faculty and student service-learning awards and honorariums. Organizationally, the administration combined the SLA with three like-minded efforts: American Humanics, the Civic Participation Project, and the American Democracy Project.

STUDENT FINDINGS AFTER INSTITUTIONAL RESPONSE

A series of Pearson's chi square tests of independence were conducted to examine the relationship between post test responses to various questions pertaining to service-learning courses across the three semesters. During the spring 2006 semester there was a total of 199 responses; 235 in fall 2006, and 236 in spring 2007. There was not a significant difference between the post test responses across the semesters for how much students agreed that the community work helped them to better understand the lectures in the course, $\chi^2(2) = 7.691$, $p = .104$. There was also not a significant difference across semesters for whether or not the objectives of the course were related to the community work for the service-learning project, $\chi^2(2) = .008, p = .644$.

There was a significant difference across semesters in the perception that community participation did not relate to the course materials $\chi^2(2)$

$= 10.095, p = .006$. Follow up comparisons found that participants had significantly lower agreement in the spring 2007 semester than the spring 2006 semester, $\chi^2(1) = 8.088, p = .004$ or the fall 2006 semester, $\chi^2(1) = 7.972, p = .005$. The spring and fall 2006 semesters did not differ significantly, $\chi^2(1) = .001, p = .971$. By the spring 2007 semester more students reported that their community work was related to the topics of the course.

There was a significant difference across semesters for students' agreement versus disagreement that they were able to discuss the community work and its relationship to the course content $\chi^2(2) = 13.270, p = .001$. Follow up comparisons found that participants had significantly higher agreement in the spring 2007 semester than the spring 2006 semester, $\chi^2(1) = 9.630, p = .002$. The fall 2006 semester also had significantly higher agreement than the spring 2006 semester, $\chi^2(1) = 9.210, p = .002$. The fall 2006 and spring 2007 semesters did not differ significantly, $\chi^2(1) < .001, p = .996$. Overall, students agreed more during the fall 2006 and spring 2007 semesters that they were able to discuss their service-learning projects and how the project experiences related to the overall course during class time. There was not a significant difference in agreement across semesters for whether the community participation helped students see the everyday use of the course material $\chi^2(2) = 2.352, p = .308$.

Students were also asked to report on the relationship of small group work and beneficial outcomes of learning. The two small group work questions were changed on the spring 2007 survey to simplify the language to not prejudice the student response and to become more similar to other Campus Compact surveys (changed "small group dynamics are detrimental to learning" to "small group dynamics made learning more difficult" and changed "working in small groups is dysfunctional" to "working in small groups is rewarding"). Because the questions on the survey for these analyses were changed, that data from the spring 2007 survey was not able to be used in the chi-square analyses. There was not a significant difference in agreement versus disagreement for whether or not small group dynamics are detrimental to learning during the spring 2006 and fall 2006 semesters, $\chi^2(2) = .531, p = .466$. There was also not a significant difference across these semesters for whether working in small groups is dysfunctional, $\chi^2(2) = .116, p = .734$. There will be better a representation of student opinions of small group work in later surveys with the improved questions.

DISCUSSION AND NEXT STEPS

As demonstrated, implementing faculty development practices may improve the practices of relating the community participation to course materials and allowing more discussion of the relationship between the service-learning project and the content of the class. Faculty were able to increase discussion of community work and its relationship to course content within their service-learning classes. Students also reported significantly higher agreement that community work was related to course material. This improvement in students' perceptions of service-learning may be attributed to the faculty development activities including teaching circles and discussions that gave faculty feedback about their service-learning projects and allowed them to adjust activities to meet the needs of students and best practices for service-learning (e.g., support).

Although the questions pertaining to understanding lectures better, the relationship of class objectives and community work, the understanding of how this participation could be used in everyday life, and small group work did not significantly improve, the student reports seem to be heading in this direction and further analyses may demonstrate these benefits to faculty development as well. A majority of students are still reporting positive perceptions to these questions; however, the views are not improving significantly across semesters. The current lack of significant findings may be explained by the ongoing process of improving and strengthening service-learning projects in classes. It is expected that as faculty receive feedback and discuss projects with the Teaching Circle and Service-Learning Academy, courses will continue to develop and students' perceptions will continue to grow in the positive direction. Also additional data needs to be collected on the small group questions following the transition in wording.

It continues to be a concern that students are reporting more agreement that community work is related to course material, but less agreement that course objectives are related to community work. Additional faculty development activities and course adjustments are needed to make course objectives and their connection to projects clear to these students. This may be accomplished through a variety of avenues including additional activities, syllabi information, or discussion. In relation, students are reporting more opportunities to discuss their service-learning activities and their relationship to the class, but are not reporting a significant difference in the connection between understanding lectures or course objectives in relationship to the service-learning projects. Perhaps gearing these increasing discussions toward difficult course topics and objectives will lead to a significant improvement in all of these areas.

Involving service-learning faculty in the analysis of the student research project was critical in the improvement of the implementation of the service-learning pedagogy. Faculty members have requested that a more formal feedback loop on student findings be established for interested faculty, thus contributing to their publishing efforts. The survey is four pages long. Continuing to refine the survey instrument is in order. The SLA recently created a newsletter. Regularly publishing some of the findings will continue to raise awareness of the benefits of service-learning. Incorporating service-learning findings with institutional research reports will provide an additional dimension. Some students in the spring 2006 group may have graduated or left the university, providing the opportunity to implement the alumni survey and collect longitudinal data for comparison. UNO will be launching a campuswide civic engagement initiative in the fall of 2009 to develop departmental objectives that further this goal of the university's strategic plan.

Further implications for research at UNO will involve developing a short survey to identify gaps in perception and experience among students, faculty, and community partners' assessment of the partnership, the benefit of the project, and the ease of implementation of the service-learning pedagogy. This will provide additional feedback for faculty development and the development of exemplary programs and courses.

IMPLICATIONS FOR PROMISING PRACTICES

P-16 Initiative Background

Whether called P-16, P-20, K-16 or K-20, as many as 30 states have made attempts to bring collaboration, connectedness, and cohesion to three typically misaligned levels of education nationwide preschool, K-12, and postsecondary (Rainwater & Van de Water, 2001; Education Commission of the States, 2006). According to Rainwater and Van Der Water, there are seven nationally popular P-16 goals: expanding access to early learning and improving readiness for school; providing seamless transitions from one level of learning to the next; closing the achievement gap between white students and sub-groups; upgrading teacher preparation and professional staff development; strengthening collaborations between families and schools; creating applied learning experiences at the secondary level; and improving college recruitment, readiness and retention (2001).

In Nebraska, the state P-16 Initiative's mission is "to increase the success rates of students at all levels of education, both public and private, to improve the prosperity and quality of life of the students themselves and to increase the education level of Nebraska's workforce to enhance the state's economic competitiveness" (Nebraska P-16 Initiative, 2001). Since launching in 1998, Nebraska's P-16 Initiative has provided opportunities for the various levels and sectors of education to communicate and to undertake curriculum-alignment projects (Nebraska P-16 Initiative,

2001). In July of 2007, Marty Mahler became the new coordinator of the Nebraska P-16 Initiative and is supportive of the UNO SLA work with service-learning at all levels of education. Mahler has committed to listening to Nebraska's youth voice throughout the phases of the current Nebraska P-16 Initiative strategic planning process.

Understanding the power of expanding the P-16 service-learning continuum and extending the opportunity for collaboration, the Omaha Public Schools (OPS) magnet schools and UNO SLA partnership was officially launched in the fall of 2005. The university initiated a project bringing UNO faculty members together with teachers from Buffett Middle Magnet School, an OPS Communications Skills & Electronic Media magnet. The Love's Jazz and Arts Center was the community partner. In the spring 2006 semester, UNO students from the School of Communication and the OPS middle school students from Buffett teamed to create promotional brochures, a Web page, and a promotional video for the center.

The collaboration between the UNO's SLA and OPS' magnet schools in the development of shared service-learning projects allows the opportunity to bring college and school-aged youth together to experience the real-world application of academic subjects and develop the habit of community engagement. This partnership within the Omaha community is growing and will become increasingly important as UNO emphasizes the civic engagement aspect of their strategic plan in fall 2009.

Initiative Goals

The success of this partnership produced significant interest among all parties in the development of continued collaborative service-learning projects totaling over 15 to date. Four overarching goals provide the foundation for the UNO SLA P-16 Initiative:

1. Through the service-learning based application of concepts, techniques, and strategies learned in the classroom, UNO and OPS students will attain a greater level of integration and mastery of particular course content.
2. Through the completion of shared service-learning projects, UNO and OPS students will gain an increased appreciation of the value of community service and consider other means in which they might serve their community.
3. Through the ongoing student-to-student collaboration provided by these shared service-learning projects, OPS students will iden-

tify with the collegiate experience and demonstrate an increased interest in pursuing higher education.

4. Through the design, implementation, and evaluation process of these service-learning projects, OPS teachers will gain training, feedback, and support to apply principles of effective practice and consider carrying the pedagogy beyond the shared projects.

PK-12 Staff Development

Committed to doing what works in PK-12 staff development, National Staff Development Council's (NSDC) framework for context, process, and content standards will provide direction for designing experiences that ensures educators acquire skills for service-learning success (NSDC, 2001). According to NSDC (2001), three context standards—learning communities, leadership, and resources—refer to the organizational environments in which adult learning occurs and is implemented. The six NSDC process standards call for staff development that is data driven, is continually informed by evaluation, is research based, is strategic in design, applies knowledge of adult learning, and equips teachers for collaboration. Process standards focus on how selected content strategies are prioritized and delivered, how adult learning is assessed, and how implementation is measured and continuously improved (NSDC, 2001). As the goal of staff development is to improve the learning of all students, NSDC's three content standards frame what adults actually learn: quality teaching, equity, and family involvement (2001). In order to be effective, the staff development offered to partnering PK-12 teachers on service-learning must be "results-based, standards-driven, and job-imbedded" (NSDC, 2001).

Critical Friends Groups as Context

The UNO SLA will bring together higher education faculty and their PK-12 service-learning project partners to form Critical Friends Groups (CFGs), comparable to teaching circles. Designed by the National School Reform Faculty (NSRF) of the Annenberg Institute for School Reform, CFGs are voluntary groups of about 8-12 educational practitioners who identify student learning goals in line with their own classroom instruction and data. CFGs look reflectively at adult best practices and strategies to achieve those goals and collaboratively examine teacher and student work (NSRF, 2006; Dunne, Nave, & Lewis, 2000). Participants in these professional learning communities can utilize their own experience and expertise and/or bring in outside experts and research to design, implement, and evaluate new service-learning experiences.

In CFGs coaches skillfully promote close reflection and "deprivatization" of practice, products, and projects with a focus on continuous improvement in mutually respectful environments (Dunne, Nave, & Lewis, 2000; NSRF, 2006). To create this culture for the service-learning partners, the SLA will have coaches trained to use the protocols available from NSRF for examining work, problem solving, discussing research and best practices, peer observing, goal setting, and team building (Dunne et al., 2000).

Process for Design and Evaluation

Consistent with NSDC's process standards for staff development, the SLA will implement for its CFG a process that is data driven, is evaluative, is research based, offers results based in design, is collaborative, and is crafted to meet the needs of the adult learner (NSDC, 2001). Utilizing adult learning strategies appropriate to producing quality service-learning will be vital for CFG success. To promote the skillful implementation of service-learning pedagogy, the study of service-learning best practices with a content expert will be combined with the design of units of instruction including a service-learning component to include rubrics for formative assessment. Teachers in the CFG will also be trained to administer the PK-12 student service-learning surveys with fidelity.

In an effort to determine the impact of this high level of intentionality, the SLA will utilize disaggregated data from these surveys to determine further staff development priorities for the CFGs, monitor progress, and help sustain continuous improvement. In addition to the PK-12 student service-learning surveys, CFG participants will provide feedback on staff development offered. Beyond the initial collection of teacher feedback, evaluation will focus on teachers' acquisition of new knowledge and skills, how that learning affects the quality of service-learning project planning and implementation, and how those changes in practice affect students' personal gains.

Principles of Effective Practice as Content

The Principles of Effective Practice for K-12 Service-Learning will provide the content of staff development for CFG participants: curriculum integration, reflection, youth voice, diversity, meaningful service, process monitoring, duration and intensity, and reciprocal partnerships (Billig,

2007; Weah, 2007). These draft national standards were reviewed during the first meeting of the UNO PK-16 CFG in November 2007. Reactor panel participants represented early childhood, elementary, middle, high school, higher education, and out-of-school-time practitioners. Responding to the national call, the proposed standards were revised for clarity, soundness, and the representation of each as an essential practice (Weah, 2007). As desired, the process utilized was consensual, allowing for facilitated participant resolution of differences and consensus on areas of agreement (Weah, 2007).

Of the eight principles, reciprocal partnerships will be chief for CFG participants' service-learning project success. If institutionalization of this collaborative P-16 service-learning undertaking is the goal for UNO SLA and OPS magnet schools, the initiative needs to be integrated into the existing initiatives for both educational partners and stake-holding community partners (Ammon, Furco, Chi, & Middaugh, 2000; Kramer, 2000). According to Ammon et al., both sides of the partnership will have to frame and provide resources to fulfill a "cohesive, long-term vision" that is also realistic and comprehensive (2001). Partnership building and maintaining is an essential component of collaboration as a function of the institutionalization process (Kramer, 2000). While increasing the number of university faculty and PK-12 teachers may be one means of sustaining this effort, all involved will be better served by building upon and maintaining established partnerships and focusing on the quality of projects through embedded staff development and ongoing support (Ammon et al., 2000). Once a foundation of quality is built, bringing in other PK-12 teachers, faculty members, and community partners to focus on an issue that has a broad appeal but can build interest through its implications for all stakeholders can be an effective approach for sustainability (Ammon et al., 2000).

CONCLUSION

In retrospect, this research has answered Stanton's call for practical interplay between service-learning investigations and practice by using student research to provide feedback for faculty development and pedagogical improvement. Serendipitous outcomes of the student survey included improvement of teaching approaches, increased collaboration with community partners, recruiting of more service-learning faculty, and supporting the institutionalization of service-learning.

Sustaining this continuous improvement approach to service-learning practices, processes, and student outcomes across the educational continuum is vital for UNO and its undertaking with collaborative PK-12 service-learning in OPS. Fostering a culture of collaboration, evidence-based practices, and continuous feedback will enable the SLA to align its day-to-day work with the needs of the students, faculty, and community partners, and to fulfill the missions of both educational institutions. Using teaching circles, and in the future Critical Friends Groups, will allow partnering service-learning practitioners to engage in ongoing, collaborative discussion informed by research through examination of results from laser-like focus on effective service-learning practice.

APPENDIX A: SERVICE-LEARNING ACADEMY SURVEY

Service Learning Academy-Post Survey Fall 2007

The purpose of the Service Learning Academy's study is to assess the impact of utilizing Service Learning as a teaching method with undergraduate and graduate students at UNO. This research protocol has been approved by the University of Nebraska Medical Center Institutional Review Board. This study has been assigned the identifying number 393-05-EX. The survey is designed to assess values, civic engagement, academic motivation and application of subject matter. The survey will be administered at the beginning of a semester, at the end, and one year after students have graduated or left the University of Nebraska at Omaha.

Responses are completely confidential. Names or other individual identifiers will not be collected and there will be no data sets in which individual identifiers could be extracted. All results will be reported as grouped data only. Students will be identified as members of a specific section of a course. There will be no connection between individual students and their responses to the survey. The class enrollment lists will be the only identifier. These lists will be submitted to the Alumni Office and retained until the students have received the final survey to complete one year after graduation or departing from the university. At that time individual names will be removed from the class list and discarded.

Participation is voluntary. Students are not required to complete the survey. There will be no consequences in the course or later if a student decides not to participate. A completed survey will indicate the respondent's willingness to participate in the study.

This is the largest service learning research project to date at UNO. Participation in this study will assist the staff of the UNO Service Learning Academy and UNO faculty members to refine and improve service learning courses offered in the future at the university.

Service Learning Academy-Post Survey Fall 2007

First we would like some information about you.

1. What is the name of the professor?*
   If you choose not to respond, please insert "No response" for your answer.

2. What course is this?*
   If you choose not to respond, please insert "No response" for your answer.

3. In which semester are you taking this course?*

   ⊂ Fall   ⊂ Spring   ⊂ Summer   ⊂ No response

   ⊂ Year, please specify

4. What is your student status?

   ⊏ Full-time   ⊏ Part-time   ⊏ No response

5. What is your class level?

   ⊏ Freshman   ⊏ Sophomore   ⊏ Junior   ⊏ Senior   ⊏ Graduate Student   ⊏ No response

   ⊏ Other, please specify

6. What is your gender?

   ⊏ Male   ⊏ Female   ⊏ No response

7. What is your age in years?
   If you choose not to respond, please enter 99. The value must be between 18 and 99, inclusive.

8. What is your ethnic background?
   Select at least 1 response and no more than 6 responses.

   ⊏ American Indian/Alaskan Native   ⊏ Hispanic   ⊏ Black (non-Hispanic)   ⊏ White (non-Hispanic)

   ⊏ Asian/Pacific Islands   ⊏ International non-US Citizen   ⊏ No response

   ⊏ Other, please specify

9. Your native language is:

   ⊏ English   ⊏ Spanish   ⊏ No response

   ⊏ Other, please specify

10. State the number of hours that you work in a week at your job.
    If you choose not to respond, please enter 99. The value must be between 0 and 99, inclusive.

Service Learning Academy-Post Survey Fall 2007

11. In which city and state do you live?

12. How would you characterize your religious/spiritual orientation?

  ○ Religious

  ○ Spiritual but not religious

  ○ None

  ○ No response

13. How would you characterize your political views?

  ☐ Far Left   ☐ Liberal   ☐ Middle-of-the-road   ☐ Conservative   ☐ Far Right   ☐ No response

14. Are you the first person in your family to go to college?

  ☐ Yes   ☐ No   ☐ No response

15. Did your high school require community service for graduation?

  ○ Yes   ○ No   ○ No response

16. Are your parents active in their faith group and/or community?

  ○ Yes   ○ No   ○ No response

17. I was already volunteering in the community before taking this course.

  ○ Yes   ○ No   ○ No response

18. This semester, how often have you:

	Frequently	Occasionally	Not at all	No response
Voted	☐	☐	☐	☐
Participated in organized demonstrations	☐	☐	☐	☐
Performed volunteer work	☐	☐	☐	☐
Discussed politics	☐	☐	☐	☐
Socialized with someone of another racial/ethnic group	☐	☐	☐	☐
Discussed religion/spirituality	☐	☐	☐	☐
Used the Internet for research or homework	☐	☐	☐	☐
Used the library for research or homework	☐	☐	☐	☐
Worked on a local, state, or national political campaign	☐	☐	☐	☐
Donated to a public cause	☐	☐	☐	☐

Service Learning Academy-Post Survey Fall 2007

Contacted a public official   ☐   ☐   ☐   ☐

Did this course meet your expectations?

19 Taking this course:
. SA = Strongly Agree, A = Agree, D = Disagree, SD = Strongly Disagree, NR = No response

	SA	A	D	SD	NR
enhanced my ability to communicate in a "real world" setting.	○	○	○	○	○
helped me develop my problem-solving skills.	○	○	○	○	○
made me more marketable in my chosen profession after I graduate.	○	○	○	○	○

20. Compared to your other classes, how much were you challenged by the material in this course?
Please note on a scale from 1-9 with 1 being much less than other classes and 9 being much more than other classes. If you choose not to respond, please enter 0 as your value. The value must be between 0 and 9, inclusive.

21. Compared to your other classes, how much effort did you put forth during this course?
Please note on a scale from 1-9 with 1 being much less than other classes and 9 being much more than other classes. If you choose not to respond, please enter 0. The value must be between 0 and 9, inclusive.

22 What is your perspective about community involvement and this course?
. Using the key below, mark the response that best fits your perspective SA = Strongly Agree, A = Agree, D = Disagree, SD = Strongly Disagree, NR = No response

	SA	A	D	SD	NR
The community participation aspect of this course helped me to see how the subject matter I learned could be used in every day life.	○	○	○	○	○
The community work I did helped me to better understand the lectures in this course.	○	○	○	○	○
The community work was not related to the materials in the course.	○	○	○	○	○
The idea of combining work in the community with university course work should be practiced in more courses at this university.	○	○	○	○	○
This course benefited the community.	○	○	○	○	○
This course showed me how I can become more involved in my community.	○	○	○	○	○
This course helped me to become more aware of the needs in my community.	○	○	○	○	○
This course enhanced my sense of responsibility to serve my community.	○	○	○	○	○
This course discouraged me from volunteering or participating in the community in the future.	○	○	○	○	○

Service Learning Academy-Post Survey Fall 2007

The next set of questions relate to your attitude toward community involvement. Please indicate your level of agreement with each of the following statements.

23. Here are some reasons for participating in community service activities. Mark to indicate how important each of these reasons is in motivating your off-campus service activities.
SA = Strongly Agree, A = Agree, D = Disagree, SD = Strongly Disagree, NR = No response

	SA	A	D	SD	NR
To test out future career plans	○	○	○	○	○
As a course requirement	○	○	○	○	○
For religious and ethical reasons	○	○	○	○	○
To develop new skills	○	○	○	○	○
To work with people different from me	○	○	○	○	○
To enhance my academic learning	○	○	○	○	○
For the feeling of personal satisfaction	○	○	○	○	○
To enhance my resume	○	○	○	○	○
To enhance my chances of acceptance to medical, law, dental, business, or graduate school	○	○	○	○	○
To learn more about other people and their experiences	○	○	○	○	○
To learn how to be effective in the area of social change	○	○	○	○	○
To help other people	○	○	○	○	○
To improve society as a whole	○	○	○	○	○
To improve the community	○	○	○	○	○
To fulfill my civic/social responsibility	○	○	○	○	○

24. Finally, we would like some of your personal reflections.
SA = Strongly Agree, A = Agree, D = Disagree, SD = Strongly Disagree, NR = No response

	SA	A	D	SD	NR
Students made a difference in their community.	○	○	○	○	○
The objectives of this course related to community work.	○	○	○	○	○
This course helped me take responsibility for my own learning.	○	○	○	○	○
I am comfortable working with diverse ethnic groups.	○	○	○	○	○
The work I did in this course helped me learn how to plan and complete a project.	○	○	○	○	○

Service Learning Academy-Post Survey Fall 2007

The other students in this class played an important role in my learning.	○	○	○	○	○
Small group dynamics were detrimental to learning.	○	○	○	○	○
The hours required for the team project (i.e., meetings, group, e-mails, travel, blackboard) were excessive.	○	○	○	○	○
Grading was not done fairly in the group project.	○	○	○	○	○
Some members on the team contributed and some did nothing.	○	○	○	○	○
Working in small groups was dysfunctional.	○	○	○	○	○
I had the opportunity in this course to periodically discuss my community work and its relationship to the course content.	○	○	○	○	○
Students should be required to provide a certain number of community service hours in order to graduate.	○	○	○	○	○
I can make a difference in my community.	○	○	○	○	○

25. Thank you for your participation. Please add any other comments you have about courses where learning takes place in a community setting.

REFERENCES

Ammon, M., Furco, A., Chi, B., & Middaugh, E. (2001). *Service-learning in California: A profile of the CalServe service-learning partnerships, 1997–2000.* Berkeley, CA: Service-Learning Research and Development Center, University of California.

Bacon, N., & Sather, P. (2001, June). *The impact of service-learning on students, faculty, and the community.* Report presented to University of Nebraska at Omaha Committee on Research.

Bligh, J. (2005). Faculty development. *Medical Education, 39,* 120-121.

Billig, S. (2007). Unpacking what works in service-learning: Promising research-based practices to improve student outcomes. In J. C. Kielsmeier, M. N. Neal, N. Schultz, & T. J. Leeper (Eds.), *Growing to greatness* (pp. 18-28). St. Paul, MN: National Youth Leadership Council.

Bringle, R. G., Phillips, M. A., & Hudson, M. (2004). *The measure of service learning: Research scales to assess student experiences.* Washington, DC: American Psychological Association.

Chadwick, S. A., & Pawlowski, D. R. (2007). Assessing institutional support for service-learning: A case study of organizational sensemaking. *Michigan Journal of Community Service Learning, 13,* 31-39.

Cruz, N. I., & Giles Jr., D. E. (2000). Where's the community in service-learning research? (Special Issue). *Michigan Journal of Community Service Learning, 7*(2), 28-34.

Driscoll, A., Gelmon, S. B., Holland, B. A., Kerrigan, S., Spring, A., Grosvold, K., et al. (1998). *Assessing the impact of service learning: A workbook of strategies and methods* (2nd ed.). Portland, OR: Center for Academic Excellence, Portland State University.

Dunne, F., Nave, B., & Lewis, A. (2000, December). CFGs: Teachers helping teachers to improve student learning. *Research Bulletin, 28*, 9-12. Retrieved April 4, 2007, from http://www.pdkintl.org/edres/resbul28.htm

Education Commission of the States. (2006). *P-16 collaboration in the states.* Retrieved April 1, 2007, from http://www.ecs.org

Furco, A. (2001). Advancing service-learning at research universities. *New Directions for Higher Education, 114*, 67-78.

Furco, A. (2002). Institutionalizing service-learning in higher education. *Journal of Public Affairs, 6*, 39-67.

Gelmon, S. B., Holland, B. A., Driscoll, A., Spring, A., & Kerrigan, S. (2001). *Assessing service-learning and civic engagement.* Providence RI: Campus Compact.

Kahne, J., Westheimer, J., & Rogers, B. (2000). Service-learning and citizenship: Directions for research (Special Issue: Strategic Directions for Service-Learning Research). *Michigan Journal of Community Service Learning, 7*, 42-51.

Kramer, M. (2000). *Make it last forever: The institutionalization of service learning in America.* Washington, DC: Corporation for National Service.

Miron, D., & Moely, B. E. (2006). Community agency voice and benefit in service-learning. *Michigan Journal of Community Service Learning, 7*, 27-37.

Nebraska P-16 Initiative. (2001). *Nebraska P-16 initiative: Nebraska's coalition for student success.* Retrieved November 11, 2005, from http://p16.nebraska.edu/

Notre Dame. (1999). *Student Life Survey: Pretest Spring 1999.* Unpublished manuscript, University of Notre Dame.

National School Reform Faculty. (2006). *CFG FAQ: What is a CFG?* Retrieved October 12, 2007, from http://www.nsrfharmony.org/faq.html#1

National Staff Development Council. (2001). *NSDC standards for staff development, revised.* Retrieved January 6, 2007, from http://www.nsdc.org/standards/index.cfm

Petras, E. M., & Porpora, D. V. (1993). Participatory research: Three models and an analysis. *The American Sociologist, 24*(1), 107-126.

Pickeral, T. (1996). Lessons from the field. In T. Pickeral & K. Peters (Eds.), *From the margin to the mainstream: The faculty role in advancing service-learning on community colleges. Models, lessons from the field, case studies.* Mesa, AZ: Campus Compact National Center for Community Colleges.

Rainwater, T., & Van de Water, G. (2001). *What is P-16 education? A primer for legislators.* Retrieved April 4, 2007, from http://www.ecs.org

Sather, P., Carlson, P., & Weitz, B. (2007). Research: Infusing service learning into research, social policy, and community-based practice. In M. Nadel, V. Majewski, & M. Sullivan-Cosetti (Eds.), *Social work and service learning: Partnerships for social justice* (pp. 93-105). Lanham, MD: Rowman & Littlefield.

Scepansky, T. (2004). *Service learning and faculty in the higher education institution.* Retrieved November 14, 2007, from http://www.newfoundations.com/OrgHeader.html

Service-Learning Academy. (2006, June). *Annual report 2005/2006* (University of Nebraska at Omaha). Omaha, NE: Sather.

Stanton, T. K. (2000). Bringing reciprocity to service-learning research and practice (Special Issue: Strategic Directions for Service-Learning Research). *Michigan Journal of Community Service Learning, 7*(2), 119-123.

Strage, A. (2004). Long-term benefits of service-learning: When and where do they manifest themselves? *College Student Journal, 38,* 257-261.

Strategic Planning Steering Committee (1997). *Strategic plan.* Omaha: University of Nebraska at Omaha.

University of Nebraska at Omaha. (2005). *UNO Freshman & Transfer Student Questionnaire.* Omaha, NE: Author.

University of Nebraska at Omaha Center for Faculty Development. (2007). *Teaching circles.* Retrieved November 26, 2007, from http://www.unomaha.edu/facdevelop/teachingcircle.php

Weah, W. (2007). Toward research-based standards for K-12 service-learning. In J. C. Kielsmeier, M. Neal, N. Schultz, & T. J. Leeper (Eds.), *Growing to greatness* (pp. 14-17). St. Paul, MN: National Youth Leadership Council.

Zlotkowski, E. (1996). Linking service learning and the academy. *Change, 28,* 20-28.

Zlotkowski, E. (1998). A service learning approach to faculty development. *New Directions for Teachers and Learning, 73,* 81-89.

CHAPTER 6

ASSESSING THE LEARNING IN SERVICE-LEARNING PROJECTS USING OUTCOME MEASURES RECOMMENDED BY THE COMMISSION ON PUBLIC RELATIONS EDUCATION

Sally Blomstrom and Hak Tam

Practitioners of service-learning are well aware of the value of service-learning, including the enriching learning experiences for students and the positive effects for the community. In order for service-learning to be sustainable, research is needed that facilitates understanding and acceptance by stakeholders. One way to undertake research of this type is to use a framework suggested by practitioners and educators in a specific discipline. Results derived from an established framework are likely to be particularly compelling. Service-learning has become a common pedagogical approach in communication; however the absence of standard methods of assessment has made it more difficult to compare service-learning with other pedagogical strategies. This chapter seeks to address that gap by suggesting a methodological approach for assessing service-learning using

Scholarship for Sustaining Service-Learning and Civic Engagement
pp. 139–160

a framework developed from the 2006 Report of the Commission on Public Relations Education (2006). Practitioners and educators identified criteria for beginning practitioners in public relations. This research demonstrates application of those criteria in 2 ways. The first involves using selected criteria to analyze reflective comments and comparing to a thematic analysis approach. The second involves developing a quantitative survey based on the criteria. Students were asked to rate their learning on each item based on their service-learning experience. They were also asked to rate their ability on each item. This professionally defined assessment method potentially allows for a more standardized assessment technique to compare projects and programs, and may help provide evidence to garner institutional support for this pedagogy.

INTRODUCTION

Practitioners of service-learning are well aware of the value of service-learning, including the enriching learning experiences for students and the positive effects for the community. In order for service-learning to be sustainable, however, research is needed that facilitates understanding and acceptance by stakeholders. One way to undertake research of this type is to use a framework suggested by practitioners and educators in a specific discipline. Results derived from an established framework are likely to be more readily accepted than more general ones. For public relations, the 2006 Report of the Commission on Public Relations Education (2006) specified knowledge, skills, and personal traits that have been adapted to the framework suggested here. The criteria recommended in the report formed the basis of a survey measuring how the students rated their learning on each item for a service-learning project, and how they rated their ability for each item.

In the instructions for the survey, students were informed that the criteria used had been generated by practitioners and educators in public relations. Students gained an appreciation for what would be expected of them as new hires in the field, and they gained awareness of how their abilities met or failed to meet those expectations. For the course instructor, the results provided feedback on the effectiveness of instruction in a structured manner. The instrument also provided a framework for course evaluation. The department chair received comments regarding areas where the students excelled and where weaknesses existed. This led to a discussion of prerequisites, course requirements, and the sequencing of courses in the curriculum. Thus, results from this instrument were of value to the students, the faculty member, and the administration. This framework of analysis also makes explicit the contributions of service-learning in the discipline of public relations, which may be an invaluable tool to draw attention and gain support from the department chair, the community partners, and the students themselves, leading to increased sustainability.

A primary purpose of service-learning is to help students meet some or all of the objectives of a course and to assist them in achieving learning outcomes. Service-learning as a pedagogical approach has grown in the field of communication in part because the approach is well suited for helping students comprehend content in the discipline. Oster-Aaland, Sellnow, Nelson, and Pearson (2004) offer support for this claim by comparing a 2001 survey with a 1995 survey of department chairs, which investigates the prevalence of service-learning in communication departments. In the 2001 survey, 90% of the respondents granted academic credit for service-learning. The proportion of students who participated in service-learning increased from 1995 to 2001. The respondents were asked to identify from a list of communication skills which they perceived were enhanced in their students who participated in their departments' service-learning programs. The skills were broadly defined as interpersonal communication, written communication, organizational communication, small group communication, public speaking, intercultural communication, mass communication, and other. With the exceptions of mass communication and other, at least 75% of respondents perceived that each area was improved through service-learning. Interpersonal communication headed the list with 95% of the administrators responding that skills in that area were enhanced through service-learning involvement.

More specific support was offered by Panici and Lasky (2002) who reported that within communication, service-learning is most commonly implemented in public relations courses. They suggest this may be the case because the subject matter of the courses lends itself to community needs. Participants in their study reported that the types of work typically produced in service-learning courses included newsletters, brochures, and pamphlets. With service-learning being a relatively common pedagogy in communication and particularly public relations, it seems stakeholders must accept its value, but how is the pedagogy being assessed? Fifteen of 32 respondents in the Panici and Lasky (2002) study reported that students, faculty, and service-learning sites were involved in the final assessment of service-learning. Sixteen of 32 respondents reported that student activity reports were used to assess learning and the same number reported that site supervisor evaluations were used.

While activity reports and supervisor evaluations provide useful data in the assessment process, the findings may lack generalizability. One study reviewing service-learning in academic accounting suggested a discipline-specific framework for assessing service-learning. Rama, Ravenscroft, Wolcott, and Zlotkowski (2000) distinguished between intellectual outcomes and personal outcomes in the literature on service-learning assessment and reported various means for assessing desired student outcomes. Intellectual outcomes included cognitive competencies such as textbook content knowledge, relationship of that knowledge to the world, and critical thinking skills. Intellectual outcomes had been assessed using grades, faculty and student self-report measures, content analysis, and multiple measures. Personal outcomes included leadership, communication, personal demeanor, and value-related competencies. Agreement had not been found on how to assess personal outcomes. Rama et al. (2000) chose to refine both types of outcomes using criteria identified from the profession, namely the American Institute of Certified Public Accountants Core Competency Framework for Entry into the Accounting Profession.

Two of the six outcomes associated with service-learning identified by Vaughn (2002) closely correspond to intellectual and personal outcomes identified by Rama et al. (2000), namely academic growth and personal growth. Vaughn cited Hamilton and Zeldin (1987) who looked at how service-learning enhanced students' cognitive development as an aspect of academic growth. Hamilton and Zeldin compared results from students engaged in internship programs with students taking conventional civics classes in several categories, including content knowledge. Among the results of their regression analysis was a significant difference for interns in terms of knowledge. Results from internships may be generalized to students engaged in substantive service-learning projects, providing reflection and feedback opportunities were included in the internship experiences. Moreover, Patterson (2004) states that public relations service-learning projects are similar to internships in that the projects are performed as part of a course in public relations; however service-learning projects usually involve less contact between students and the organization than do internships. As for the variable of personal growth, Vaughn presented findings from the literature, including greater self knowledge, increased confidence, tolerance for diversity, and the development of realistic skills.

Additional support for academic (intellectual) growth and personal growth was offered by Eyler and Giles (1999). Students reported that they were able to apply their knowledge to real problems, suggesting higher-order processing and a deeper understanding of the material. Further, students reported improvements in greater self knowledge and in their ability to work with others. Astin and Sax (1998) looked at student development in terms of three domains. Within the domain of academic development, 9 out of 10 outcomes showed positive effects from education-related service. Within the domain of life skills, service participation was associated with increases in 13 life skills. These included social self-confidence, interpersonal skills, ability to work cooperatively, and relevance of coursework to everyday life.

Practical skills, interpersonal skills, citizenship, and personal responsibility were represented by the 12 items in the SELEB (Service-learning
Benefit) Scale developed by Toncar, Reid, Burns, Anderson, and Nguyen
(2006). The scale was tested by comparing results from students in a public relations course with students in a senior-level marketing course. Both
courses involved service-learning components. Students in the public
relations course reported higher rankings in all four areas with the highest ranking in the area of practical skills. The practical skills identified by
Toncar et al. (2006) correspond in part with intellectual outcomes identified by Rama et al. (2000), and similarly the interpersonal skills and personal responsibility identified by Toncar et al. correspond with the
personal outcomes identified by Rama et al.

The idea of assessing intellectual outcomes and personal outcomes for
service-learning has support in the literature, but the items within those
categories need to be discipline specific. Stacks, Boton, and Van
SlykeTurk (1999) surveyed practitioners and educators to evaluate the
skills, attitude, and content knowledge that public relations students
should possess to be successful on the job. Those were defined as desired
outcomes. Of the 102 items included on the questionnaire, 24 resulted in
a combined score for practitioners and educators of 6 or higher on a 7-
point scale. Top-ranked desired items with a score of 6.30 or higher
included writing news releases, being a self starter, organizational skills,
critical thinking and problem solving skills, interpersonal skills, word pro-
cessing/e-mail skills, knowledge of and interest in current events, flexibility, understanding of protocol with the mass media, basic knowledge of
the mass media, understanding business practices, and taking criticism.
Only three outcomes were reported as "found" in entry-level personnel.
These outcomes, which had a score above 5.0, were word processing/
email, good attitude, and typing. Respondents were also asked to evaluate
the skills required for hiring. Those included writing skills, ability to communicate publicly, interpersonal skills, and practical experience.

In a similar vein, responses from both practitioners and educators were
incorporated in the November 2006 Commission on Public Relations
Educations report titled, "The Professional Bond-Public Relations Education and the Practice." An extensive set of recommendations was presented in the report, which spanned practice, education, and research.
The criteria specified in these recommendations will be employed in this
paper to refine and measure intellectual and personal outcomes for
assessment of the learning that resulted from service-learning projects in
public relations (Appendix A). Specifically, this paper will analyze the
reflections and survey responses from students involved in three service-
learning projects. We will proceed by discussing the projects, presenting
the analytical framework for outcome measurements and looking at how

the reflective comments from students fit within these outcome measurements qualitatively and quantitatively, and we will present and review a quantitative survey instrument based on the framework along with the results obtained from its use. This paper suggests using criteria developed by professionals in the discipline to assess service-learning projects and bring visibility to the broad range of learning outcomes that this pedagogy produces. Our example of assessment criteria is specific to the discipline of Public Relations.

DESCRIPTION OF SERVICE-LEARNING PROJECTS

Chadron State College is part of the Nebraska State College system. It offers a 4-year program for a wide range of academic majors, serving over 2,500 students in the western Nebraska region. Public relations (PR) was added as an option (i.e., field of specialization) in communication arts beginning in the fall of the 2005-06 academic year. All students in the department complete the core requirements for a comprehensive major in communication arts and then take additional courses to complete one of three options or specializations. The three options include public relations, journalism, and communication. The courses below were the first offered for the PR option.

For a practice-oriented focus, the first author, as the primary faculty member for the PR option in the Communication Arts Department, elected to incorporate service-learning as a way of introducing real world exposure to the students. This study examines three service-learning projects completed during the 2005-07 academic years. In all three cases, most of the students had chosen the public relations option.

The first service-learning project involved students in public relations techniques (CA 250, fall semester of the 2005-2006 academic year, $n = 13$), who developed promotional materials for the Nebraska Museum Association. One year later the second project involved students in public relations multimedia (CA 350, fall 2006-2007, $n = 12$), who developed promotional materials and ideas for the Applied Sciences Department. The next semester (spring 2006-2007) a third service-learning project took place involving students from research methods (CA 430, $n = 7$), who wrote a survey, gathered data, and conducted a focus group for a project with Indian Health Service. Each project will be reviewed in some detail.

Promotional Package for the Nebraska Museum Association

A representative from the Nebraska Museum Association inquired as to whether students in the public relations techniques class would undertake designing and developing promotional materials for their organization.

The outcomes desired by the community partner fit well with the content of the course. The students worked in teams to design bookmarks, T-shirts, a Web site, posters, brochures, promotional items, and public service announcements for the association. The teams met with the representative on two separate occasions and presented their work at the last meeting with her. Team presentations were videotaped for viewing by another association representative, and all materials were submitted for consideration by the two representatives. Feedback was given by the association representative on the presentations and the deliverables and by the faculty member. At the end of the course students responded to reflective questions.

Public Relations Package for the Applied Sciences Department

The students in the public relations multimedia class were asked to develop materials for the Applied Sciences Department at the college. The students again worked in teams to create brochures, print ads, radio ads, Web ideas, and promotional suggestions to attract potential students to the programs offered by the department. The course content dealt with creating these deliverables along with how their use could be incorporated within a larger promotional effort. The teams met with a graduate assistant from applied sciences to learn what the Applied Sciences Department was looking for and to learn what already had been done. The graduate student, a technical writer by profession, presented initial information, reviewed materials developed by the teams, and gave feedback. Later the chair of the department heard student presentations and provided feedback. The faculty in the department also heard presentations revised according to the feedback received from the chair, and they gave additional input to the students on the presentations and deliverables. The materials were also graded by the faculty member. Throughout the project students were encouraged to talk about their experiences. At the end of the course, all students responded to the same reflective questions used in the first course. Students were able to see the work created by other groups of students as they progressed through each stage of feedback with the client, and they learned from each other.

Survey and Focus Group for Indian Health Service

The third service-learning project consisted of applying course concepts from a research methods class to a dental health project undertaken by Indian Health Service. Students viewed a videotape and designed and implemented a survey to measure the effectiveness of its content. They gathered data. They also organized and conducted a focus group. After the focus group, they wrote a report with recommendations for the client. Additionally they got the PR Club involved with the project. Club members wrote and illustrated a coloring book to accompany the video. Another student designed brochures and fliers to promote the health message. The client representatives met with the faculty member on several occasions but did not meet with the students directly. The students worked together as a class rather than as teams because of the nature of the tasks. Feedback was given by the Indian Health Service representative and the tasks were graded by the faculty member. Students responded to the reflective questions and completed the survey.

Students anecdotally reported satisfaction with the "real world" experiences gained through the service-learning projects. These experiences were important because faculty reasoned that as a new offering by the college, practical experience would help prepare students for work in the area after graduation.

METHOD

In the literature, service-learning outcomes had been assessed using a variety of means including test scores, standardized and self-report surveys, content analysis, grades, interviews, focus groups, and exam scores (Rama et al., 2000). The lack of consistency in instruments and methods used in assessing the learning makes comparisons between pedagogies and among service-learning projects difficult.

In order to implement an instrument that could be used more generally in the discipline, the researchers chose a frame from the practitioner/educator's perspective. PR is a practice-oriented specialization. Preparing students for their careers in the field is a goal of the program. The Commission on Public Relations Education published a report (2006) titled, "The Professional Bond—Public Relations Education and the Practice." In the report trends affecting PR practice are identified, and a set of recommendations is given for what a PR curriculum should include. The report also listed the attributes new entrants into the profession should possess (Appendix A).

There was considerable agreement between educators and practitioners on the skills needed for practitioners at the entry level. These included writing skills, critical thinking and problem-solving skills, a good attitude, an ability to communicate publicly, and initiative. Drawing on the work by Rama et al. (2000), the two categories of outcomes examined were intellectual skills and personal skills. The categories were segmented into components that were applicable to these service-learning projects. The individual items were drawn from the criteria recommended by the commission's report. For purposes of this study the skills are broken down as follows:

- Intellectual Skills in the following areas:
  - Research methods and analysis
  - Informative and persuasive writing
  - Technological and visual literacy
  - Message production
  - Public speaking and presentation
- Personal Skills in the ability to do the following:
  - Maintain a positive attitude
  - Demonstrate creativity
  - Demonstrate the ability to work in groups (respect and empathy)
  - Demonstrate the ability to take criticism

In each of the three classes described, after completing the service-learning projects, students were asked to complete reflective exercises during class time. Standard questions, with modified prompts on the third question, were used in part because enrollments in the classes were small with $N_1 = 7$, $N_2 = 12$, $N_3 = 13$, $N_{total} = 32$. The following prompts were used to guide the reflections:

1. What did you do for the project? Please include research, item(s) produced, and presentation components.
2. What are your reactions to working on the project? What did you learn about yourself? For example, did you employ a new creative skill, do you see yourself as more confident in the area than you did when the term started, did you become aware of assumptions you held, were you aware of any biases you held, what did you feel as a result of the project?
3. How did the experience better help you understand what you learned in the course? (Prompts for this question varied with the course depending on the content. Sample prompts for the writing courses are written here.) Please address audience analysis, writing press (news) releases, developing brochures, print ads, radio ads, Web applications, promotional ideas, and presenting your work.

These handwritten reflections were collected for data analysis. First the data was interpreted using thematic analysis commonly employed in qualitative research. Reflective comments from the students were coded and analyzed for underlying themes (Nespor, 2006; Marshall & Rossman, 1996). In addition, the reflections were coded using relevant criteria selected from the commission's report. Qualitative findings from these alternate techniques were compared to illustrate how the professional frame made visible the learning outcomes that would otherwise be overlooked.

In addition to qualitative data using reflective comments, students in the research methods course ($N = 7$) took a survey after completing their service-learning project. The instrument consisted of all items specified in the Commission on Public Relations Education report. The students were asked to respond to each item in two ways. They were asked to rate their learning in each area based on the service-learning project just completed, and they were asked to rate their overall ability in each area. A five-point Likert-type scale was used for the survey instrument. Quantitative information based on the PR Commission's attributes was collected.

RESULTS

Qualitative data based on the reflective comments were analyzed in two different ways as described in the Methods section above. Two trained coders participated in the data analysis using an iterative process to cross-validate the analysis. Five intellectual parameters and four personal parameters were selected as being most pertinent to the learning outcomes of these service-learning projects.

Theme identification yielded the following results:

- Self-awareness/self-discovery was the most frequently described response. They discovered their strengths, their creative side, and their sensitivity to others.

- Learning how to work in a group setting was the next highest ranked comment. They found out how to make themselves heard, how to play to each others' strengths, and how to contribute to the team effort.

- Confidence was another dominant theme. They gained confidence in themselves through the work they produced.

- In terms of task skills, students primarily reported learning in the areas most directly related to their tasks and their roles. They learned about audience analysis and about understanding the client's environment and needs. They worked on the deliverables and developed the message and the graphics, and prepared the public service announcements, PR packages, and promotional materials.

- They also learned that their work may not be accepted as initially presented and that being able to take criticism is important.

Quantitative analysis based on the intellectual skills and personal skills attributes described in the Commission on Public Relations Education

2006 report yielded complementary information. These findings are summarized in Exhibits 6.1 and 6.2

Overall the responses from students reinforced the outcomes taken from the Commission on Public Relations Education 2006 report that were selected as appropriate for these projects. Eight of the nine outcomes were mentioned by 50% or more of the respondents in their reflections.

Quantitative data from the survey of the students in the research methods course shows yet another way to use the PR commission's attributes in learning-outcome assessment. Students were asked to rate the learning they gained from their service-learning experience for each of the items from the commission's report. The criteria identified are categorized according to skills, knowledge, or personal traits. In the area of skills, stu-

Exhibit 6.1.   Categorical Outcomes for Intellectual Skills

Class	Total	Research Methods and Analysis	Informative and Persuasive Writing	Technological and Visual Literacy	Message Production	Public Speaking and Presentation
CA430	7	7	0	6	4	1
CA350	12	11	9	12	11	9
CA250	13	3	9	8	8	6
Total		21	18	26	23	16
				Percentages		
CA430	7	100%	0%	86%	57%	14%
CA350	12	92%	75%	100%	92%	75%
CA250	13	23%	69%	62%	62%	46%
Total	32	66%	56%	81%	72%	50%

Exhibit 6.2.   Categorical Outcomes for Personal Skills

Class	Total	Positive Attitude	Creative	Work in Groups	Take Criticism
CA430	7	6	3	5	2
CA350	12	12	5	7	2
CA250	13	8	9	5	1
Total	32	26	17	17	5
			Percentages		
CA430	7	86%	43%	71%	29%
CA350	12	100%	42%	58%	17%
CA250	13	62%	69%	38%	8%
Total	32	81%	53%	53%	16%

dents rated their learning as 4.0 or higher on 9 out of 22 items. Those items were cross-cultural sensitivity, sensitive communication, critical listening, research methods, current issues, public speaking, ethical decision making, professional public relations community, and audience segmentation. Students rated their learning in the category of knowledge as 4.0 or higher on 4 out of 14 items. The four items were diversity, relationships, ethical issues, and multicultural global awareness. Students rated their learning as 4.0 or higher in the category of personal traits on 11 out of 12 items. These items included being responsible, having the ability to adapt while retaining individual identity, showing respect and empathy, being flexible, having a positive attitude, self management, integrity, intellectual curiosity, being a self starter, being creative and pragmatic, and thinking conceptually. Overall students rated their learning as four or higher out of five rankings on more items (11) in the personal traits category than in the categories of knowledge (4) or skills (9). A higher percentage of items in the personal traits category received a score of four or higher. Percentage of items ranked with a 4.0 or higher for each category is represented in Exhibit 6.3, which demonstrates the relative self-reported learning in each area resulting from the service-learning experience.

Students were also asked to rate their abilities in each of the areas. Exhibit 6.4 below indicates how students evaluated their abilities for each of the items from the commission's report using a 5-point scale with 1 indicating poor and 5 indicating excellent.

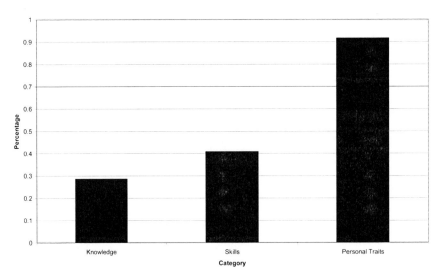

Exhibit 6.3.   Responses of 4.0 greater indicating what students perceived they learned as a result of the service-learning project.

Since service-learning is an interactive and highly contextual experience, these results apply to these students working on these projects with these specific community partners, and they provided useful information. The attributes presented by the commission allow for a vigorous description of learning outcomes that can be implemented to compare learning across projects.

To test if this instrument can be used as a standardized instrument, the researchers undertook a pilot study at another institution with non-PR majors participating in service-learning assignments ($N = 60$). Most of these students were either engineering or aviation majors. Students

Exhibit 6.4.   Public Relations Students' Self Rating of Their Ability

Skills	M	Knowledge of	M
Sensitive communication	4	Relationships	4
Critical listening	4	Diversity	3.86
Cross cultural sensitivity	4	Ethical issues	3.71
Public speaking	3.86	Organizational change	3.57
Persuasive writing	3.71	Research forecast	3.57
Research methods	3.57	Concept strategy	3.43
Community relationship	3.57	Multicultural and global issues	3.43
Ethical decision making	3.57	Social trends	3.43
Prof. PR community	3.57	Public relations theories	3.29
Current issues	3.57	World frameworks	3.14
Problem solving	3.43	Management concepts	3
Information management	3.29	Public relations history	3
Mastery of language	3.29	Marketing and finance	2.57
Management communication	3.29	Legal issues	2.43
Technological literacy	3.29	**Knowledge item average**	**3.32**
Strategic planning	3.14		
Message production	3.14	**Personal Traits**	
Issues management	2.86	Demonstrate respect and empathy	4.67
Audience segmentation	2.86	Responsible	4.57
Environmental monitoring	2.86	Flexible	4.43
Managing people & resources	2.83	Adaptive to situation while retaining identity	4.29
Foreign language	1.14	Positive attitude	4.14
Skills item average	**3.31**	Integrity	4.14
		Self-management	4
		Intellectually curious	4
		Self-starter	4
		Being creative while being pragmatic	4
		Think conceptually	3.86
		Take criticism	3.43
		Personal Traits item average	**4.13**

Exhibit 6.5.   Category Means and Differences Between PR Majors with Non-PR Majors on Self-Reported Abilities

	PR Majors	Non-PR Majors	Differences
Knowledge	3.316	3.152	0.164
Skills	3.311	3.358	−0.048
Personal traits	4.127	3.995	0.132

responded to the survey as a pretest before they engaged in the service-learning projects. As compared to the PR students at the first institution, this instrument revealed some significant differences. In general, the non-PR majors rated their personal traits higher than skills or knowledge, which was consistent with the PR majors. The self rankings by the non-PR majors for personal traits and knowledge items were lower on average than the averages of the PR majors. The non-PR majors rated their skills as slightly higher than the PR students. The largest difference between the means for the two groups was in the area of knowledge, as can be seen in Exhibit 6.5.

T tests were performed to examine differences on individual items and significance at $< .05$ was found for foreign language, diversity, legal issues, public speaking, and managing people and resources. While this comparison is outside of the scope of this paper, the researchers would like to point out the potential for using a standardized instrument for assessing learning outcomes in different service-learning situations.

DISCUSSION

Rama et al. (2000) summarized a broad cross-section of research articles in service-learning including outcome measures for each. The summary illustrates the problem of the lack of reliable, valid, replicable instruments used in current research. Each study addressed some selected attributes using specific operative parameters. The results leave a fragmented picture of what service-learning has accomplished. In some cases, these studies showed conflicting results on similar measures. Part of the problem is the highly contextual and interactive nature of service-learning, which undermines reproducibility. Compounding the problem is the intrinsic difference between quantitative versus qualitative studies. Qualitative data is highly delimited and contextualized, thus making it difficult to compare studies even when the same parameter is studied.

In this study, the researchers struggled with a question originally posed by Dr. Judith Green in the context of K-12 education in the era of outcome accountability mandated by the No Child Left Behind Act, namely, what counts as learning and what learning counts? (Green & Lusk, 2007). Learning outcomes can be assessed from various perspectives including that of the student (Toncar et al., 2006), the faculty (Hesser, 1995), and the employer/professional's perspective (Rama et al., 2000; Stacks et al., 1999). For the same service-learning event, one might get different results from each of the various constituents. The model suggested by Driscoll, Holland, Gelmon, and Kerrigan (1996), involves the constituencies of students, faculty, community, and institution, which provide a more comprehensive assessment.

Compared to many other forms of pedagogy, service-learning is a relatively resource-intensive way to affect student learning. For service-learning to be sustainable, the case must be made for how investing these resources will yield worthwhile results. Support is required from stakeholders. The model presented here provides both a frame and content for discussion with stakeholders. The frame was readily acknowledged and accepted because of the credibility of the Commission on Public Relations Education. Results from implementing the model informed the students, the administration, and the faculty member. Students gained an appreciation of how they stood relative to expectations in the field; administrators gained evidence of what students were learning in the program and how that learning related to job requirements; and the faculty member gained valuable feedback on instructional effectiveness. Since PR was offered as an emphasis within a communication major, and since the offering was less than 2 years old, this structure provided the department with a framework that could be used to rethink course requirements and sequencing.

Institutional support is critical for service-learning sustainability (Bringle & Hatcher, 1996; Holland, 1997). Pritchard (2002) noted:

> The goals of community service-learning do not automatically coincide with the education system at large.... If people with no allegiance to community service-learning control the education system, institutional support for community service-learning may be weak, sporadic or undermined because of other institutionalized commitments. (p.14)

While it is appropriate to conduct service-learning research from the students' or the instructors' perspectives, Pritchard's concern can be addressed by interpreting student and instructor responses within the professional perspective suggested by the Commission on Public Relations Education, which reflects criteria from both practitioners and educators. This particularly applies to public relations and communication education, because both are practice-oriented fields. Using a set of measures grounded in the expectations of professionals combined with expectations of educators, this method introduces the possibility of using a set of common measures that are applicable to the field and that allow for comparisons among different studies. Furthermore, rather than measuring student learning outcomes specific to a project, this assessment approach allows for measuring what the students learned from service-learning involvement, including personal trait development, that exceeds the stated outcomes for the project. It provides indications of job-market readiness and can help inform curriculum improvements.

In this report, the difference in outcome findings is demonstrated using two different methods to analyze the same set of students' reflections, specifically the theme-deduction approach commonly practiced in qualitative research and the outcome measures approach defined by the commission. Meanwhile, a quantitative study using the commission's outcome measures provides a more vigorous display of learning outcomes with a high level of specificity. From a research standpoint, this scale of measurement allows for comparing the results of different service-learning projects. From a practice standpoint, this measurement scale can readily demonstrate to administration the value of this pedagogy, especially when related to course and program outcomes. In this case, service-learning was well received and has been implemented in other courses offered by the department. Results from use of the instrument opened the door to discussion about program requirements. For example, graphic design courses are encouraged earlier in the program so that students are prepared to create deliverables required in upper division courses.

Overall, the results indicate that involvement in service-learning projects had value for students. The qualitative and quantitative methods provided information that both complemented and reinforced each other. When looking at assessment at the course level, these results are consistent with the feedback from community partners and with the grades assigned by the faculty member. Participation in service-learning resulted in students meeting course objectives that corresponded to the project tasks undertaken. Additionally, students gained personal traits that are expected in new hires yet are often not specifically spelled out in program or course objectives. These personal traits can make a difference when graduates interview for positions in the field.

LIMITATIONS OF THE STUDY

The number of subjects in each of the case examples is quite small. While they describe the outcomes in the specific contextual settings, they do not necessarily point to generalizable findings about these service-learning project designs. The case examples presented are intended to illustrate how these criteria might be used to extract a richer set of learning outcomes and can be contrasted against the findings derived from using a more conventional interpretation of reflective comments. In this sense, the paper suggests a methodological approach to enhance the richness of findings in service-learning research.

IMPLICATIONS FOR PRACTICE AND RESEARCH

From a PR program assessment perspective, this framework can be used to indicate areas in which the program has met objectives of the profession and areas where the program might be modified. This instrument provides valuable information to the department, which can be used in reviewing whether or not to modify courses and how to improve the program of study. The assessment of technological and visual literacy, for example, could suggest to the program directors they might look at prerequisite and co-requisite courses in graphic design and Web page development in the suggested program of study. It can also be used for possible course requirement considerations to better prepare students for entry-level positions in public relations. For example, a foreign language requirement might be considered or recommended for students in the program under study here.

Using the instrument to measure communication outcomes for non-PR groups has potential. Currently the instrument is being adapted in another study using only the items relevant to the service-learning project to compare learning outcomes before and after the service-learning project. The preliminary data suggest that the instrument can be adapted to make it applicable for service-learning projects outside of public relations. The pretest findings are particularly useful in understanding these non-PR majors enrolled in communication courses as they arrive with different ranges of skills. This would be helpful in selecting service-learning projects to suit these students and in planning the structure of the service-learning projects. Additionally the results can be used to inform development of appropriate reflective skills and tools for processing the experiences.

In public relations courses, faculty can choose the criteria that most directly apply to the service-learning project. For example, some assignments require persuasive writing, some require teamwork, other assignments require neither. The faculty member can choose the items from the model that best fit the assignment. Assessing the learning on selected parameters still allows for comparisons between similar projects. Depending on the amount of involvement students will have in a project, the instrument could be used to see how students rate their abilities at the start, during the project, and at the completion of the service-learning project. If tailored for a specific service-learning project, it can be used at the start to inform students about the skills and abilities the instructor is looking for in much the same way a rubric is used. The instrument can inform students about the criteria that will be used in evaluation and serve as a guide for them (Vaughn, 2002). Explaining that the instrument was designed with criteria identified by a professional entity sends the message that some objectives of the service-learning project and the course are included to prepare students for the job market. The students gain realistic experience in service-learning and this instrument can help reinforce those real world connections. For example, if students know that taking criticism will be an important aspect of the service-learning project, they will better understand why the opportunity for critical feedback is given and how they can respond to the comments and implement suggestions for their personal development. Receiving negative feedback in a professional manner can be discussed prior to and after feedback is received from the community partner.

Certainly a main benefit of service-learning is that students interact with members of the larger community. Hopefully participants see the opportunities and rewards that can come from engagement of this type. We recognize that a sense of "aha" or wonder occurs with some frequency during service-learning experiences. We cannot measure all of what happens. What we can attempt is to assess the learning that the service-learning project was designed to achieve. The model presented here offered support that student learning outcomes were met for the course. The researchers were somewhat surprised by the extent to which students improved their abilities in the area of personal traits. Those soft skills were not addressed in the course objectives, but certainly are valuable characteristics for graduates when they look for positions in the field.

CONCLUSION

Service-learning involves multiple stakeholders. While student reflections have been an integral part of service-learning assessment and are the most commonly used source of data, service-learning research can be more dynamic if one uses a broader assessment frame. Multiple perspectives in outcome assessment may be performed to provide a more comprehensive view of service-learning. Driscoll et al. (1996) identified and gathered assessment information from four perspectives.

1. The faculty perspective is well documented in the literature (Abes, Jackson, & Jones, 2002; Eyler & Giles, 1999). Faculty may assess the students' prior knowledge, current content taught in the cur-

riculum, question(s) posed with the assignment, quality of the students' products, and how that quality compares to the expectation of the faculty member.

2. Community partner perspectives are less well documented, but are receiving attention (Panici & Lasky, 2002; Worrall, 2007). Community partners may assess various components including students' work. This feedback is both useful and appreciated. It can, however, be difficult to assess the assessor's reference points as these depend on prior experience; expectations of input and deliverables; and impressions of personal interaction, technical competence, and professionalism.

3. The students themselves often provide the perspective used in assessment (Rama et al., 2000). They can assess their skills, abilities, the project, and their learning. Students' reflective statements and survey responses were utilized in this study.

4. The institution offers another perspective. Institutions benefit from assessing service-learning as a pedagogical strategy. Service is important for many institutions in their outreach to the community, and because of this, tools are needed that provide useful feedback on the effectiveness of that service (Driscoll et al., 1996; Oster-Aaland, 2004).

5. An additional angle of vision presented here is that of the professionals, the future employers of these students. They form an important constituent because employers give external feedback on the overall effectiveness of educational programs. Employers, represented by practitioners in the report, are an essential stakeholder because they hire graduates (Rama et al., 2000; Stacks et al., 1999).

Under each of these scenarios, the common theme is that assessment requires prudent selection of measurement parameters and reference perspectives. Instruments that are discipline specific make the assessment process more readily understood and accepted by stakeholders. This paper shows how the researchers constructed methodological grounding using the parameters described in the 2006 Commission on Public Relations Education Report as the measurement construct. This framework may serve as a more consistent way to measure and report outcomes from different service-learning projects in public relations and related areas. By nature, service-learning is a moving target due to the interactive and contextual variables. A consistent model of assessment based on criteria specific to the discipline may increase the comparability and reproducibility of service-learning research within that discipline.

ACKNOWLEDGMENT

We want to thank Chadron State College for awarding a grant from Learn and Serve America to implement the service-learning project with Indian Health Service.

APPENDIX A:
THE PROFESSIONAL BOND—
PUBLIC RELATIONS EDUCATION AND THE PRACTICE

Knowledge	*Personal Traits*
• Communication and persuasion concepts and strategies	• Responsible
• Communication and Public Relations theories	• Flexible
• Relationships and relationship-building	• Professionally oriented self-managers
• Societal trends	• Respond and adapt without giving up personal identity
• Ethical issues	• Intellectually curious
• Legal requirements and issues	• Think conceptually
• Marketing and finance	• Positive attitude
• Public Relations history	• Take criticism
• Uses of research and forecasting	• Organized self-starters who take initiative
• Multicultural and global issues	• Creative and pragmatic
• The business case for diversity	• Integrity
• Various world social, political, economic and historical frameworks	• Respect and empathy
• Organizational change and development	
• Management concepts and theories	

Skills	
• Research methods and analysis	• Managing people, programs, and resources
• Management of information	• Sensitive interpersonal communication
• Mastery of language in written and oral communication	• Critical listening skills
• Problem solving and negotiation	• Fluency in a foreign language
• Management of communication	• Ethical decision making
• Strategic planning	• Participation in the professional public relations community
• Issues management	• Message production
• Audience segmentation	• Working with current issues
• Informative and persuasive writing	• Environmental monitoring
• Community, consumer and employee relations and other practice areas	• Public speaking and presentation
• Technological and visual literacy	• Applying cross-cultural and cross-gender sensitivity

REFERENCES

Abes, E. S., Jackson, G., & Jones, S. R. (2002). Factors that motivate and deter faculty use of service-learning. *Michigan Journal of Community Service Learning, 9*(1), 5-17.

Astin, A. W., & Sax, L. J. (1998). How undergraduates are affected by service participation. *Journal of College Student Development, 39*(3), 251-263.

Bringle, R. G., & Hatcher, J. A. (1996). Implementing service-learning in higher education. *The Journal of Higher Education, 67*(2), 221-239.

Commission on Public Relations Education. (2006). *The 2006 Report of the Commission on Public Relations Education: A Professional Bond.* Retrieved March 20, 2007, from http://www.commpred.org/report/

Driscoll, A., Holland, B., Gelmon, S., & Kerrigan, S. (1996). An assessment model for service-learning: Comprehensive case studies of impact on faculty, students, community, and institution. *Michigan Journal of Community Service Learning, 3*, 66-71.

Eyler, J., & Giles, D. E. (1999). *Where's the learning in service-learning?* San Francisco: Jossey-Bass.

Green, J., & Luke, A. (2007). Rethinking learning: What counts as learning and what learning counts. *Review of Research in Education, 30*, xi-xiv.

Hamilton, S. F., & Zeldin, R. S. (1987). Learning civics in the community. *Curriculum Inquiry, 17*(4), 407-420.

Hesser, G. (1995). Faculty assessment of student learning: Outcomes attributed to service-learning and evidence of changes in faculty attitudes about experiential education. *Michigan Journal of Community Service Learning, 2*, 33-42.

Holland, B. (1997). Analyzing institutional commitment to service: A model of key organizational factors. *Michigan Journal of Community Service Learning, 4*, 30-41.

Nespor, J. (2006). Finding patterns with field notes. In J. Green., G. Camilli, & P. Elmore (Eds.), *Complimentary methods for research in education* (pp. 297-308). Washington, DC: American Educational Research Association/Erlbaum.

Marshall, C., & Rossman, G. (1995). *Designing qualitative research* (2nd ed.). Thousand Oaks, CA: Sage Publications.

Oster-Aaland, L. K., Sellnow, T. L., Nelson, P. E., & Pearson, J. C. (2004). The status of service learning in departments of communication: A follow-up study. *Communication Education, 53*(4), 348-356.

Panici, D., & Lasky, K. (2002). Service-learning's foothold in communication scholarship. *Journalism and Mass Communication Educator, 57*(2), 113-125.

Patterson, S. A. (2004). How service-learning enhances your PR program. *Public Relations Tactics, 11*(4), 23.

Pritchard, I. A. (2002). Community service and service-learning in America: The state of the art. In A. Furco & S. Billig (Eds.), *Service-learning: The essence of the pedagogy* (pp. 3-22). Greenwich, CT: Information Age.

Rama, D. V., Ravenscroft, S. P., Wolcott, S. K., & Zlotkowski, E. (2000). Service-learning outcomes: Guidelines for educators and researchers. *Issues in Accounting Education, 15*(4), 657-692.

Stacks, D. W., Botan, C., & Van Slyke Turk, J. (1999). Perceptions of public relations education. *Public Relations Review, 25*(1), 9-28.

Toncar, M. F., Reid, J. S., Burns, D. J., Anderson, C. E., & Nguyen, H. P. (2006). Uniform assessment of the benefits of service-learning: The development, evaluation, and implementation of the SELEB scale. *Journal of Marketing Theory and Practice, 14*(3), 223-238.

Vaughn, P. M. (2002). *Enhancing student development in service-learning with performance-based assessment rubrics.* Unpublished doctoral dissertation, Arizona State University (UMI Microform 3043835).

Worrall. L. (2007). Asking the community: A case study of community partner perspectives. *Michigan Journal of Community Service Learning, 14*(1), 5-17.

PART IV

SERVICE-LEARNING AND ETHICS EDUCATION

CHAPTER 7

BUILDING ETHICAL CITIZEN SCHOLARS

Student Success in Service-Learning

Susan Waters and Elizabeth Carmichael Burton

This research investigates the extent to which service-learning impacts the moral development of college students, and in particular their personal interests, concern for humanity, and beliefs about justice. Using a quasi-experimental design, survey responses of 56 students who participated in a service-learning course were compared to 35 students who did not participate in a service-learning course to determine if there were differences in moral reasoning and ethical standards applied to a set of prompts representing ethical dilemmas. In addition, the study compared students' responses to the survey with responses provided by community members and business partners to compare moral development levels of the 3 groups. Results indicated that service-learning had a positive impact on students' sense of ethics, community partners were highly developed in postconventional moral reasoning, and business leaders were highly developed in conventional reasoning.

Scholarship for Sustaining Service-Learning and Civic Engagement
pp. 163–183
Copyright © 2008 by Information Age Publishing
All rights of reproduction in any form reserved.

INTRODUCTION

In the university environment, student success is often equated with student retention. Several authors, however (Berkowitz & Fekula, 1999; Evenbeck & Hamilton, 2006; Kuh, 2007; Kuh, Kinzie, Schuh, & Whitt, 2005; Pascarella & Terenzini, 1991); take a larger view of student success in higher education, citing the importance of the university in fostering multiple aspects of student development, including academic, moral, and social-emotional development. Factors such as the external learning environment and interactions within the community can facilitate this kind of student success and increase the university's effectiveness. Studies have shown, for example, that institutions of higher education that have integrated curricula and offer students opportunities to participate in civic engagement or service-learning demonstrate a positive influence on the students, including expected gains in overall moral development, judgment, values acquisition and reasoning, and contributing to the success of the student (Kenny, Simon, Kiley-Brabeck, & Lerner, 2002; Pascarella & Terenzini, 1991). Not enough is known about how this type of student success can be nurtured and the role that service-learning can play in fostering students' moral development.

The purpose of this research is to examine whether students in a United States public 4-year, comprehensive university show changes in their moral reasoning, judgment, and values acquisition as a result of their engagement in service-learning activities within their college. In addition, the research investigates ethical perspectives of community partners and business leaders. The present study is an example of students participating in service-learning who acquired new views resulting in an increase in moral judgment, especially the acquisition of more sophisticated thinking and rejection of simplistic thinking, while a comparison group of students only increased to the stage of understanding the necessity of laws and a sense of duty. This chapter starts with a review of the literature, then includes a presentation of the methods used, and finally the results of the study. Discussion of results and suggestions for future research are presented at the end of the chapter.

Service-Learning at Missouri State University

Bringle, Philips, and Hudson (2004) define service-learning as a "course based, credit-bearing educational experience in which students (a) participate in an organized service activity that meets identified community needs and (b) reflect on the service activity in such a way as to gain further understanding of course content, a broader appreciation of the discipline, and an enhanced sense of civic responsibility" (p. 5). Service-learning offers experience in multiple contexts for solving complex issues in the community (Eyler & Giles, 1999) and helps attain two goals: benefit to the community (agency, clients, city, neighborhood, etc.) and benefit to the instructor in helping him or her reach specific educational objectives. Service-learning allows students to apply theories learned in the class-room to real-life situations. Reflection activities such as journals or small group discussions enable the students to connect their community service activities to their academic activities, thereby providing experiences that can be further explored, studied, and analyzed (Bringle et al., 2004).

Learning through "hands-on" experience is beneficial to students because this enables them to utilize the knowledge learned in the class-room and teaches them how to resolve and respond to real issues. Critical reflective thought can add new meaning to service experiences, enrich the academic content of the course, and develop students' abilities to take informed actions in the future (Dewey, 1916, 1933; Hatcher & Bringle, 1997). As students engage in humanitarian projects, they not only acquire relevant work experience related to their studies, but also attain a higher level of ethical principles and personal satisfaction of achievement. Even-beck and Hamilton (2006) recognize that students participating in service-learning increased in their overall classroom knowledge and skills, and enhanced overall student learning and engagement. These authors believe that "service-learning has become one of the most powerful peda-gogies in undergraduate education. It not only fuses attitude, behavior, and cognition, but also builds for citizenship" (p. 19).

The Office of Citizenship and Service-Learning (CASL) at Missouri State University was created to have a central role in helping the univer-sity fulfill its mission in public affairs and obligations as a metropolitan university. The state general assembly granted our university its statewide mission in public affairs in 1995 and CASL was adopted in 1996 with a mission requiring a campuswide commitment to foster competence and responsibility in the common vocation of citizenship and "developing educated persons." In supporting faculty, students, and community part-ners in service-learning, the CASL office seeks to enhance experiential learning that results in engaged citizenship and advances teaching peda-gogy to improve student learning in all participating disciplines. Beyond this, CASL helps the university share its resources (i.e., faculty, staff, and students), with the community, impacting the community in a positive manner. The primary rudiments of the CASL program are the courses taught by faculty, each of which feature service-learning as a significant pedagogical approach. The CASL Oversight Committee, comprised of one faculty member from each college, monitors and evaluates the CASL program.

Students interested in earning academic credit for meaningful and productive community service have two options: the (1) component course or the (2) integrated service-learning course. In the component course, students earn an additional credit in selected courses in exchange for the learning acquired by completing 40 hours of service that is relevant to course content and benefits an external government or nonprofit agency. A student who desires the service-learning option will simultaneously register for the service-learning designated course and the service-learning component course. The service-learning credit is awarded for the demonstration of learning that results from the service rather than the service itself. A reflection component is key to the critical thinking that a student will engage in during the experiential learning with the community partner.

The second option, the integrated service-learning course, has all of the aspects of experiential education, reflection, and assessment integrated into the substance of the course. The community service experiences of the students are an integral part of the course. Credit is assigned for both the customary academic learning as well as for a minimum of 15 hours of service with a community partner. The student's grade is for the quality of learning as identified through reflection mechanisms determined by the course instructor. The integrated service-learning option treats service-learning as another academic project in the course, on par with an exam, research paper, or other such project.

Community partners, students, and faculty engage in what Boyer (1990) has termed *the scholarship of engagement* at Missouri State University. For 11 years, the CASL program has supported faculty in their careers of scholarship, community partners with agency needs, and students in their academic and civic goals. The public affairs theme at our university nurtures a learning environment where civic virtue is celebrated and practiced, where citizenship obligations are explored and encouraged, and where the capacity and commitment to think about the public implications of private behavior is cultivated.

The Promise of Service-Learning as a Strategy for Moral Development

Service-learning is connected to moral development because it extends students' concerns beyond themselves as they fulfill the needs of an organization (Markus, Howard, & King, 1993). Service-learning work is typically with a not-for-profit organization and thus students are taking care of others and working toward a selfless cause, an "education in citizenship." Students work in teams and strive to exercise professional ethics

that coincide with the moral standards of the university and the organization with which the students are engaged. Students represent the university and ideally embody the university's mission while applying skills
taught in the college setting (Kirk & Riedle, 2005). Service-learning during college exposes students to a broader world and thus nurtures moral
development (Gorman & Duffy, 1994; Markus et al., 1993).

In a pilot study conducted at Boston College, students who engaged in
a service-learning course increased in their moral reasoning compared to
a comparison group (Gorman & Duffy, 1994). The study had flaws, however, since the pretest was administered at mid-semester, rather than at
the beginning of the course and effects may have already occurred. In
addition, the students who participated in community projects were all
enrolled in a social responsibility course that discussed social injustice and
philosophical theories in contrast to the comparison group of students
who were enrolled in a Western culture course.

In a similar study, Boss (1994) tested students' moral development as a
class requirement during an ethics course, comparing one class of students engaged in community service work to another class with no intervention. Boss found that there was a significant gain in the moral
reasoning of the students who served within the community and no gain
in the comparison group. She included a discussion of relevant moral
dilemmas in the classroom, which developed cognitive reasoning and
indicated this discussion was necessary for a change from conventional to
post-conventional moral reasoning.

Through exposure to service-learning, students continue to increase
moral development and reasoning through their new civic responsibilities
and social interactions (Pascarella & Terenzini, 1991; Schaffer, Paris, &
Vogel, 2003). By combining outreach scholarship, moral development,
and personal satisfaction (derived from the acquisition of skills during
external engagement), a student is motivated to involve himself or herself
in purposeful civic activities throughout his or her post-college career
(Kenny et al., 2002).

Mentkowski and Associates (2000) indicate that some critics propose
university students are too old to be taught ethics (see also Bebeau, 2002);
however, the present study illustrates this is not the case. Skoe and von
der Lippe (2002) offer the following explanation as to why moral development continues throughout college:

> As people grow older, they likely go though various experiences that initiate
> thinking and re-evaluation of life, self, and relationship. For example, in the
> beginning of young adulthood people usually encounter life issues with
> which they have to deal as independent adults without direct parental medi-
> ation or support. This is generally the period in which home leaving is
> achieved, serious career decisions must be confronted, and long-term rela-

tionships may be established for the first time ... [these] crises both reveal and create character. (p. 487)

The rationale for how and why service-learning promotes moral development may be found in cognitive development literature. Piaget (1932) claimed that children have two primary types of moral judgment: a young child will value authoritarianism and an older child will develop a concern for society. He believed that the "child should act on his environment" (Ginsberg & Opper, 1969, p. 230), and conducted multiple studies whose results supported Dewey's (1963) "philosophy of experience," that shows that morality is developed through experience (Brandenberger, 2005).

According to Kohlberg's theory of moral development (1971, 1981), college subjects an individual to an array of new experiences, new social relationships, a new independent lifestyle, and a need for self-reliance. These factors can generate positive cognitive moral conflict from new perspectives, resulting in a greater influence on a student's moral development (Pascarella & Terenzini, 1991). Kohlberg developed a six-stage model with three levels (1971) based on Piaget's ideas that describes the development of moral reasoning and illustrates how rationale for moral choices grows over time (Cabot, 2005). In this theory, Kohlberg notes that individuals advance at their own rate, not necessarily finishing at the highest stage (Callery, 1990). Stage one is the lowest stage establishing the preconventional level where individuals focus on themselves and conduct moral action merely to avoid punishment. Stage two is concerned with satisfying one's own needs and how fairness affects an individual personally. Stage three initiates the conventional level and equates good behavior with pleasing and helping others, whereas stage four emphasizes showing respect for authority as one's duty. Stage five starts the principled level and allows the individual to choose what is right based on societal consensus. Stage six is the highest level where individuals abide by collective principles, having a strong sense of personal ethics (Cabot, 2005; Good, 1998; Turiel & Rothman, 1972).

The present study utilizes Rest, Cooper, Coder, Masanz, and Anderson's adaptation (1974) of the Kohlberg typology. Rest was a student of Kohlberg and developed the Neo-Kohlbergian approach, arguing that Kohlberg's six-stage model failed to address issues of moral sensitivity or incentives for individuals to act morally (Cabot, 2005). Rest (1979a) defined moral reasoning as "a particular type of social value, that having to do with how humans cooperate in the service of furthering human welfare and how they adjudicate conflict among individual interests" (p. 3).

STUDY DESIGN

This research seeks to inform the higher educational community about the benefits of service-learning for the development of moral reasoning of students. The study investigates the hypothesis that students will increase in their ethical development after participating in a service-learning intervention during one semester as compared to students without the intervention. As an exploratory analysis, the study also investigated the extent to which student scores in both the treatment and comparison groups were similar to or different from directors/leaders in the nonprofit or profit arena. The rationale for examining these issues is to understand whether not-for-profit directors can possibly influence students' ethical development. A secondary rationale was to distinguish if the nonprofit directors' moral development was similar to or different than leaders in the for-profit business community, given that service-learning students are typically placed with a nonprofit organization rather than a for-profit organization.

Method

Sample

The pool from which the service-learning student sample for this study was drawn was comprised of university students enrolled in a service-learning course in any subject matter during the fall of 2006. Six hundred eighty-one students participated in component or integrated service-learning courses in each of the university's six colleges during that semester. The Office of Citizenship and Service-Learning randomly selected courses in which sophomores and seniors were enrolled and several instructors administered the survey in upper level integrated service-learning courses. A total of 56 students completed the pre- and postsurvey out of the 153 component and integrated service-learning students who were asked to participate, with a 37 percent response rate. No lecture or discussion of ethics or morality was provided in any of the classes and the students were not aware of the hypotheses of the study.

A comparison group of university students not enrolled in any service-learning courses was randomly selected from sophomores to seniors across all six colleges. A total of 35 students out of a total of 51 students from three different classes completed the pre- and postsurvey, with a 69 percent response rate. Faculty members were briefed not to discuss the hypotheses of the study and the comparison group of students had no ethical discussion or training in their classes.

The survey was also mailed to 150 directors of not-for-profit organizations with whom the university partners. Thirty-nine directors of non-profit organizations completed the survey, with a 26% response rate. The Office of Citizenship and Service-Learning (CASL) obtained the list of the Springfield Area Chamber of Commerce's 1,970 members. In addition, a random list of 200 businesses was selected to receive the survey. Thirty-eight business leaders in the community completed the survey with a 19% response rate.

Measures

To measure ethical development, the Defining Issues Test 2 (DIT2) survey instrument was used, revised from the former 30-year-old DIT. The Defining Issues Test (Rest et al., 1974) was a written paper and pencil test created to measure moral comprehension (Narvaez & Bock, 2002) based on Kohlberg's theory (1971, 1981). The original moral judgment interviews developed by Kohlberg were long, and respondents had difficulty staying on track with moral issues. In addition, assessing the interviews was a lengthy process and hampered by the difficulty for researchers to objectively assess participants' varied responses (Rest et al., 1974). The DIT and DIT2 allow for standardized responses rooted in recognition (Gorman & Duffy, 1994; Rest et al., 1974; Rest, Narvaez, Thoma, & Bebeau, 1999c).

The DIT2 is shorter in length than the DIT with five moral scenarios instead of six. The measure, retaining more participants through participant reliability checks, does not sacrifice validity, and contains more detailed instructions than those in the DIT (Rest, Narvaez, Bebeau, & Thoma, 1999b). Beyond these differences, the tests function in highly similar fashion (Cabot, 2005). Both tests analyze moral reasoning and moral judgment by presenting theoretical moral dilemmas. The DIT and DIT2 allow researchers to gather information on the personal construction of respondents (i.e., the participant's ideas on values, rights, civic obligations, integrity, and social structure). Changes in ratings of ethics are viewed as linear development that is fluid and continuous, and moral stages are not labeled as better or worse (Rest et al., 1999b).

Narvaez and Bock (2002) assert that Rest provides greater support for stages five (social contract orientation) and six (universal ethics principle) in Kohlberg's model than earlier measures that were used. Thoma, Barnett, Rest, and Narvaez (1999) claim that the tests also have the potential to determine one's political affiliation, religious beliefs, class, ethnic background, standards of work ethic, geographic region, and social background, although the tests primarily assess moral development.

Interpretation of the DIT2

Respondents interpret the DIT2 by comparing the scenarios listed to preexisting mental structures called schemas. Schemas are knowledge structures that exist to help individuals to compare current stimuli to past experience and are necessary to organize incoming cognitive data and stimuli gathered empirically (Narvaez & Bock, 2002). Schemas set standards that help individuals in moral decision making and are stored in long-term memory (Rest, Narvaez, Bebeau, & Thoma, 1999a). The DIT2 measures shifts in three types of moral schemas that take place during early adulthood, contributing to moral judgment development.

The first schema measured is the *Personal Interest Schema*, which is derived from Kohlberg's stages two and three, conveying individualism and exchange (stage two) and good interpersonal relationships (stage three). The Personal Interest Schema reflects underdeveloped thinking in which individuals are concerned with self-preservation and reacting to impulses. Individuals are considering micromorality as a whole, but have not yet advanced to take society into account (Narvaez & Bock, 2002; Rest et al., 1999a). Kohlberg's stage one of obedience and punishment orientation was not used.[1]

The *Maintaining Norms Schema* emerges during adolescence and reflects Kohlberg's stage four—maintaining the social order. Young adults begin to have concern for humanity outside of friends and family. How people should be treated is considered and a newfound respect for authority develops (Rest et al., 1999a). Individuals begin to need rules and norms to function effectively and understand the necessity of laws; moreover, a sense of duty emerges (Narvaez & Bock, 2002).

The *Postconventional Schema* is the third schema examined and reflects Kohlberg's stage five—social contract and individual rights, and also stage six—universal principles. The Postconventional Schema involves making the world just and sharing the universal ideal. Individuals are presented the opportunity to become advocates of change based on their sense of morality and beliefs in human rights. For this schema, the individual considers the validity of laws and rules. Macromorality comes into play as individuals progress from self-concern to awareness of others to awareness of society as a whole (Narvaez & Bock, 2002; Rest et al., 1999a). This is the peak of moral judgment development (Derryberry & Thoma, 2005) as described by Rest et al. (1999a):

> The defining characteristic of postconventional thinking is that rights and duties are based on sharable ideals for organizing cooperation in society, and are open to debate and tests of logical consistencies, experience of the community, and coherence with accepted practice. (p. 41)

Finally, the *N2 index* combines two schemas: the *Postconventional Schema* and the *Personal Interest Schema*. The N2 score investigates "the degree to which Postconventional items are prioritized ... plus the degree to which Personal Interest items (lower stage items) receive lower ratings than the ratings given to Postconventional items (higher stage items)" (Bebeau & Thoma, 2003, p. 19). Two effects are evident from the N2 score: acquisition of a more sophisticated thinking and rejection of simplistic thinking.

The survey has reliability checks integrated into the system. Cronbach alpha for the P score and the N2 score is in the upper .70s to low .80s with test-retest reliability about the same. Further, the DIT2 shows discriminant validity from verbal ability/general intelligence; that is, the information in a DIT2 score predicts to the validity criteria above and beyond that accounted for by verbal ability. The DIT2 is equally valid for males and females (Bebeau & Thoma, 2003).

Data Analysis

To compare the ethical developmental levels of service-learning students and the comparison students, one-way analysis of variance (ANOVA) and paired samples *t* tests were used. Difference scores between the two groups on ethical development levels were determined. Differences between genders were also explored. The dependent variable was moral development defined as four schemas: personal interest, maintaining norms, postconventional, and N2.

RESULTS

The means and standard deviations for the service-learning and nonservice-learning participants are presented in Exhibit 7.1. The results for the ANOVA indicated a significant time effect, Wilk's Λ = .83, $F(4, 52)$ = 2.76, $p < .05$, partial η^2 = .18 for the service-learning participants. Four paired-samples *t* tests were computed to assess differences between moral development schemas at the two time intervals. A difference in mean rating of moral development between the pre- and postsurvey was significantly different for the N2 index, $t(55) = -2.16$, $p < .05$, partial η^2 = .08.

The results for the ANOVA for students who did not participate in service-learning indicated no difference over time, Wilk's Λ = .74, $F(4, 27) = 2.40$, $p > .05$, partial η^2 = .27. On the four paired-samples *t* tests used to assess differences between moral development schemas at the two time intervals, differences in mean rating of moral development between the pre- and post-survey were significantly different for the personal interest schema, $t(30) = 2.91$, $p < .01$, partial η^2 = .22, and the maintain-

Exhibit 7.1.   Service-Learning (SL) Students' Schemas' Ratings at Beginning and End of Semester (n = 56 matched pairs) Compared to Control (C) Students' (n = 31 matched pairs) Ratings

Schema	Mean at Beginning	Mean at End	Mean Difference	SD	t	Sig.
SL Personal interest	25.43	23.79	1.64	12.56	0.98	0.33
C Personal interest*	30.00	24.15	5.85	11.19	2.91	0.01
SL Maintaining norms	38.24	38.48	−0.24	15.93	−0.11	0.91
C Maintaining norms*	32.97	38.00	−5.03	12.72	−2.20	0.04
SL Post-conventional	30.73	30.90	−0.16	15.33	−0.08	0.94
C Post-conventional	31.48	32.68	−1.20	12.99	−0.51	0.61
SL N2* index	28.93	34.27	−5.35	18.49	−2.16	0.03
C N2 index	29.46	31.65	−2.19	12.01	−1.01	0.32
SL Total	30.83	31.86	−1.03	5.60	−1.36	0.18
C Total	30.98	31.62	−0.64	3.67	−0.97	0.34

Note: *Means for pre- and posttest results differ significantly, $p < 0.05$.

ing norms schema, $t(30) = -2.20$, $p < .05$, partial $\eta^2 = .14$. A comparison of the total gain of both the service-learning and comparison group using a repeated measures multivariate analysis of variance (MANOVA) showed no significant differences, $F(8, 76) = 3.71$, $p < .05$, partial $\eta^2 = .28$.

As shown in Exhibit 7.1, the comparison students had a statistically significant decrease in scores of 5.85 on the personal interest schema, when compared to the service-learning students who reported a decrease of 1.64 in the personal interest schema. The comparison students made a statistically significant gain of 5.03 on the measure of maintaining norms, compared to the service-learning students with a gain of .24. These results are similar to Boss's (1994) findings that showed comparison students moved to a higher level of conventional reasoning rather than moving toward postconventional reasoning.

The service-learning and control group of students were similar in their gains in the postconventional schema; however, the service-learning students had a significant gain of 5.35 in the N2 index when compared to the control group, which only experienced a slight gain. The hypothesis that ethical variables will be stronger among the service-learning students was thus partially supported because of the significant increase in the N2 index of the service-learning students when compared to no increase in the N2 index by the nonparticipating group of students.

Gender was found to be not a significant influence for ethical development of any of the groups, although females were significantly represented more than males in all groups. A one-way within subjects ANOVA indicated a significant main effect for personal interest, Wilk's $\Lambda = .83$, $F(2,34) = 3.50$, $p < .05$, partial $\eta^2 = .17$, with a significant linear effect, $F(1, 35) = 6.69$, $p < .05$, partial $\eta^2 = .16$; and a significant main effect for maintaining norms, Wilk's $\Lambda = .84$, $F(2,34) = 3.27$, $p = .05$, partial $\eta^2 = .16$, with a significant linear effect, $F(1, 35) = 5.20$, $p < .05$, partial $\eta^2 = .13$.

An additional one-way within subjects ANOVA was calculated to evaluate the difference between the students participating in service-learning and the community partners and business leaders on ethical development schema ratings without the independent variable of gender. The results for the ANOVA indicated a nonsignificant personal interest multivariate effect, Wilk's $\Lambda = .88$, $F(2, 35) = 2.36$, $p > .05$, partial $\eta^2 = .12$, with a significant linear effect, $F(1, 36) = 4.86$, $p < .05$, partial $\eta^2 = .12$; a significant maintaining norms multivariate effect, Wilk's $\Lambda = .80$, $F(2, 35) = 4.42$, $p < .05$, partial $\eta^2 = .20$, with a significant linear effect, $F(1, 36) = 6.58$, $p < .05$, partial $\eta^2 = .15$; a non-significant postconventional multivariate effect, Wilk's $\Lambda = .88$, $F(2, 35) = 2.37$, $p > .05$, partial $\eta^2 = .12$, with a significant quadratic effect, $F(1, 36) = 4.85$, $p < .05$, partial $\eta^2 = .12$; and a non-significant N2 index multivariate effect, Wilk's $\Lambda = .97$, $F(2, 35) = 2.36$, $p > .05$, partial $\eta^2 = .03$.

The linear and quadratic effects necessitated computing 12 paired-samples t tests to assess differences of moral development schema ratings among the three groups. As displayed in Exhibit 2, the results indicate that the mean for service-learning students' personal interest schema ($M = 23.42$, $SD = 12.37$) was significantly greater than the mean for business leaders' (BL) personal interest schema ($M = 17.19$, $SD = 10.72$), $t(36) = 2.21$, $p < .05$; the mean for the BL maintaining norms schema ($M = 43.96$, $SD = 14.57$) was significantly greater than the mean for service-learning students maintaining norms schema ($M = 36.51$, $SD = 13.33$), $t(36) = -2.56$, $p < .05$; the mean for the BL maintaining norms schema ($M = 43.96$, SD = 14.57) was significantly greater than the mean for community partners (CP) maintaining norms schema ($M = 35.14$, $SD = 15.38$), $t(36) = -2.40$, $p < .05$; the mean for the CP postconventional schema ($M = 41.18$, $SD = 14.41$) was significantly greater than the mean for the service-learning students postconventional schema ($M = 33.28$, $SD = 15.90$), $t(38) = -2.29$, $p < .05$; and the mean for the CP postconventional schema ($M = 41.38$, $SD = 14.77$) was significantly greater than the mean for the BL postconventional schema ($M = 32.88$, $SD = 14.87$), $t(36) = 2.11$, $p < .05$.

The community partners were found to be significantly higher in their moral development of the postconventional schema than were both students and business owners/directors. This may indicate that these com-

Exhibit 7.2. Means and Standard Deviations of Service-Learning Students' (SL) Schemas Ratings at End of Semester (n = 56 Matched Pairs), Business Leaders' (BL) Ratings (n = 38), and Community Partners' (CP) Ratings (n = 39) in Paired Samples

Schema	Mean	SD	Schema	Mean	SD
Pair 1			*Pair 7**		
SL Personal interest	23.61	12.07	SL Postconventional	33.28	15.90
CP Personal interest	20.18	11.29	CP Postconventional	41.18	14.41
Pair 2			*Pair 8**		
BL Personal interest	17.19	10.72	BL Postconventional	32.88	14.87
CP Personal interest	20.12	11.39	CP Postconventional	41.38	14.77
Pair 3*			*Pair 9*		
SL Personal interest	23.42	12.37	SL Postconventional	34.47	15.42
BL Personal interest	17.19	10.72	BL Postconventional	32.88	14.87
Pair 4			*Pair 10*		
SL Maintain norms	37.04	13.63	SL N2 index	36.99	17.38
CP Maintain norms	35.05	14.98	CP N2 index	38.28	14.78
Pair 5*			*Pair 11*		
BL Maintain norms	43.96	14.57	BL N2 index	34.95	13.63
CP Maintain norms	35.14	15.38	CP N2 index	38.75	14.88
Pair 6*			*Pair 12*		
SL Maintain norms	36.51	13.33	SL N2 index	37.89	17.39
BL Maintain norms	43.96	14.57	BL N2 index	34.95	13.63

Note: *The means for two groups differ significantly, $p < 0.05$.

munity partners possibly can serve as highly ethical role models for students. The business leaders were found to be significantly higher in the maintaining norms schema than were both students and community partners, demonstrating that they understood the necessity of laws and a sense of duty. Finally, the students who participated in service-learning were found to be significantly higher in personal interest than the business leaders, indicating that they were concerned with self-preservation.

DISCUSSION

This study examined moral judgment development in students who were enrolled in service-learning courses for one semester compared to a group of students not enrolled in such a course at a large midwestern university. The DIT2 survey instrument was used to measure moral judgment development and utilized Rest's (1979b) ethical stages taken from Kohlberg's theory, which Rest identified as the Personal Interest Schema, Maintaining Norms Schema, Postconventional Schema, and the N2 Index. Gender was explored as a confounding factor and was found to have no significant effect on outcomes.

The hypothesis that service-learning participation will impact students' moral development was partially supported by the significant rise in the N2 index after the service-learning intervention when compared to the nonparticipating group. The N2 index demonstrates the increase from the Personal Interest Schema, the lowest stage, to the Postconventional Schema, the highest stage, and illustrates the acquisition of a more sophisticated thinking (i.e., moving toward Postconventional) and rejection of simplistic thinking (i.e., moving away from Personal Interest) by the students who participated in service-learning. This increase in N2 index scores did not occur with the comparison students; instead, they showed a significant rise in the Maintaining Norms Schema, the middle stage, which is not as highly developed as the Postconventional Schema. They also had a significant drop in the Personal Interest Schema, which suggests these students function most effectively with rules, norms, and laws. Moreover, the community partners were significantly higher in the Postconventional Schema, the highest stage, than either the business leaders or the students.

Moral Development of Not-For-Profit Directors Versus For-Profit Directors

The not-for-profit community partners were found to be significantly more ethically developed than any of the other groups that were examined. This might be the case because employees in the nonprofit sector form a shared culture of values, norms and beliefs, which identifies what is morally acceptable in the organization (Agarwal & Malloy, 1999). Nonprofits act as vehicles from which employees can promote personal ethics and societal ideals, consequently, reporting great job satisfaction, and tending to feel as if their work contributes to the organizational mission (Brower & Shrader, 2000; Mirvis & Hackett, 1983). It is generally assumed that nonprofit directors typically focus on the betterment of society (Wang & Coffey, 1992) and have a "heightened sense of accountability to the community and the clients to act honestly and in their best interest" (Brower & Shrader, 2000, p. 148). This selfless attitude of employees may be linked to postconventional thinking that concentrates on problem solving strategies to handle ethical issues and awareness of moral problems that can influence the reasoning and judgment process with the opportunity to become an advocate of change. Furthermore, perhaps adults self-select their careers based on their moral values. This explanation could provide one reason for the difference in this study of the findings of medium moral ethical standards of business leaders when compared to the high ethical standards of nonprofit directors.

On the other hand, Brower and Shrader (2000) found that agency theory suggests for-profit organizations have conflicting demands from stakeholders such as generating profits, being a good citizen, taking care of employees, and delivering a high quality product. The authority lies with the directors who act on the behalf of the stakeholders, those being the shareholders and managers (Monks & Minnow, 1989) and brings extrinsic rewards. Stewardship theory is in contrast to agency theory and in this theory directors are presumed to act by intrinsic motivation in the best interests of the organization (Davis, Schoorman, & Donaldson, 1997). Brower and Shrader examined a very small sample of not-for-profit board members and for-profit board members using the DIT to measure their ethical reasoning and found that the two groups of board members did not differ significantly in their levels of moral reasoning (see also Jeffrey & Weatherholt, 1996). Also, as an extra measurement section for the DIT, Brower and Shrader created several business scenarios that reflected real life situations and named this the Moral Response Survey. Different from the DIT results, the Moral Response Survey yielded higher moral reasoning levels for the for-profit directors than for the not-for-profit directors. Therefore, evidence is inconclusive as to whether for-profit or not-for-profit directors are higher in moral reasoning levels.

Service-Learning Makes a Difference in Moral Development

From this study, it is evident that university students are not too old to be taught ethics; as Skoe and von der Lippe (2002) noted about college students at the beginning of this chapter, "Serious career decisions must be confronted, and long-term relationships may be established for the first time … [these] crises both reveal and create character" (p. 487). While in college, students may be confronted with knowledge that challenges current thinking and forces students to correct contradictions by developing new views that often result in a moral adjustment (Skoe & von der Lippe, 2002). Challenges allow students to rely on postconventional moral schemas to reason through situations.

Determining why service-learning has the capacity for growth in moral development requires more research. One initial theory would be that the mentoring of a student by a potentially moral nonprofit director provides the student with a real world role model to emulate. Or this capacity for growth in moral development may have occurred because students experienced solving complex issues in multiple contexts in the community (Eyler & Giles, 1999) and as a result, developed "an increased awareness of one's personal values" (Astin, Vogelgesang, Ikeda, & Yee, 2000, p. iv). The student discovers a world beyond him/herself and considers the rights of others less fortunate than him or her, moving away from a culture of narcissism and toward postconventional thinking (Cabot, 2005). This factor that drives students to look beyond themselves and care for others could be the same dynamic that contributes to nonprofit directors possibly having higher moral development than business leaders as found in this study, and represented by their sense of caring about the rights and problems of others.

Past research has shown that students prefer to be helping in what is referred to as the charity orientation rather than working toward societal change (Moely & Miron, 2005), which could explain service-learning students moving toward the postconventional schema, but not reaching it, since the postconventional schema consists of social justice and understanding universal ethical principles. "The charity paradigm involves 'giving of the self, expecting nothing in return, and with no expectation that any lasting impact will be made'" (p. 63, as cited in Morton, 1995, p. 20). Morton (1995) maintains that teachers' assumptions give way to clear goals. The continuum of service that starts with helping behaviors can continue to an interest in social justice and change, similar to the postconventional schema, allowing the student to advocate for social change and social justice within the social structure in which the student has been placed. In the present study, students who participated in service-learning moved away from personal interest toward a sophisticated thinking, rather than just maintaining norms. According to Morton, this movement away from simplistic thinking could possibly continue to move toward postconventional morality by guidance from a knowledgeable teacher who energizes the student toward understanding universal principles of a society. If this study had continued for several semesters with students guided by high quality teachers, the students might have achieved postconventional morality.

LIMITATIONS OF THE STUDY

This study utilized a small regional convenience sample with the possibility of a self-selection bias. All of the participating students and organizations live in one town in the Midwestern United States, so these results cannot be considered as typical of other areas of the country. Other limitations include too few controls on the types of students' service-learning experiences; no measures of quality; a short amount of time for the research to take place, not allowing for a significant difference to occur; a small sample size; and bias that may have been introduced by the administrators of the surveys. Therefore, results must be interpreted carefully, without the possibility of making generalizations to classify all service-learning students' ethical development and results by this one study. Future research could possibly verify these results. Also, it is possible that persons from organizations that chose to participate were confident of their ethical standards, and this could have increased bias toward higher moral development. This study should be considered exploratory, and further research is essential to yield more conclusive results.

CONCLUSION

This study contributes scholarship pertaining to the development of moral reasoning and judgment of service-learning students who took part in service-learning as an intervention in a college course during one semester. These students acquired more sophisticated thinking and rejected simplistic thinking, suggesting a positive impact of service-learning on their moral development, which may be related to working with moral employees of not-for-profit organizations. The ethical benefit for students, derived from taking service-learning in their courses on campus, is an educational advantage that can drive faculty to support and bring "service-learning from the margins to the mainstream" (Furco, 2002, p. 47). More research is needed in the area of moral development of college students who have participated in a service-learning component of a course. Positive results would support university and colleges' responsibility of building ethical scholars and achieving an ethical aspect of student success.

ACKNOWLEDGMENTS

This research was supported in part by grants from Missouri Campus Compact and was presented at the Seventh International Research Conference on Service-Learning and Community Engagement in Tampa, Florida. We thank Melissa Mace, executive director of Missouri Campus

Compact, for her support and also those who kindly volunteered to participate in the study.

NOTE

1. Respondents must possess a 12-year-old reading level to participate in both the DIT and DIT2, and thus these tests cannot assess development that takes place in the stages of childhood (i.e., level one) (Narvaez & Bock, 2002). By the time individuals take the DIT, the Personal Interest Schema is commonly regarded as having already developed, because respondents passed this schema during early adolescence (Rest et al., 1999a).

REFERENCES

Agarwal, J., & Mallory, D. C. (1999). Ethical work climate dimensions in the non-for-profit organization: An empirical study. *Journal of Business Ethics, 20*, 1-14.

Astin, A. W., Vogelgesang, L. J., Ikeda, E. K., & Yee, J. A. (2000). *How service-learning affects students.* Los Angeles: University of California, Higher Education Research Institute.

Bebeau, M. J. (2002). The defining issues test and the four components model: Contributions to professional education. *Journal of Moral Education, 31*(3), 271-295.

Bebeau, M. J., & Thoma, S. J. (2003). *Guide for the DIT2: A guide for using the Defining Issues Test, Version 2 (DIT2) and the scoring service of the Center for the Study of Ethical Development.* Minneapolis: University of Minnesota.

Berkowitz, M. W., & Fekula, M. J. (1999). Educating for character. *About Campus, 4*(5), 17-22.

Boss, J. A. (1994). The effect of community service on the moral development of college ethics students. *Journal of Moral Education, 23*(2), 183-198.

Boyer, E. (1990). *Scholarship reconsidered: Priorities of the professorate.* New York: Jossey-Bass.

Brandenberger, J. (2005). College, character, and social responsibility. In D. K. Lapsley & F. C. Power (Eds.), *Psychology and education* (pp. 305-334). Notre Dame, IN University of Notre Dame Press.

Bringle, R. G., Philips, M. A., & Hudson, M. (2004). *The measure of service-learning: Research scales to access student experiences.* Washington, DC: American Psychological Association.

Brower, H. H., & Shrader, C. B. (2000). Moral reasoning and ethical climate: Not-for-profit vs. for-profit boards of directors. *Journal of Business Ethics, 26*, 147-167.

Cabot, M. (2005). Moral development and PR ethics. *Journal of Mass Media Ethics, 20*(4), 321-332.

Callery, P. (1990). Moral learning in nursing education: a discussion of the usefulness of cognitive-developmental and social learning theories. *Journal of Advanced Nursing, 15*, 324-328.

Davis, J. H., Schoorman, F. D., & Donaldson, L. (1997). Toward a stewardship theory of management. *Academy of Management Review, 22*(1), 20-47.

Derryberry, W. P., & Thoma, S. J. (2005). Functional differences: comparing moral judgment developmental phases of consolidation and transition. *Journal of Moral Education, 34*(1), 89-106.

Dewey, J. (1916). *Democracy and education.* New York: The Free Press.

Dewey, J. (1933). *How we think.* Boston: Heath.

Dewey, J. (1963). *Experience and education.* New York: Collier Books.

Evenbeck, S., & Hamilton, S. (2006). From "my course" to "our program": Collective responsibility for first-year student success. *Peer Review, 8*(3), 17-19.

Eyler, J., & Giles, D. E., Jr. (1999). *Where's the learning in service-learning?* San Francisco: Jossey-Bass.

Furco, A. (2002). Institutionalizing service-learning in higher education. *Journal of Public Affairs, 6*(Suppl.1), 39-67.

Ginsburg, H., & Opper, S. (1969). *Piaget's theory of intellectual development: An introduction.* Englewood Cliffs, NJ: Prentice-Hall.

Good, J. L. (1998). Development of moral judgment among undergraduate university students. *College Student Journal, 32*(2), 270-276.

Gorman, M., & Duffy, J. (1994). Service experience and the moral development of college students. *Religious Education, 89*(3), 422-522.

Hatcher, J. A., & Bringle, R. G. (1997). Reflection. *College Teaching, 45*(4), 153-158.

Jeffrey, C., & Weatherholt, N. (1996). Ethical development, professional commitment, and rule observance attitudes: A study of CPAs and corporate accountants. *Behavioral Research in Accounting, 8*, 8-31.

Kenny, M. E., Simon, L. A. K., Kiley-Brabeck, K., & Learner, R. M. (Eds.). (2002). *Learning to serve, promoting civil society through service learning.* Boston: Kluwer Academic.

Kirk, R., & Riedle, L. (2005). Creating lifelong learners and lifelong givers. *Delta Kappa Gamma Bulletin, 71*(4), 32-36.

Kohlberg, L. (1971). Stages of moral development as a basis for moral education. In C. M. Beck, B. S. Crittenden, & E. V. Sullivan (Eds.), *Moral education, interdisciplinary approaches.* New York: Newman Press.

Kohlberg, L. (1981). *The meaning and measurement of moral development.* Worcester, MA: Clark University Press.

Kuh, G. D. (2007). What student engagement data tell us about college readiness. *Peer Review, 9*(1), 4-8.

Kuh, G. D., Kinzie, J., Schuh, J. H., & Whitt, E. J. (2005). Never let it rest: Lessons about student success from high-performing colleges and universities. *Change, 37*(4), 44-51.

Markus, G. B., Howard, J. P., & King, D. C. (1993). Integrating community service and classroom instruction enhances learning: Results from an experiment. *Education Evaluation and Policy Analysis, 15*(4), 410-419.

Mentkowski, M., & Associates (2000). *Learning that lasts: Integrating learning, development, and performance in college and beyond*. San Francisco: Jossey-Bass.

Mirvis, P. H., & Hackett, E. J. (1983). Work and work force characteristics in the nonprofit sector. *Monthly Labor Review, 106*(4), 3-12.

Moely, B. E., & Miron, E. (2005). College students' preferred approaches to community service: Charity and social change paradigms. In S. Root, J. Callahan, & S. H. Billig (Eds.), *Improving service-learning practice: Research on models to enhance impacts: Vol. 5. Advances in service-learning research* (pp. 61-78). Greenwich, CT: Information Age.

Monks, R. A., & Minnow, N. (1989). The high cost of ethical retrogression. *Directors and Boards, 13*, 9-12.

Morton, K. (1995). The irony of service: Charity, project development, and social change in service learning. *Michigan Journal of Community Service Learning, 2*, 19-32.

Narvaez, D., & Bock, T. (2002). Moral schemas and tacit judgment or how the defining issues test is supported by cognitive science. *Journal of Moral Education, 31*(3), 298-314.

Pascarella, E. T., & Terenzini, P. T. (1991). *How college affects students*. San Francisco: Jossey-Bass.

Piaget, J. (1932). *The moral judgment of the child* (M. Gabain, Trans.). New York: Harcourt, Brace & World.

Rest, J. R. (1979a). *Development in judging moral issues*. Minneapolis: University of Minnesota Press.

Rest, J. R. (1979b). *Revised manual for the defining issues test: An objective test of moral judgment development*. Minneapolis, MN: Minnesota Moral Research Projects.

Rest, J., Cooper, D., Coder, R., Masanz, J, & Anderson, D. (1974). Judging the important issues in moral dilemmas an objective measure of development. *Developmental Psychology, 10*(4), 491-501.

Rest, J. R., Narvaez, D., Bebeau, M. J., & Thoma, S. J. (1999a). *Postconventional moral thinking: A neo-Kohlbergian approach*. Mahwah, NJ: Erlbaum.

Rest, J. R., Narvaez, D., Bebeau, M. J., & Thoma, S. J. (1999b.). A Neo-Kohlbergian approach: The DIT and schema theory. *Educational Psychology Review, 11*(4), 291-324.

Rest, J. R., Narvaez, D., Thoma, S. J., & Bebeau, M. J. (1999c.). DIT2: Devising and testing a revised instrument of moral judgment. *Journal of Educational Psychology, 91*(4), 644-659.

Schaffer, M. A., Paris, J. W., & Vogel, K. (2003). Ethical relationships in service-learning partnerships. In S. H. Billig & J. Eyler (Eds.), *Deconstructing service-learning: Research exploring context, participation, and impacts: Vol. 3. Advances in service-learning research* (pp. 147-168). Greenwich, CT: Information Age.

Skoe, E. A., & von der Lippe, A. L. (2002). Ego development and the ethics of care and justice: The relations among them revisited. *Journal of Personality, 70*(4), 485-508.

Thoma, S., Barnett, R., Rest, J., & Narvaez, D. (1999). What does the DIT measure? *British Journal of Social Psychology, 38*, 103-111.

Turiel, E., & Rothman, G. R. (1972). The influence of reasoning on behavioral choices at different stages of moral development. *Childhood Development*, *43*(3), 741-756.

Wang, J., & Coffey, B. S. (1992). Board composition and corporate philanthropy. *Journal of Business Ethics, 11*, 771-778.

CHAPTER 8

A RESEARCH STUDY INVESTIGATING THE IMPACT OF SERVICE-LEARNING ON ETHICAL DECISION MAKING

Brian R. Hoyt

This study evaluated the potential impact of service-learning on ethics education by comparing student scores in Ethical Decision-Making Abilities (ED-MA) before and after a service-learning experience. An important next question for the field is whether a project-based ethics-education model can be developed and used to predict resulting impacts on ethical decision making. The findings of this study suggest that service-learning has a positive impact on Ethical Decision-Making Abilities (ED-MA). However, statistically significant higher mean differences in ED-MA were reported only when students participated in particularly intense and engaged service experiences. The study included a pre- and posttest of more than 800 students involved in service-learning experiences at 21 universities. The study has implications for the understanding of and application of best-practice models in ethics education and service-learning when using James Rest's construct explaining ED-MA.

Scholarship for Sustaining Service-Learning and Civic Engagement
pp. 185–205
Copyright © 2008 by Information Age Publishing
All rights of reproduction in any form reserved.

INTRODUCTION

Despite a significant increase in service-learning scholarship over the past 15 years, research on moral development and ethics education is not proportionately represented with that body of work beyond early reports that service-learning has a positive impact on moral development of college students (Howard, Marcus, & King, 1993). Pascarella (1997) described the connection between experiential learning and moral development in his report on college experiences and concluded that specific experiences could foster growth in a receptive and reflective individual if the experience (service) is accompanied by other experiences (college) in a cumulative and mutually reinforcing pattern. Pascarella's later 2005 (Pascarella & Terenzini, 2005) study concluded that prominent experiences influence growth in moral development. A meta-analysis conducted by Rest and Narvaez (1994) concluded that purposeful course interventions appear to stimulate the use of principled reasoning in judging moral issues. Service-learning has been reported to be a purposeful course intervention impacting moral reasoning, which is a component of ethical development (Boss, 1994; Fenzel & Leary, 1997). Research further suggests that service-learning experiences have an effect on learning and moral development in higher education. Service-learning emphasizes hands-on tasks that address real-world concerns as a method of teaching and learning. The service experience provides a context for observing and testing discipline-based theories, concepts, skills, values, or beliefs. The academic context enhances the service experience by addressing questions about real-world concerns and provides opportunities to examine those concerns in depth.

Although experiential learning, active learning, and community service have been around for a long time, service-learning has become a major pedagogical tool only in the past 15-20 years (Ehrlich, 1997, as cited in Ikeda, 1999) and has only recently been considered as a valuable strategy for teaching ethics. Kolenko, Porter, Wheatley, and Colby's (1996) meta-analysis of service-learning in business education set up the discussion for the use of service-learning in ethics education. Fleckenstein's (1997) examination of the efficacy of service-learning in business ethics, as compared to traditional ways of integrating ethics education into a curriculum, stressed active learning and a focus on others as advantages of service-learning.

Thorne-LeClair and Ferrell's (2000) study concluded that experiential approaches that incorporate behavioral simulation are effective in ethical development. Other studies report greater impact on students' abilities to address ethical issues as a result of educational experiences including experiential action-based activities (Hartog & Frame, 2004; Fleckenstein, 1997; Weber & Glyptis, 2000). The study by Weber and Glyptis (2000) found that a business ethics course using community-service experience had a positive effect on students' values and opinions as related to ethical decision making. Sims (2002) focused his examination on experiential learning including service-learning's potential effectiveness in business ethics. He describes a powerful form of teaching where participants acquire new knowledge, skills, and abilities by internalizing theory through guided practice. Weber and Sleeper (2003) focused on the project-based aspects of service-learning relating to business ethics and social responsibilities of corporations.

Additional support for investigating the connection between service-learning and ethical decision making in ethics education is based on reported results that experiential courses are effective environments for improved ethical development. Ethical development represents the increased capacity in establishing standards of conduct that guide attitudes and behavior. Service-learning is reported to be likely to produce stronger effects on students' thinking processes in regard to ethical issues (Izzo, Langford, & Vitell, 2006).

A well-developed body of research addressing moral reasoning in ethics education is based on Kohlberg's theory of cognitive moral development (Bebeau, 2002; Bouhmama, 2001; King, 2002). The cognitive development view expresses that, through social experiences, people develop concepts of how to organize assistance when making future decisions. Along with these different concepts are different senses of fairness (the stages of moral reasoning). The stage schemes are part of long-term memory and aid the decision maker in arriving at a judgment when making sense of problematic social situations. The stage schemes direct an individual to attend to certain considerations and to prioritize claims so as to sponsor one or another line of action. The stage schemes serve as "rules of thumb," or schemas, in solving moral or ethical problems (Kohlberg, 1984; Rest, 1986). Deborah Wells's (2001) meta-analysis examined over 20 studies specific to the cognitive moral development construct and ethical decision making in the field of human resources. Loe, Ferrell, and Mansfield's (2000) meta-analysis reviewed 188 studies on ethical decision making constructs including the cognitive moral development model. King's (2002) study reviewed 172 studies on ethics education including cognitive moral development studies.

Other studies connecting moral reasoning with ethics education were expanded by Rest and Navarez' (1994) construct (Polman & Rea, 2001; Weber, 2006; Zion & Slezak, 2005). Rest's work moved beyond Kohlberg's focus on moral reasoning alone as a representation of moral development and said that moral development is best represented by a set of ethical decision making abilities and the effectiveness of ethics education can be measured by the development of those abilities (Rest, Narvaez, Bebeau, &

Thoma, 1999; Strain, 2005). Rest recognized that ethical decision making involved more than reasoning alone (Rest et al., 1999) and subsequent work focused on other processes that individuals would use in addition to reasoning that contribute to ethical decision making and ultimately ethical behavior. Rest's work culminated in a descriptive model, the four-component model, which identifies four integrated abilities as necessary conditions for effective moral functioning (as moral conduct). The four integrated abilities include the following: moral reasoning, ethical sensitivity, moral motivation and identity formation, and ethical implementation. The four-component model posits that an individual who decides and then intends to behave ethically must have performed these four basic psychological processes.

The first component, ethical sensitivity, involves the interpretation of situations by imagining what courses of action are possible and projecting the consequences of action in terms of how each action option would affect all parties involved. Moral reasoning, the second component of Rest's four-component model, is solidly based on Kohlberg's conception of cognitive stage development. The stage schemes (preconventional, conventional, and postconventional) provide heuristics in solving ethical problems. Individuals at different stages of development assess fairness and their ethical judgments in different ways, accounting for both the different lines of potential actions as well as the certainty each shares in regard to his or her reasoned judgment. Component three, moral motivation, infers that individuals recognize ethical values (e.g., fairness) as well as other values (e.g., achievement), and sometimes those value sets are in conflict. Moral motivation is a process that contributes to ethical decision making and posits that individuals will prioritize between values and ethical options based on their motivation to select an ethical value over another value. The intensity of their desire to act ethically is assessed when reviewing competing values and subsequent choices of action. Component four, ethical implementation, involves determining the sequence of specific actions while overcoming barriers and difficulties in implementing a desired decision outcome. Bebeau's (2002) meta-analysis of the four-component model contributed to understanding ethical decision making in the professions by describing the fourth component as competence to act on a decision. An individual may be ethically sensitive, make sound ethical judgments, and place high priorities on ethical values, but if that same individual is distracted from their plan to act or there is a deficiency in abilities, ethical failure will occur.

The four-component model identifies four decision-making processes that individuals must have the ability to execute in order to behave ethically. It recognizes the complexity of ethical decision making and conduct by highlighting the importance of the interaction of each component (no one component alone is enough to explain or influence ethical intent) and asserts that concentrated efforts in one component can diminish attention to another component (Bebeau, 2002; Rest, 1986; Narvaez & Rest, 1995). Studies exploring and applying the four-component model to ethical decision making are more recent and numerous. Loe et al.'s meta-analysis (2000) reviewed and categorized 188 studies including several studies directly measuring components of the four-component model. Bebeau's meta-analysis (2002) specifically reviewed studies using the four-component model as a more complete perspective on ethical decision-making processes. Miner and Petocz's meta-analysis (2003) of models of ethical decision making included studies based on the four-component model. O'Fallon and Butterfield's meta-analysis (2005) reviewed 174 research studies between 1996 to 2003 on ethical decision making, including a group of studies using Rest's four-component model.

The moral-intensity model of Jones (1991) incorporates individual and environmental factors that influence ethical decision making. The Jones model is based on Rest's four-component model and posits that the moral intensity of a situation has an impact on an individual's ethical decision-making intentions. Jones identified six categories of ethical intensity: (1) magnitude of consequences, (2) probability of effect, (3) temporal immediacy, (4) concentration of effect, (5) proximity, and (6) social consensus. Subsequent studies have supported Jones's work that ethical-intensity experiences influence ethical decision making as Rest's construct presents (Harrington, 1997; Singer & Singer, 1997, Singhapakdi, & Franke, 1999). Paolillo and Vitell's study (2002) found moral intensity, as defined by the Jones model, to significantly influence ethical decision-making intentions of managers. Loe et al.'s meta-analysis (2000) on ethical decision making suggests that more research be conducted on ethical decision-making intentions and moral intensity.

Studies in ethics education report contradictory effects on the ethical development of undergraduate college students. Barrow (2006) addressed these contradictions by suggesting that a disconnect exists between teaching ethics and anticipated behavioral changes. Barrow first identified a distinction between a dilemma and a problem. Problems imply that some kind of ethical difficulty is solvable, whereas a dilemma is by definition unsolvable. Barrow then identified the inadequacies of higher education's attempts to resolve or impact ethical dilemmas. She compared the weak influence that higher education (a college experience) has on ethical behavior to the power of family, media, and peer group pressure. She concluded that the task of ethics training is to develop expectations of society and the workplace and to provide a framework within which practical decisions must be made.

Sims and Felton (2006) investigated whether business ethics education can actually be taught, addressing whether learning ethics can take place in the higher education environment when factors such as objectives, the learning environment, learning processes, and roles of students are not clearly addressed. McDonald and Donleavy's report (1995) on the objections to teaching business ethics is a well-cited point of reference for the weak support of ethics education and training. This report identifies studies that vary as to the positive impact on ethical awareness and reasoning after ethics courses. Some research studies indicate a positive impact (Glenn, 1992) while others demonstrate a lack of impact (Wynd & Mager, 1989). McDonald (2004), in her case study report article, summarized the contradicting deliberations of the efficacy of ethics education (Loeb, 1991; Marnburg, 2003) but then concluded that effective ethics training is primarily a factor of effective integration of ethics training into a curriculum. Marnburg's analysis of ethics-education studies provides an overview of the differences in both research efforts and perspectives of practitioners relative to the orientation of ethics classes.

Ritter's (2006) study of ethical decision making reviewed the range of delivery methods that are used to facilitate the introduction of ethics content in undergraduate education. Ritter agreed with Sims and Felton's (2006) suggestion that three basic options exist for delivery of ethics training in the university setting: (1) establish a core course that focuses solely on ethics, (2) integrate ethics content as a thread among several classes, or (3) establish a core course in ethics and intentionally intersperse ethics content throughout other major courses. Peppas and Diskin's study (2001) found no significant ethical value development after participation in one ethics course. Their findings reported that a more intense exposure of ethics training for students using a curriculum approach had stronger effects than a single course. Other studies concluded that a more robust curricular approach had stronger effects than single courses (Louma, 1989; McDonald, 2004; Wynd & Mager, 1989). Still other studies concluded that a core course offers effective ethics training (Meinhardt, 2003; Wu, 2003).

Ritter's (2006) study concluded with a perspective on single course versus ethics curriculum that addresses the student's initial ethics schema before participating in either a course or a more robust curriculum. Ritter suggests further research is needed to determine course-versus-curriculum impacts depending on whether a student's ethical schema is highly developed. She suggests that a course or curriculum approach may be evaluated relative to the assumption of student readiness (creation of schema or activating an existing schema to apply in ethical situations). While some studies suggest that ethics education is only valuable to individuals with an existing mental schema that enables them to consider ethical strategies and related moral values (Cragg, 1997; Ritter, 2006), other studies suggest that an ethics-education intervention can also begin establishing a schema that can be activated and used for future decision making (Smith & Queller, 2000). The broad direction of this study was intended to examine the impact of service-learning as an active-learning methodology on students' ethical decision-making schema.

Another selection of research studies in university environments on ethics education examines the relationship between the level of learner participation and ethical development. One subset of studies suggests that more passive approaches such as theoretical and case discussions impact ethical development (Green, 1994; Klugman & Stump, 2006), while other researchers have examined the extent to which active learning is a requirement for ethical development. Izzo et al. (2006) found that active learning was associated with improved moral development and posited that particularly active and participative approaches to ethics education were more likely to produce stronger effects on students' ethical thinking. Thorne-LeClair and Ferrell's study (2000) concluded that techniques using active learning approaches are more effective when students are evaluating alternatives, outcomes, and consequences. Other studies that report similar positive impact on students' abilities to address ethical issues as a result of more interactive experiences include the use of decision-making models (Ritter, 2006; Trevino, 1992; Wittmer, 1992, 2000), role playing (Jurkiewicz, Giacalone, & Bittick, 2004; Sanyal, 2000), and experiential (Fleckenstein, 1997; Hartog & Frame, 2004; Weber & Glyptis, 2000).

THE STUDY

This project used a quantitative design to examine the impact service-learning has on the dependent variable ethical decision-making abilities framed in Rest's four-component model. Findings may lead to a better understanding of the relationship between service-learning and ethical development within ethics education. The findings may also lead to the development of more effective ethics-training interventions that then can be explored directly in workplace settings. The study tested the following hypotheses:

Hypothesis 1:   Ethical Decision-Making Abilities will be positively impacted by a service-learning experience.

Hypothesis 2a: Ethical Decision-Making Abilities will be positively impacted when the service-learning experience is particularly intense/engaged as a result of individual factors.

Hypothesis 2b: Ethical Decision-Making Abilities will be positively impacted when the service-learning experience is particularly intense/engaged as a result of environmental factors.

Methods

This study used a pre- and postsurvey design. Two surveys, one addressing values and behavior and another addressing the participants' service-learning experiences, were administered at the beginning of the academic term and then again at the end of the term following a service-learning experience. Courses in the study, with the exception of a control group, incorporated service-learning activities. Surveys completed by respondents were mailed to the principal investigator.

Institutional participants were recruited and selected based on their involvement in service-learning. Participation in service-learning was independently confirmed by viewing statements identified on the institutions' Web sites and membership in Campus Compact. The institutions represented in the study included 21 colleges/universities, including 15 faith-based institutions and six non-faith-based institutions. Faith-based participants represented colleges and universities from Christian liberal arts, Bible colleges, and Catholic traditions. Each selected faith-based institution clearly identified itself as a faith-based school through its mission statement, promotional literature, Web site messages, or faculty and/or student statement of faith requirement. Non-faith-based colleges and universities were represented by private colleges, private liberal arts schools, and public universities.

The sample was comprised of 72% female (601) and 28% male (234) participants. Students in the sample were from 32 majors with grade levels represented by 27% seniors, 24% juniors, 21% sophomores, and 28% freshmen. Most students in service-learning classes (78%) were in class sizes between 11-30 students with 80% of the participating courses requiring service-learning activities. Service-learning experiences included 60% work on community-agency activities, 28% on agency improvements, and 4% on agency planning. Most of the community interaction (44%) was with the general community, 13% in health care, 13% in education, 9% in not-for-profit, 5% in elderly care, 3% in children services, and 12% miscellaneous. The average number of orientation interventions used was 3.1 and the average number of course reflection interventions was 3.6. Courses assigned different weights to the service-learning component with 38% of the courses requiring between 5-25% of the course workload on the service activities, 35% of courses requiring service-project activities between 26-50%, and 19% requiring over 50% of the workload to be on the service project. Just over half (51%) of the study's participants were in classes that projected a service-time commitment between 11-20 hours for the term, 26% between 21-50 hours, and 13% between 5-10 hours.

Survey Measures

This study used Braithwaite and Law's values inventory as the primary measure of ethical development. The survey measures three domains: personal goals, modes of conduct, and social goals. Personal-goals scales measure values that people use as guiding principles in their lives. Modes-of-conduct scales measure values that people use as ways of behaving as a guiding principle in life. The social-goals scale measures values people use as standards to make judgments that may be used to guide action. The goal and mode values inventory as adjusted has 78 items with a 7-point asymmetrical response format. Responses are given on a scale anchored by "I reject this" and "I accept this as of the greatest importance." The instrument takes between 15 and 20 minutes to complete. The median reliability values for the three main scales are Goals that People use as Guiding Principles for Life (.71), Principles that Guide Judgments and Actions (.77), and Ways of Behaving as Guiding Principles for Life (.73) (Braithwaite & Law, 1985).

Ethical Decision-Making Abilities were measured with adjustments to the Braithwaite and Law goal and mode of behavior survey. The Positive Orientation to Others scale is an appropriate index of how service has deepened students' regard for others in terms of descriptors such as tolerant, forgiving, considerate, trusting, and generous (Bringle, Phillips, & Hudson, 2003).

The adjustment to the Braithwaite and Law values and mode of behavior survey was based on validity exercises including concept mapping and affinity analysis with students not part of the study. The inventory, as adjusted, measures the Ethical Decision-Making Abilities Key Indicators for this study and uses the set of subscales based on Rest's four-component moral-conduct construct including ethical sensitivity (28 items with Cronbach alpha = .92), moral motivation (19 items = .88), moral reasoning and identity (21 items = .86), and ethical implementation (8 items= .74).

The service-learning course inventory was designed to assess the cognitive, behavioral, and affective changes in learning and commitment that students experience as a result of a service-learning activity. The instrument's design was based on identifying the strength and types of learning as well as aspects of commitment. The measures focus on service-learning engagement experiences. The inventory uses a 5-point Likert-style agreement scale. The learning subscales include 29 items measuring content and application knowledge and 55 items measuring commitment. The service-learning inventory asks respondents to provide information on 12 demographic categories such as age, major, and gender, and several items about their service-learning experience including service project, time and load allocation, and volunteer experience. The inventory takes approximately 20 minutes to complete.

The test for reliability on the service-learning inventory was based on a subgroup of university students surveyed by the principal investigator and not part of the actual study. The Cronbach's alpha for the 5-week test-retest reliability was .69 for learning subscales and .74 for commitment subscales. Both were considered to be within the acceptable range. Researchers using these subscales reported Cronbach alpha reliability ranges from .64 to .72 (Shiarella, McCarthy, & Tucker, 2000). Factor analysis included the identification of six learning subscales and four commitment subscales confirmed by concept mapping.

Results

The impact of service-learning on the four components of Ethical Decision-Making Abilities is represented by the increase in mean score after the service-learning experience. Exhibits 8.1 through 8.6 represent the impact service-learning had on Ethical Decision-Making Abilities. The paired T test for pre-/postdifferences showed increased means for all four components of ED-MA (Exhibit 8.1). Three of the four differences were statistically significant including differences on the measures of ethical sensitivity ($p \leq .05$), moral motivation ($p \leq .001$), and ethical implementation ($p \leq .001$). No differences were found for moral reasoning.

Exhibit 8.2 presents the independent T test that was calculated to determine if there are any statistical differences in mean ED-MA scores between students who participated in service-learning and those who did not participate in service-learning. The T test reported increased means for service-learning students but none of the four components of ED-MA was statistically significant.

Exhibit 8.3 presents an analysis of the effects of individual engagement levels in service-learning on the Ethical Decision-Making Abilities measure. An independent T test was calculated to determine if there were any statistical differences in means between two groups who differed in individual engagement intensity factors and the impact on ED-MA. The analysis compared outcomes scores for those who scored higher than average and lower than average on the individual engagement measure service-attitude intensity. The service attitude was represented by the "Positive Orientation Toward Others" construct set in the Braithwaite and Law

Exhibit 8.1.   Paired T-Test Analysis to Determine Differences Comparing Pre- and Post-ED-MA Scores

		Mean	SD	t	df	Sig. (2-tailed)
Pair 1	Rest's Ethical Sensitivity Pre 2 - Rest's Ethical Sensitivity Post 2	−1.54717	14.48869	−2.199	423	.028*
Pair 2	Rest's Mortal Reasoning Pre 2 - Rest's Moral Reasoning Post 2	−1.00238	11.81793	−1.738	419	.083
Pair 3	Rest's Moral Motivation Pre 2 - Rest's Moral Motivation Post 2	−2.35934	10.31419	−4.705	422	.000***
Pair 4	Rest's Ethical Implementation Pre 2 - Rest's Ethical Implementation Post 2	−1.55399	5.11911	−6.266	425	.000***

Note: *$p \leq .05$. **$p \leq .01$. ***$p \leq .001$.

Exhibit 8.2.   Independent *T*-Test Analysis to Determine Mean Differences Between Groups Experiencing Service-Learning With Those Students Who Did Not Participate in Service-Learning

		t	df	Sig. (2-tailed)	Mean Difference	Std. Error Difference
Rest's Ethical Sensitivity Diff 2	Greater mean score for students engaged in s-l	−.447	422	.655	−.99291	2.22284
Rest's Moral Reasoning Difference 2	Greater mean score for students engaged in s-l	−1.183	418	.237	-2.14315	1.81162
Rest's Moral Motivation Difference 2	Greater mean score for students engaged in s-l	−.627	421	.531	−.98347	1.56814
Rest's Ethical Implementation Difference 2	Greater mean score for students engaged in s-l	−.449	424	.654	−.34927	.77811

Note: *$p \leq .05$. **$p \leq .01$. ***$p \leq .001$.

values and modes inventory. The Positive Orientation Toward Others's 13 items describe values toward others that influence behavior and the Cronbach alpha reliability score for the 13 items was .90. The average service

**Exhibit 8.3.   Independent *T* Tests to Determine Differences
Between Two Groups in ED-MA When Individual
Engagement Factor Service-Attitude Intensity is Examined**

		t	*df*	Sig. *(2-tailed)*	Mean *Difference*	Std. Error *Difference*
Rest's Ethical Sensitivity Diff 2	Greater mean score for students with higher service intensity	14.396	422	.000***	16.62501	1.15487
Rest's Moral Reasoning Difference 2	Greater mean score for students with higher service intensity	9.084	417	.000***	9.61017	1.05788
Rest's Moral Motivation Difference 2	Greater mean score for students with higher service intensity	9.711	420	.000***	8.82190	.90845
Rest's Ethical Implementation Difference 2	Greater mean score for students with higher service intensity	8.138	423	.000***	3.76282	.46235

Note: *$p \leq .05$. **$p \leq .01$. ***$p \leq .001$.

attitude score was calculated and used as the cut point to separate the above average service attitudes from below average service attitudes. The *T* test reported that students who scored above average in service attitudes had higher mean differences than those students who scored below average in service attitudes in all four Ethical Decision-Making Ability areas. All differences between service intensity means were higher with more intense service attitudes (> than average score) and statistically significant on measures of ethical sensitivity, moral reasoning, moral motivation, and ethical implications.

Exhibit 8.4 presents a second analysis of the effects of individual engagement intensity factor in service-learning on Ethical Decision-Making Abilities (ED-MA). An independent *T* test was calculated to determine, as a more intense individual engagement factor, if there were mean-score differences between students who had future service-career aspirations and students who are not planning to be in service-related careers in ED-MA. The *T* test reported that students with future service-career aspirations had higher mean scores than those students without service-career aspirations in four of four components of Ethical Decision-Making Abilities. Two of the four differences were statistically significant

Exhibit 8.4.   Independent *T* Tests to Determine Differences Between Two Groups in ED-MA When Individual Engagement Factor Career-Aspiration Intensity is Examined

		T Test for Equality of Means			
		t	*df*	*Sig. (2-tailed)*	*Mean Difference*
Rest's Ethical Sensitivity Diff 2	Greater mean for students with service career aspirations	1.275	376	.203	1.94771
Rest's Moral Reasoning Difference 2	Greater mean for students with service career aspirations	2.207	371	.028*	2.72374
Rest's Moral Motivation Difference 2	Greater mean for students with service career aspirations	1.903	374	.058*	2.04015
Rest's Ethical Implementation Difference 2	Greater mean for students with service career aspirations	1.320	377	.188	.70877

Note: $*p \leq .05$. $**p \leq .01$. $***p \leq .001$.

including differences on the measures of moral reasoning and moral motivation.

Exhibit 8.5 presents an analysis of the effects of individual engagement intensity in service-learning on Ethical Decision-Making Abilities (ED-MA). The independent *T* test was calculated to determine if there were mean score differences in Ethical Decision-Making Abilities between students who self reported higher engaged-learning outcomes from those students who self reported lower learning outcomes. The self-reported learning outcomes were composed of 50 items on the service-learning inventory representing a variety of learning-outcome dimensions including basic knowledge, application knowledge, and learning to learn. The *T* test reported that students with higher than average learning-outcome scores had higher mean scores in Ethical Decision-Making Abilities than students with lower than average learning-outcome scores. Four of four components in ED-MA were also statistically significant including differences on the measure of ethical sensitivity, moral reasoning, moral motivation, and ethical implementation.

Exhibit 8.6 presents the last analysis of individual engagement intensity factors in service-learning on Ethical Decision-Making Abilities (ED-MA). The independent *T* test was calculated to determine if there were mean score differences in ED-MA between students who have previous

Exhibit 8.5.   Independent _T_ Tests to Determine Differences Between Two Groups in ED-MA When Individual Engagement Factor Learning Outcomes Intensity is Examined

		t	df	Sig. (2-tailed)	Mean Difference	Std. Error Difference
Rest's Ethical Sensitivity Diff 2	Greater mean score for students self reporting higher learning	2.47	372	.014*	3.7	1.49
Rest's Moral Reasoning Difference 2	Greater mean score for students self reporting higher learning	2	372	.018*	2.9	1.22
Rest's Moral Motivation Difference 2	Greater mean score for students self reporting higher learning	1.9	369	.05*	2.01	1.05
Rest's Ethical Implementation Difference 2	Greater mean score for students self reporting higher learning	1.9	372	.047*	1.05	.527

Note: $*p \leq .05. **p \leq .01. ***p \leq .001.$

volunteer service experience with those students who do not have previous volunteer service experience. The _T_ test reported greater mean scores in ED-MA for those students without previous volunteer experience in four of four ED-MA components with none of the greater means statistically significant.

Environmental factors such as institutional commitment to community service, service project types, service orientation, and reflection opportunities were analyzed to determine the impact on service-learning intensity and resulting effect on ED-MA. There were no statistically significant relationships between the extent to which students were environmentally engaged and outcomes on the Ethical Decision-Making Abilities measures.

The analysis of variance (ANOVA) presented differences in mean scores on the ED-MA between groups who served different community populations, with those students who provided services for children, education, and health care showing the highest means. None of the differences, however, was statistically significant. There were also no statistical differences between service project types (strategy projects, improvement projects, and activity-based projects) and ED-MA outcomes, though activity-based projects showed the highest mean differences. Students from

Exhibit 8.6.   Independent *T* Tests to Determine Differences Between Two Groups in ED-MA When Individual Engagement Factor of Previous Service Experience Intensity is Examined

		t	df	Sig. (2-tailed)	Mean Difference	Std. Error Difference
Rest's Ethical Sensitivity Diff 2	Greater mean scores for students without previous service experience	−.727	376	.468	−1.16461	1.60249
Rest's Moral Reasoning Difference 2	Greater mean scores for students without previous service experience	−.204	371	.838	−.26646	1.30382
Rest's Moral Motivation Difference 2	Greater mean scores for students without previous service experience	−.104	374	.917	−.11772	1.13007
Rest's Ethical Implementation Difference 2	Greater mean scores for students without previous service experience	−.795	377	.427	−.44868	.56423

Note: *$p \leq .05$. **$p \leq .01$. ***$p \leq .001$.

institutions with higher commitment to community service had higher mean scores than those whose institutions had less commitment, but again differences were not statistically significant in ED-MA outcomes.

ANOVAs were also conducted to determine the differences in ED-MA outcomes associated with eight different types of orientations (e.g., agency representative visits to campus, tour of agency facility, review of brochures, faculty explanation). Mean differences were reported in ED-MA between orientation types but none was statistically significant. Service-learning reflections were measured using the ANOVA with mean differences calculated between eight different types of reflection interventions (e.g., journaling, in-class small-group discussion, class discussion, written paper). Higher mean differences were reported for written paper and small-group discussions in ED-MA but none was statistically significant.

Finally, differences in institutional tradition relative to community service were analyzed to determine environmental impact on service-learning and any resulting effects on Ethical Decision-Making Abilities. An independent *T*-test analysis found higher mean differences between students from faith-based traditions and those from other institutions, but these differences were not statistically significant in ED-MA outcomes. An additional ANOVA was conducted to determine differences among seven types of academic traditions (faith-based liberal arts, Bible colleges, Catholic institutions, public, private faith based, community colleges, and liberal arts). Stronger mean scores in ED-MA were reported for liberal arts, faith-based liberal arts, and Catholic institutions, but none was statistically significant.

DISCUSSION

Overall, findings of the study revealed a positive impact on Ethical Decision-Making Abilities of students involved in service-learning activities. However, results suggest that the effects of service-learning experiences on students are mixed, and predictive power about this pedagogy is more limited than expected. Service-learning participation affected three of the four components of the Ethical Decision-Making Abilities in a positive way as measured by a pre/post analysis. The comparison between the ED-MA of students who participated in service-learning and those students who did not engage in service-learning did not indicate a statistical difference in ED-MA outcomes.

The broad findings might be explained by the work of Pascarella (1997), indicating that the college experience itself, not withstanding specific interventions such as service-learning, is enriched enough to have an impact on ethical decision making of students. As Colby, Ehrlich, Beaumont, and Stephens (2003) found, the college experience may increase student awareness of unquestioned interpretive schemas, expose biases, or highlight the ambiguity of moral/ethical situations that previously were considered clear. It is also possible that the reflection component of service-learning was not intense enough as explained by Colby et al.'s discussion (2003) that acknowledges that the reflective component of service-learning could be a viable intervention. This service-learning intervention could change students' cognitive schema and influence interpretations if it involves reflection on their moral interpretations and discussion of them with others over time. This perspective also offers an explanation as to how any intervention, overall college experience, or service-learning experience needs to reach a level of intensity to "trigger" a change in moral/ethical decision-making schemas.

The second prediction of this study, that a particularly intense service-learning experience would positively impact students' Ethical Decision-

Making Abilities, was supported by the data analysis. The individual factors (attitude toward service, service-career aspirations, and self-reported learning outcomes) that represented intensity levels of student engagement were found to be significant conditions for increased Ethical Decision-Making Abilities. When service attitude scores, service-career aspirations, and self-reported learning outcomes were more intense, students reported greater changes in ED-MA measures. These findings support other researchers who have suggested the intensity of a service experience and the issues the service activity addresses raise the level of moral imperative in a situation and will impact ethical decision making (Jones, 1991; Loe et al., 2000; Paolillo & Vitell, 2002).

This study did not address the nature of the intensity factor. Service-learning was measured as an "aggregate" intensity factor influencing ED-MA without measuring Jones's (1991) six specific components of moral intensity. Jones's research posits that six components impact moral intensity and ethical decision making: magnitude of consequences (total sum of harm/benefit of the decision), social consensus (extent of social agreement that the decision is either good or bad), probability of the effect (the likelihood that the decision will cause harm/benefit), temporal immediacy (the amount of time before consequences either good/bad are realized), proximity (the social distance between the decision maker and those impacted by the decision), and concentration of effect (the number of people affected by the decision). The sources of intensity could certainly provide additional insights as to what types of service-learning projects are more intense and which of the six intensity factors may further explain why some students' service experiences are more meaningful than other students' experiences.

It is also possible that students experience service-learning differently, and that the experience may be more intense for some individuals than others. A study by Ritter (2006) suggests that ethics education is only agreeable to individuals already primed to consider ethical issues and action strategies. Studies that control for priming have included timing (Lowry, 2003) and previous experiences (Cragg, 1997; Weber & Glyptis, 2000). ED-MA is one schema that could characterize this stage of priming Ritter discusses and might best explain how individual factors of intensity influence that priming schema.

The findings of this study can provide suggestions for future research directed at the measuring of the important construct of ethical decision-making abilities. An important next step for the studies on the effects of participation in service-learning on ethical development may also be a focus on the logistics as factors to predict positive outcomes. This study found that with more intense individual engagement, service-learning has a greater impact on ethical decision-making. However, the study did not illuminate what logistic efforts (types of reflection, orientation, service projects, etc.) will have the greatest impact on more intense engagement. Future studies that measure the variation between service-learning interventions (e.g., effectiveness of orientation and reflection) will be necessary to more accurately gauge the success of service-learning as an ethics education delivery intervention.

Finally, the field could benefit from an investigation of the extent to which current ethical decision-making abilities predict the intention to act ethically in the future. Extending this study by examining service-learning as an intervention in ethics education could use the theory of planned behavior (Ajzen, 1987, 2005) to explain how service-learning might influence students' ethics schema so that the schema becomes activated in future decision making. The application of this theory would posit that intentions to make ethical decisions can be predicted from the antecedent perceived behavioral control with respect to acquiring the abilities for ethical decision making (ED-MA).

REFERENCES

Ajzen, I. (1987). Attitudes, traits, and actions: Dispositional prediction of behavior in personality and social psychology. In L. Berkowitz (Ed.), *Advances in experimental social psychology* (Vol. 20, pp. 1-63). San Diego, CA: Academic Press.

Ajzen, I. (2005). *Attitudes, personality and behavior* (2nd ed.). Berkshire, England: Open University Press.

Barrow, R. (2006). Moral education's modest agenda. *Ethics and Education, 1*(1), 3-13.

Bebeau, M. (2002). The Defining Issues Test and the Four Component Model: Contributions to professional education. *Journal of Moral Education, 31*(3), 271-295.

Boss, J. (1994). The effect of community service work on the moral development of college students. *Journal of Moral Education, 23*, 183-191.

Bouhmama, D. (2001). Relation of formal education to moral judgment development. *The Journal of Psychology, 122*(2), 155-158.

Braithwaite, V. A., & Law, H. G. (1985). Structure of human values: Testing the adequacy of the Rokeach Value Survey. *Journal of Personality and Social Psychology, 49*, 250-263.

Bringle, R., Phillips, M., & Hudson, M. (2003). *The measure of service learning: Research scales to assess student experiences.* Washington DC: American Psychological Association

Colby, A., Ehrlich, T., Beaumont, E., & Stephens, J. (2003). *Educating citizens.* San Francisco: Jossey-Bass.

Cragg, W. (1997). Teaching business ethics: The role of ethics in business and in business education. *Journal of Business Ethics, 16*, 231-245.

Ehrlich, T. (1997, Summer/Fall). Civic learning: Democracy and education revisited. *Educational Record, 78*(3 & 4), 57-65.

Felton, E., & Sims, R. (2005). Teaching business ethics: Targeted outputs. *Journal of Business Ethics, 60,* 377-391.

Fenzel, L., & Leary, T. (1997). *Evaluating outcomes of service-learning courses at a parochial college.* Presented at the annual meeting of American Education Research Association, Chicago.

Fleckenstein, M. (1997). Service learning in business ethics. *Journal of Business Ethics, 16,* 1347-1351.

Glenn, J. (1992). Can a business and society course affect the ethical judgment of future managers? *Journal of Business Ethics, 11,* 217-223.

Green, R. (1994). *The ethical manager: A new method for business ethics.* New York: MacMillan.

Harrington, S. (1997). A test of a person-issue contingent model of ethical decision making in organizations. *Journal of Business Ethics, 16*(4), 363-375.

Hartog, M., & Frame, P. (2004). Business ethics in the curriculum: Integrating ethics through work experience. *Journal of Business Ethics, 54,* 399-409.

Howard, J. P., Marcus, G. B., & King, D. C. (1993). Integrating community service and classroom instruction enhances learning: Results from an experiment. *Educational Evaluation and Policy Analysis, 15,* 410-419.

Ikeda, E. (1999). How does service enhance learning? Toward an understanding of the process. Unpublished doctoral dissertation, University of California Los Angeles.

Izzo, G., Langford, B., & Vitell, S. (2006). Investigating the efficacy of interactive ethics education: A difference in pedagogical emphasis. *Journal of Marketing Theory and Practice, 14*(3), 239-248.

Jones, T. (1991). Ethical decision-making by individuals in organizations: An issue-contingent model. *Academy of Management Journal, 42,* 479-485.

Jurkiewicz, C., Giacalone, R., & Bittick, R. (2004, Summer). The squeaky wheel approach to teaching ethics. *Public Integrity, 6,* 249-262.

King, P. (2002). Moral judgment development in higher education: Insights from the Defining Issues Test. *Journal of Moral Education, 31*(3), 247-270.

Klugman, C., & Stump, B. (2006). The effect of ethics training upon individual choice. *Journal of Further and Higher Education, 30*(2), 181-192.

Kohlberg, L. (1984). *Essays on moral development, Vol. 2: The psychology of moral development.* San Francisco: Harper & Row.

Kolenko, T., Porter, G., Wheatley, W., & Colby, M. (1996). A critique of service learning projects in management education: Pedagogical foundations, barriers, and guidelines. *Journal of Business Ethics, 15,* 133-142.

Loe, T., Ferrell, W., & Mansfield, P. (2000). A review of empirical studies assessing ethical decision making in business. *Journal of Business Ethics, 25*(3), 185-204.

Loeb, S. (1971). A survey of ethical behaviors in the accounting profession. *Journal of Accounting Research, 9,* 287-306.

Loeb, S. (1991). The evaluation of outcomes of accounting ethics education. *Journal of Business Ethics, 10*(2), 77-84.

Louma, G. (1989). Can ethics be taught? *Business & Economic Review, 3*(1), 3-5.

Lowry, D. (2003). An investigation of student moral awareness and associated factors in two cohorts of an undergraduate business degree in a British university: Implications for business ethics curriculum design. *Journal of Business Ethics*, *48*(1), 7-13.

Marnburg, E. (2003). Educational impacts on academic business practitioner's moral reasoning and behavior: Effects of short courses in ethics or philosophy. *Business Ethics: A European Review*, *12* (4), 403-413.

McDonald, G. (2004). A case example: Integrating ethics into the academic business curriculum. *Journal of Business Ethics*, *54*, 371-384.

McDonald, G., & Donleavy, G. (1995). Objections to the teaching of business ethics. *Journal of Business Ethics*, *14*, 839-853.

Meinhardt, J. (2003). Survey shows MBA programs. *The Business Journal*, *2*, 24.

Miner, M., & Petocz, A. (2003). Moral theory in ethical decision making: Problems, clarifications and recommendations from a psychological perspective. *Journal of Business Ethics*, *42*, 11-25.

Narvaez, D., & Rest, J. (1995). The four components of acting morally. In W. Kurtines & J. Gewirtz (Eds.), *Moral behavior and moral development: An introduction* (pp. 213-224). New York: McGraw-Hill.

O'Fallon, M., & Butterfield, K. (2005). A review of the empirical ethical decision-making literature: 1996-2003. *Journal of Business Ethics*, *59*, 375-413.

Paolillo, J., & Vitell, V. (2002). An empirical investigation of the influence of selected personal, organizational and moral intensity factors on ethical decision making. *Journal of Business Ethics*, *35*, 65-74.

Pascarella, E. (1997). College's influence on principled moral reasoning. *The Educational Record*, *78*, 47-55.

Pascarella, E., & Terenzini, P. (2005). *How college affects students, Vol. 2: A third decade of research*. San Francisco: Jossey-Bass.

Peppas, S., & Diskin, B. (2001). College courses in ethics: Do they really make a difference? *The International Journal of Education Management*, *15*(7), 347-353.

Polman, J. & Pea, R. (2001). Transformative communication as a cultural tool for guiding inquiry science. *Science Education*, *85*(3), 223-238.

Rest, J. (1984). Research on moral development: Implications for training counseling psychologists. *The Counseling Psychologists*, *12*, 19-29.

Rest, J. (1986). *Moral development: Advances in research and theory*. New York: Praeger.

Rest, J., & Narvaez, D. (1994). *Moral development in the professions*. Hillsdale, NJ: Erlbam.

Rest, J., Narvaez, D., Bebeau, M., & Thoma, S. (1999). *Postconventional moral thinking: A neo-Kohlbergian approach*. Mahwah, NJ: Erlbaum.

Ritter, B. (2006). Can ethics be trained? A study of ethical decision-making process in business students. *Journal of Business Ethics*, *68*, 153-164.

Sanyal, R. (2000). Teaching business ethics in international business. *Teaching Business Ethics*, *4*, 137-149.

Shiarella, A., McCarthy, M., & Tucker, M. (2000). Development and construct validity of scores on community service attitudes scale. *Educational and Psychological Measurement*, *60*, 286-300.

Sims, R. (2002). Business ethics teaching for effective learning. *Teaching Business Ethics*, 6, 393-410.

Sims, R. & Felton, E. (2006). Designing and delivering business ethics and learning. *Journal of Business Ethics*, 63(3), 297-313.

Singer, M., & Singer, A. (1997). Observer judgments about moral agents' ethical decisions: The role of scope of justice and moral intensity. *Journal of Business Ethics*, 16(5), 473-484.

Singhapakdi, A., Vitell, S., & Franke, G. (1999). Antecedents, consequences, and mediating effects of perceived moral intensity and personal moral philosophies. *Journal of the Academy of Marketing Science*, 27(1), 19-36.

Smith, E., & Queller, S. (2000). *Mental representations*. In A. Tesser & N. Schwarz (Eds.), *Blackwell handbook in social psychology, Vol. 1: Intraindividual process* (pp. 111-133). Oxford, United Kingdom: Blackwell.

Strain, C. (2005). Pedagogy and practice: Service-learning and students' moral development. *New Directions for Teaching and Learning, 103*, 61-72.

Thorne-LeClair, D., & Ferrell, L. (2000). Innovation in experiential business ethics training. *Journal of Business Ethics*, 23(3), 313-322.

Trevino, L. (1992). Experimental approaches to studying ethical-unethical behavior in organizations. *Business Ethics Quarterly*, 2(2), 121-136.

Weber, J. (2006). Business ethics training: Insights from learning theory. *Journal of Business Ethics, 70*, 61-85.

Weber, J., & Glyptis, S. (2000). Measuring the impact of a business ethics course and community service experience on students' values and opinions. *Teaching Business Ethics, 4*, 341-358.

Weber, P., & Sleeper, B. (2003). Enriching student experiences: Multi-disciplinary exercises in service learning. *Teaching Business Ethics, 7*, 417-435.

Wells, D. (2001). Ethical development and human resource training: An integrative framework. *Human Resource Management Review, 11*, 135-159.

Wittmer, D. (1992). Ethical sensitivity and managerial decision-making: An experiment. *Journal of Public Administration Research and Theory, 2* (4), 443-462.

Wittmer, D. (2000). Ethical sensitivity in management decisions: Developing and testing perceptual measure among management and professional student groups. *Teaching Business Ethics, 4*, 181-205.

Wynd, W., & Mager, J. (1989). The business and society course: Does it change student attitudes? *Journal of Business Ethics, 8*, 486-491.

Wu, C. (2003). A study of the adjustment of ethical recognition and ethical decision-making of managers-to-be across the Taiwan Strait before and after receiving a business ethics education. *Journal of Business Ethics, 45*, 291-307.

Zion, M., & Slezak, D. (2005). It takes two to tango: In dynamic inquiry, the self directed participant acts in association with the facilitating facilitator. *Teaching and Facilitator Education, 21*(7), 875-894.

ABOUT THE CONTRIBUTORS

Shelley H. Billig is vice president of RMC Research Corporation in Denver, Colorado. She serves as principal investigator of multiple studies in service-learning and educational reform and evaluator of multiple interventions designed to impact academic and social-emotional learning and civic engagement.

Sally Blomstrom, PhD, is an associate professor of communication at Embry-Riddle Aeronautical University. She started incorporating service-learning pedagogy in 1994. Her research interests include creativity, assessment and service-learning in STEM education.

Melody A. Bowdon, PhD, is an associate professor of English at the University of Central Florida, where she teaches service-learning courses in technical and professional writing and conducts community-based research on communication practices in the nonprofit sector. Since 2005 she has served as senior research fellow for Florida Campus Compact.

Robert G. Bringle, PhD, PhilD, is Chancellor's Professor of Psychology and Philanthropic Studies at Indiana University-Purdue University Indianapolis. His work as director of the IUPUI Center for Service and Learning has resulted in numerous national recognitions for his campus and himself, including the Ehrlich Faculty Award for Service Learning, being recognized at the International Service-Learning Research Conference for outstanding contributions, and receiving an honorary doctoral degree from the University of the Free State, South Africa.

R. Marc Brodersen is a research associate at RMC Research Corporation in Denver, Colorado. He serves as project director of several Learn and Serve evaluations and character education evaluation projects and has expertise in quantitative analysis.

Elizabeth Carmichael Burton is the associate director of the Office of Citizenship and Service-Learning (CASL) at Missouri State University. She developed the Student Service-Learning Leaders (S2L2) program to train students in leadership roles to further develop the program in student voice, reflection and faculty support.

Patti Clayton, PhD, is founding director of the Center for Excellence in Curricular Engagement in the Office of the Provost and executive vice chancellor at NC State University. She also serves as a senior scholar with the Center for Service and Learning at IUPUI and consults with universities around the country.

Barbara Dewey, LCSW & LMHP served as the initial researcher for the University of Nebraska at Omaha Service-Learning Academy. She facilitated the focus groups, developed the survey instrument, analyzed the initial findings, and worked collaboratively with service-learning faculty and community partners to improve outcomes for students.

Megan Fair is a graduate student worker in the Service-Learning Academy at the University of Nebraska at Omaha. She is seeking an educational specialist degree in school psychology.

Michelle Grimley is the director of the Partnership in Character Education project for the School District of Philadelphia.

Barbara Holland, PhD, is director of the National Service-Learning Clearinghouse, a senior scholar with Indiana University-Purdue University Indianapolis in their Center for Service and Learning, as adjunct professor of the University of Western Sydney, executive editor of *Metropolitan Universities* journal. Most recently she has served as pro vice chancellor engagement on the Campbelltown Campus at the University of Western Sydney in Australia.

Shelley M. Henderson, MSEd, former secondary Language arts teacher, now serves the University of Nebraska at Omaha's Service-Learning Academy as P-16 coordinator connecting higher education and PK-12 practitioners to engage and empower students of all ages in meeting real community needs through their learning. She is also an officer on the Nebraska Staff Development Council, on the Nebraska Department of Education's Comprehensive System of Personnel Development Advisory Committee, and a member of the National School Reform Faculty.

Brian R. Hoyt is an associate professor of management at Ohio University, where his teaching responsibilities include courses in management and marketing. His scholarship addresses ethics education, ethical decision-making, service-learning, and the integration of interactive technology into project management activities. Professor Hoyt has been awarded teaching and research awards at Ohio University and has been recognized nationally for his work in service-learning. His expertise in continuous improvement methodology and practice has been developed into a national reputation including selection as a National Malcolm Baldrige Award Examiner.

Dan Jesse is a senior research associate at RMC Research Corporation in Denver, Colorado. He serves as project director for several studies in civic engagement, character development, reading, and other education-related issues.

Jessica Katz Jameson, PhD, is an associate professor and an associate head for undergraduate studies in the Department of Communication at NC State University. She serves on the academic council of the NC State Institute for Nonprofits and has provided leadership in the design of an integrated service-learning curriculum for a multidisciplinary minor in nonprofit studies. She is a civically engaged scholar and serves on the advisory council for the Center for Excellence in Curricular Engagement.

Marjori Maddox Krebs, EdD, is an assistant professor in teacher education at the University of New Mexico, primarily teaching preservice teachers. She is a member of the fundraising/communications committee for the International Association of Research in Service-Learning and Community Engagement

Paul Sather, MSW, ABD, serves both as the director of the Service-Learning Academy and the American Humanics program at the University of Nebraska at Omaha. He coordinates UNO's effort to increase the relationship between UNO students and community partners, as well as support faculty to develop and improve service-learning courses.

Trae Stewart, PhD, is an assistant professor in the College of Education at the University of Central Florida. His primary areas of research include service-learning and queer issues in education.

Hak Tam, MSEE, MBA, is currently pursuing a PhD in educational leadership and organizations at the University of California, Santa Barbara.

His research interests are in learning outcome assessment, experiential learning, international business, and entrepreneurship education.

Susan Waters, PhD, is an assistant professor in the Department of Communication at Missouri State University and primarily teaches public relations courses. She is a member of the fundraising/communication committee for the International Association of Research in Service-Learning and Community Engagement.